99

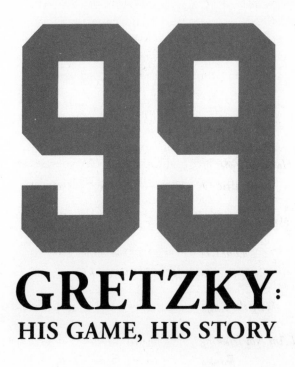

GRETZKY:
HIS GAME, HIS STORY

AL STRACHAN
Assisted by WAYNE GRETZKY
Foreword by ROY MACGREGOR

FENN

M & S

Library and Archives Canada Cataloguing in Publication

Strachan, Al
99: Gretzky: his game, his story / Al Strachan ;
foreword by Roy MacGregor.

ISBN 978-0-7710-8329-7

1. Gretzky, Wayne, 1961-. 2. Hockey players – Canada – Biography.
3. Hockey coaches – Canada – Biography. I. Title.
II. Title: Ninety-nine, his game, his story.

GV848.5.G78S77 2013   796.962092   C2013-900689-3

Library of Congress control number: 2013931565

Typeset in Garamond

Printed and bound in the United States of America

Fenn/McClelland & Stewart,
a division of Random House of Canada Limited
A Penguin Random House Company
One Toronto Street
Toronto, Ontario
M5C 2V6
www.randomhouse.ca

1   2   3   4   5   17   16   15   14   13

For the lovely Vivienne

CONTENTS

FOREWORD
By Roy MacGregor

"Come on! – you'll have a great time!"

And I did. It was late fall, 1994. The National Hockey League owners had just locked out its players in what would, over the years, become a virtual ritual, but this was the very first and, without Twitter and endless talking-head panels, there wasn't much for hockey journalists to do but wait it out and find something else to fill in the time.

Al Strachan suggested I join him and a handful of other hockey writers – Tony Gallagher of the *Vancouver Province*, Kevin McGran of Canadian Press (now with the *Toronto Star*) – who were going to follow Wayne Gretzky on a barnstorming "Grand Tour" of Europe. The "Ninety-Nine All Stars," put together by Gretzky, his agent Mike Barnett and (I would not know until I read this book) Al Strachan, would play exhibition matches against club teams in Finland, Sweden, Norway and Germany. "Strach" was going for the Sun chain. I was then with the *Ottawa Citizen*, part of the then-powerful Southam empire. If hockey superstars like Gretzky, Brett Hull, Mark Messier, Paul Coffey, Steve Yzerman and Sergei Fedorov were going to be wearing jerseys rather than suits and playing real games rather than head games, then Southam certainly wouldn't want the Sun to own it. They happily agreed that both Tony, another Southam employee, and I could go along.

Strach, whom I did not know very well then, was far more welcoming than I had expected. I knew his reputation for caustic remarks and quick dismissals but I had to learn for myself that the sarcasm and jibes come with such joyous wit that he is, in fact, a delight to be around. I knew he and Tony had long been friends but I had no real concept of how close he was with Gretzky, the organizer, funder and main attraction of the trip.

At first, this bothered me, as I'm sure it bothered others. Strachan, and Tony, as well, had an access that McGran and I simply could not match. Neither of us had covered Gretzky in his heyday, as both Tony and Al had. The worry proved completely unfounded, as Al made sure that each game was run roughly as real NHL games were, with a semi-formal scrum with Gretzky and other players at the end of each match. The rest of the time, we all travelled together as one delightful group, sightseeing during the days and playing exhibition games – several of them excellent – at night. The travelling band included various wives and girlfriends and several of the players took along their fathers, including the incomparable Walter Gretzky. Sergei Fedorov, perhaps because his father wasn't available, brought along a stripper.

This was my first real encounter with Gretzky and the friendship that began on that trip eventually became a "partnership" after his retirement in 1999. The *National Post* had started up just the year before and, wanting to make a big splash in sports, arranged for Wayne to write a weekly column for them. He agreed but asked that I, having transferred to the *Post* from the *Citizen*, "assist" him with it. I then got to know the Wayne Gretzky that Al Strachan knew and admired – though I would never know him as well as Al.

The incredible friendship between the game's greatest player and the game's most controversial commentator was something to behold. Gretzky is renowned for his diplomacy on all matters concerning hockey.

He has always been careful to avoid controversy, endlessly polite and quick to offer the benefit of the doubt. Not so Strach. Al is one of those people with no built-in governor. He says whatever he is thinking, and usually in a low-but-penetrating voice that is impossible not to pick up. Most people built like that, though, are not very bright and could well use a governor. Not Al. He is one of the brightest brains in sports journalism – erudite, well-read, with an incredible grasp of history and events. His politics might make some cringe, but if they wish to debate him they had better know their file – because he will rip it to shreds.

Those who get to know his humorous side, however, soon come to treasure it. He can be hilarious. I sometimes think this is why Gretzky is so fond of him. Al not only knows his sports on a level that can keep up to the encyclopedic Gretzky, but Al is more than happy to say, aloud, things that Gretzky might only be thinking. He also makes Gretzky laugh. At himself, as well.

Today's journalists cannot possibly get to know athletes as they once could. When Al Strachan started out, hockey dressing rooms were quiet places where reporters could sit alone with a player and chat about everything from the game at hand to the world at large. Television cameras and radio microphones were rare. Today, it is impossible to speak alone with a professional athlete. The moment his mouth opens, small hand-held recorders and iPhones press in on him to vacuum up every word, many of the recorder holders not paying the slightest attention or, for that matter, even bothering to look at the player. Whatever he says, even the most utterly meaningless – "the first goal is important," "we have to play desperate hockey" – is instantly sent out on Twitter. It has made players retreat to clichés, avoid all talk that might be misconstrued. Idle chatter is a dead art.

It is because of this that this book is so telling. It is not just about feats and records – though they are there, as well – but about a very special relationship between a superstar athlete and a star reporter.

Wayne Gretzky and Al Strachan, both richly deserving of their rightful places in the Hockey Hall of Fame.

E ven though Wayne Gretzky began his National Hockey League career in 1979, it wasn't until the 1981 Canada Cup that I really got to know him. Our paths had crossed a couple of times in post-game scrums, but in circumstances of that nature, you don't get much of a chance to interact.

However, in an event like the Canada Cup, where the players have lots of free time and the same reporters are coming back day after day, relationships begin to form.

The reporter, naturally enough, will revisit the players with whom he feels he is developing a rapport. Similarly, the players will either increase or decrease their level of cooperation as they get to know the people with whom they are dealing.

A couple of factors led to my becoming friends with Wayne Gretzky. One was that both James Christie and I were covering the tournament for the *Globe and Mail*. We were both about the same height. We were both overweight and we both had moustaches. Jim's was a bit more luxuriant than mine, but whose wasn't? During a chat just after the training camp opened, Gretzky called me "Jim." I pointed out the error of his ways and we laughed about it. The next day, I teased him about it.

When you're Wayne Gretzky, most people, with the exception of most of your teammates, treat you like royalty. To have someone make fun of you, however lightly, opens a new door in the relationship. You can get angry and slam that door, or you can laugh and go marching through it. Gretzky opted for the latter.

Face to face, I have often made fun of him. He makes fun of himself. Once, after he was hit in the ear with a deflected slapshot and had to leave the game to get stitches, he grinned and said to me, "That's the first time in my life I ever blocked a shot."

But I never made fun of him in print. I have always considered him to be the greatest player in hockey history. I have heard all the arguments made on behalf of other candidates, and as I respect every one of those guys, I will not enter into a debate on the matter because such debates always end up in a recitation of shortcomings.

If other people want to see Gordie Howe or Mario Lemieux or Bobby Orr as the greatest ever, that's fine. A case can be made for every one of them.

But my own choice is Gretzky, and I've never made any secret of it. Because we had come to know each other, he made sure that he read my columns and he liked what he saw, not only in what I wrote about him but also in what I wrote about hockey.

Not long after the 1981 tournament, we were on a long charter flight together for some reason. He came and sat beside me for what I initially assumed was just a brief courtesy visit. But he stayed for the entire flight and it transpired that we agreed not only about hockey, but about many other things in life as well. A firm friendship was formed.

I was very fortunate in that the *Globe and Mail* sent me all over the continent covering hockey, and as a result, whenever I encountered Gretzky, I had lots of hockey gossip to pass along. He loved that because he had become a prisoner of his fame. If he went out, he would be mobbed, so he spent a lot of time talking on the phone to his friends in hockey. The primary currency in those conversations was inside information.

Wayne and I became close friends. He would often phone just to chat, and likewise, I would phone him when I had learned something I thought might interest him. There were no cellphones in those days, but he always made sure that I had his most recent private numbers and knew what alias he would be using to register at a hotel.

If we were in the same town, we would invariably go out for dinner on the off-nights. On game nights, we would meet for a beer or two afterwards.

When he left Edmonton in 1988, we drifted apart somewhat. For one thing, he got married, and like everyone else in those circumstances, he altered his lifestyle. Janet is a wonderful lady, and we get along famously, but it stands to reason that when you're a married man with children, the relationships you had as a bachelor get altered.

Another factor in the change was that he was no longer based in Canada. Both the *Globe and Mail* and subsequently the *Toronto Sun*, which I joined in 1994, focused on Canadian teams more than American teams.

For the rest of his career, we maintained a close relationship and spent time together when our paths crossed, but nonetheless, it must be conceded that the calls were no longer as frequent.

Even so, whenever I needed to talk to him, he was available, and there were occasions when we saw each other on a daily basis for extended periods—the Scandinavian goodwill tour in 1994, for instance, and during a number of playoff series in which he was participating. Because my editors knew that Wayne and I were good friends, I was invariably assigned to the series in which he was playing.

To this day, we still talk regularly, and when it came time to finalize this book in 2013, we spoke at length about his career.

The book was intended to be much shorter than it is, but with so much material at hand, it was impossible to keep it at the prescribed length. There are still some leftovers that simply wouldn't fit, but I feel safe in saying that this book contains thousands of pieces of information about Wayne Gretzky that you didn't know and an equal number of his quotes that you have never heard before.

There are even some that he says he had forgotten about.

CHAPTER ONE

More than a decade after Wayne Gretzky's 1999 retirement as an active player, there is still a gaping hole in hockey.

The National Hockey League continues to feature skilled players, and there are even those—Sidney Crosby comes to mind—who may eventually do as much for the game as Gretzky did over the years.

But Gretzky, despite his most common nickname, was much more than great. He was magnificent. His feats are legendary. When he retired, he held no fewer than sixty-one NHL records, most of which stand today and some of which will stand for at least our lifetimes. Perhaps they will last forever, and hockey will move on to a "modern era" in which the Gretzky standard is set aside as unattainable.

Gretzky holds every offensive record worth holding. He won ten scoring titles. He won the Hart Trophy as the most valuable player in the league nine times and twice won the Conn Smythe Trophy as playoff MVP. He also won the Lady Byng Trophy five times, was a first-team all-star eight times and a second-team all-star seven times. He was on four Stanley Cup–winning teams.

He not only broke records, he shattered them, so much so that even *Sports Illustrated,* a magazine that for a number of years was notorious for its anti-hockey stance, had to concede he was the most dominant athlete ever—in any sport.

Today, and for the foreseeable future, the fifty-goal season is a rarity. Gretzky once scored fifty goals in the first thirty-nine games of the season.

Today, a 100-point season is the benchmark of excellence. Gretzky had a 215-point season and a 212-point season. Only four times has an NHL player cracked the 200-point barrier. It was Gretzky all four times.

But there is so much more to Wayne Gretzky than his hockey skills, superb though they were. Anyone who knows him always makes the same observation: no matter how great he might have been as a hockey player, he is every bit as great as a human being.

You could ask Jean Anderson, for instance. Just hours before Gretzky announced his retirement in New York—a hectic time in his life, to say the least—he called Jean's husband, the Brantford, Ontario, sports broadcaster Arnold Anderson.

Arnold Anderson was the first person to conduct a radio interview with Gretzky, a ten-year-old hockey prodigy at the time. Gretzky called to wish him well as he battled cancer. "That says something about the man—on a day like today that he would call," said Jean. "We were moved."

On that same weekend, I was wandering around Madison Square Garden and a security guard volunteered the information that when he was at his previous post, he'd had access to the players and had mentioned to Gretzky that he would like a stick. He was transferred to a different post where players did not normally go, but Gretzky sought him out and gave him a stick.

I told that story to Gretzky's former coach and general manager, Glen Sather. He was not surprised and said that one of his fondest memories of Gretzky, still a teenager, was that he had insisted that Joey Moss, who has Down syndrome, be hired as a clubhouse attendant in Edmonton. "Here was something he could do to help a young guy," Sather said. "He turned Joey's whole life around. That was seventeen or eighteen years ago. That kid still is around and he even signs autographs. I have millions of memories of Wayne, and they aren't so much what he did on the ice as what he did off the ice."

Long after he had been traded away from the Oilers, Gretzky continued to buy a season ticket to Oilers games for Moss, who otherwise would have had to stay in the dressing room and watch the game on television—if it was televised. (In 2012, Joey Moss was awarded the Queen Elizabeth II Diamond Jubilee Medal.)

When Gretzky was traded to the Los Angeles Kings in 1988, the opening game was seventy tickets short of being a sellout. Gretzky bought the seventy tickets and donated them to an orphanage. That information came from team owner Bruce McNall. Gretzky never mentioned it.

During the late stages of his playing career, Gretzky lived in a gated community just north of Los Angeles. One day when I arrived for a pre-arranged meeting, the guard at the massive electronic gate was unfailingly polite but firm. He explained that he would be glad to admit me as soon as he had called Gretzky and obtained clearance. He said he hoped I understood, but it was his job to make sure that only welcome visitors are allowed in, and he intended to do his job.

"I'm sorry, sir," he said, "I can't let you in until Mr. Gretzky calls. I might do it for some people, but Mr. Gretzky is the nicest person in this entire community and I wouldn't want to do anything to upset him."

Throughout his career, Gretzky gave away approximately seven hundred sticks a year, which he paid for himself. He signed approximately two hundred autographs a day. His large dining-room table is usually covered with all kinds of memorabilia that fans, his personal assistant, his father, Walter, charities and so on have sent for him to sign. Every time he goes past the table, he'll sign ten or so, then continue on to wherever he was going.

"I don't know what my dad does with all of them," he told me once. "I think he must stand down on the street corner, asking if anybody wants one." When we were chatting in 2013, I reminded him of that and he laughed.

"Nothing has changed," he said. "I just sent him a box of about a thousand that I signed over a two-week period and I stuck in a note saying, 'Happy Father's Day.'

"He'll call and he'll say, 'I don't have any pictures,' and I'll say, 'I just sent you five hundred or a thousand. What do you mean, you don't have any?'

"'Well, they go fast,' he says."

Even though Gretzky no longer plays, his father still loves hockey and Wayne makes sure he can see games in person.

"I get him two season tickets to the Leafs," Gretzky said, "and I think he goes to 90 per cent of the games. He goes down to the restaurant before the games and he says hello to everybody and then he goes to the game. He loves it. It keeps him young. It's actually really good for him. He's an interested NHL fan. He doesn't really root for one team or another, but he still likes to see the players."

In an era when sports stars are known for their arrogance and their disdain for their fans, not to mention their criminal lifestyles in too many cases, Gretzky always exceeded every expectation—in a positive sense. For years, even though he was recognized as the greatest hockey player in the world, he did interviews in every city on the NHL circuit. Naturally enough, he was always the one the local TV rights-holder wanted to talk to between periods. He would stand patiently in front of microphones and cameras, answering questions and promoting hockey, often in areas where the game badly needed promoting. He never skipped a morning skate, even on those rare occasions when he didn't go on the ice, because he knew that no matter what might be happening in hockey that day, the media would be looking for his perspective.

He spent his entire professional career—two decades as an active player—in the harshest of spotlights, and there was never once a justified hint of impropriety on his part. There were no suspensions, no court cases, not even a temper tantrum. The so-called "scandal" regarding his involvement in a betting ring that came after his playing career had concluded was a 100-per-cent fabrication, 90 per cent of it created by the media, the other 10 per cent by NHL commissioner Gary Bettman.

Instead, Gretzky's magnificent career is studded with honours, awards and adulation—Hart Trophies, Art Ross Trophies, Lady Byng Trophies, Conn Smythe Trophies and Stanley Cups, followed by the inevitable Hall of Fame induction. He is the only player in NHL history to be so esteemed that the league retired his number. No NHL player will ever again wear the famous 99.

In 1998, when he was thirty-seven and feeling his age a bit, he turned down an opportunity to play in the world championship, the annual tournament in which Canada competes using players whose NHL teams are out of the playoffs. But until then, on every single occasion for nineteen years, Gretzky answered every call to play for his country. He never was too busy to play for Canada in Canada Cups or the World Cup or the Olympics. He never was too tired to make the transatlantic trip to play in earlier editions of the world championships. He never developed mysterious back or groin ailments that prevented him from participating in all-star games.

In 1994, the first of the three hockey seasons curtailed by a Bettman-imposed lockout, he organized a European barnstorming tour that caused mob scenes wherever it went in Scandinavia and Germany, raising the NHL's profile accordingly.

He even had a hand in the Stanley Cup triumphs of the Dallas Stars, Carolina Hurricanes, Anaheim Mighty Ducks and Tampa Bay Lightning. Were it not for Gretzky, it is almost certain that the NHL would not be established throughout the American Sunbelt.

Even the Los Angeles Kings, Stanley Cup winners in 2012, might not exist. Before Gretzky arrived in L.A. in 1988 and made the Kings the darlings of the southern California sporting scene, the team had filed for bankruptcy. There was considerable speculation that the Kings would either fold or move.

But Los Angeles is the glitter capital of the world, and when Gretzky arrived on the scene and was embraced by all the beautiful people, he brought hockey the California acceptance it had long coveted. In turn, the Los Angeles media machine trumpeted the Kings' success, thereby making NHL expansion into other locales in the southern United States a viable proposition. In a more direct example of Gretzky's impact, Michael Eisner, the head of the Walt Disney Company, spurred by his son's adulation of the Kings and Gretzky, had Walt Disney Studios make the movie *The Mighty Ducks*. Then Eisner bought an expansion franchise for Anaheim and named the team after the film.

About the only criticism of Gretzky to surface regularly is that he is too revered by the media. It's a strange criticism. Why is it wrong to consistently praise someone who rightly, and equally consistently, deserves it? It is easy to be negative, but if the critics were able to come up with one single serious flaw exhibited by Gretzky in his life, then their arguments might be taken seriously.

Where has he gone wrong? He was not only an outstanding hockey player, he is also an outstanding Canadian. He was instrumental in getting the 2010 Olympics for Vancouver, partly because wherever he has gone, he has represented his country with grace, dignity and eloquence. If spreading the truth about a great man is somehow unacceptable, then there is something tragically wrong with the media business. If there has ever been a superstar who is as thoughtful, personable and humble, he has not come to the attention of people who cover sports today.

Someday, far down the road, there may be another player who can match Wayne Gretzky's achievements. But there almost certainly will never be another player who can match his achievements and do it with his class.

CHAPTER TWO

I n North American sports, the great players sooner or later find their way to New York. Hollywood makes the movies, but New York makes the news. So it was only fitting that Wayne Gretzky would end his career with the Rangers.

He had done Hollywood with the Los Angeles Kings and, in the process, changed the face of the National Hockey League.

Now he would do New York.

It was to be a three-year stint, the winding down of a glorious career, and even though this period wasn't as productive as earlier stretches, it was perhaps the most eventful. He was embraced by the notoriously fickle New York fans; he was reunited with his buddy Mark Messier; he suffered an injury that appeared to be serious enough to put a premature end to his career; and finally, despite the pleas of family and friends, he decided that it was time to retire.

When he arrived in New York in 1996, he was thirty-five, and indisputably no longer what he had been in his best days. He was still a dominant player and among the league's top point-getters, but when you've been head and shoulders above everyone else in the world, merely being one of the best is cause for introspection.

He was still the league's reigning statesman, the ultimate authority on all things related to hockey. He was the one who was sought out for an opinion whenever a contentious issue surfaced—which it often did in the NHL. It was his presence in Los Angeles that had convinced entrepreneurs of the merits of hockey and had, as a result, spawned NHL franchises throughout the American Sunbelt.

Gretzky's idol had always been Gordie Howe, the man known as Mr. Hockey. But Howe had earned that title in an earlier era. Now, as the twentieth century neared its end, Wayne Gretzky had become Mr. Hockey to fans all over the world. He had set record after record, not merely edging past the previous mark but leaving it in the dust. He was a child prodigy who, unlike many such youngsters, had lived up to his billing as an adult. In fact, he had not only fulfilled all early expectations of him, he had surpassed them.

Yet in 1996–97 incredible though it may seem, he started to lose confidence in his ability. Halfway through his first season with the Rangers, after having been laid low for a while with a particularly virulent strain of flu, he said, "I don't think there's an athlete in the world that plays at the top of their game who has not had a problem with their confidence level at some point. When I came here, I was nervous. If you hear it enough and see it enough, that people don't think you can play, subconsciously, you may start to believe it."

The funk didn't last long. A few chats with Messier restored his confidence, and his switch back to a wooden stick—a Hespeler—helped him regain his touch. Also, travel with the Rangers, whose divisional rivals were all nearby, was such a breeze that he was usually well rested.

For most of his days with the Oilers, Gretzky had flown on commercial flights. To avoid being pestered, he would sit in the window seat in the last row and either sleep or pretend to do so. The Kings had their own plane, but because of their location in southwestern California, the players often felt that the only way to rack up more air miles was to be an astronaut.

Once he settled in, Gretzky enjoyed New York. He lived in an apartment at Madison Avenue and 63rd Street, within easy reach of the best that Manhattan has to offer—the fine restaurants, the theatres, the museums and all the other attractions.

The proprietor of a friendly nearby delicatessen reserved a booth for Gretzky, and most mornings he'd drop in for breakfast in relative anonymity. The booth was hidden from street view, and usually he was able to eat without being disturbed. Occasionally, a fan would engage him in a chat—which he didn't mind—but he was never mobbed.

"New Yorkers are great," he said as we were having our deli breakfast not long after he had joined the Rangers. "Out on the street, they'll recognize me and they'll usually shout or say something, but then they just go on their way. There are lots of celebrities in New York, so they don't get too excited."

Even so, the New York experience was never quite what Gretzky had hoped it would be. After the first year, Messier left for a windfall contract in Vancouver. The Canucks' management tried to atone for the mistakes they'd made a year earlier when they failed to sign Gretzky by offering Messier a fantastic deal. It was so good that he collected his final payment—which was based on an appreciation in the team's value—in 2012.

Without Messier or a comparable replacement, the Rangers missed the playoffs the next year, which didn't please Gretzky in the least. But it was in the third year that his hockey world started to crumble. The Rangers were playing some of the best hockey of his tenure, but for a full month, he was on the sidelines with a serious back injury.

It was the second major back injury of his career. The other had been caused when Gary Suter ran him into the boards during a Canada Cup game, and he was out of action for half of the 1992–93 season.

The latest back injury was unrelated. "The one in L.A. was a T6 [vertebra]," Gretzky explained. "This is a C5. This is more upper back, lower neck. It's a different part of the back."

This one was also different in that it wasn't the result of one specific check. It was the result of repeated abuse. Throughout Gretzky's career, a goal scorer often received a cross-check in the back when he raised his arms in celebration. This was so much the norm that when one of Gretzky's teammates, Craig Simpson, asked for a penalty to be assessed, the referee said, "What are you complaining about? You scored, didn't you?"

Gretzky's back had been bothering him for a long time, but in typical hockey fashion, he had done his best to play through the pain. Finally, in late February 1999, he could do so no longer and had to come out of the lineup.

"Yeah, that's why I'm mad at myself," he said after watching from the sidelines for three weeks. "I didn't get it checked. I had it all year and I didn't know it. I would have missed games then, and not now."

The Rangers had climbed back into the playoff hunt while Gretzky was out of action, and naturally enough, he would have loved to have been a part of it.

"Depressing?" he said, repeating a question I had put to him. "It's the worst—especially now our team is playing so well.

"It hit me about once a month, for about a six- or seven-day cycle," he said. "My neck and the right side of my body were really sore. I just thought it was one of those things. You know when you get a good night's sleep but maybe sleep on it wrong and get a stiff neck? That's what I thought I had. We played in Edmonton on a Sunday (February 21), and I got up Sunday morning and I couldn't move the right side of my body. I almost didn't play in Edmonton, but I said, 'Jeez, I've got to play here.' So we just heated it all day Sunday and Monday [before that night's game in Calgary], but both games, I had to play with one arm because I couldn't move the right side of my body."

Two days later, in New York the problem was worse than ever. Gretzky approached coach John Muckler and said, "John, I can't even hold my stick. I had better get this checked."

The team doctors put him on a three-stage plan. "I was on an oral anti-inflammatory for two weeks," he said. "That was the first step. That was the plan all along. The team went away, and I couldn't do anything anyway, so I went to Florida."

But when he came back in mid-March, tests showed that there had been no improvement. At that point, the medical staff gave him a steroid injection. Despite the general bad name that steroids have in the sporting world, in this case they were administered by a team physician and certainly weren't intended to be performance-enhancing, but rather, performance-enabling. They were meant to get Gretzky back in the lineup.

"It's a steroid that they hope will eat away at the inflammation," said Gretzky after the first injection. "Now I have to wait until next Tuesday, and if I still have the same kind of symptoms, I get another shot. I guess you can do these shots three times over three weeks."

Despite being in constant pain, he hadn't lost his sense of humour. "If it doesn't take after three weeks," he said, "then I guess we're on to Plan C—and I don't know what Plan C is.

"Hopefully, these shots will work. The doctor says he has had worse cases that the shots have worked on, and he has had easier cases where it hasn't taken, so we don't know."

As it happened, two steroid injections did the job and Gretzky came back, but not before he had missed a month of action and twelve games.

To Gretzky, it was clear that his career was coming to an end. First, there was no guarantee that the pain would not return. Second, the person he most trusted to evaluate his playing skills—his father, Walter—wasn't saying much. He knew that his son was harbouring thoughts of retirement, and he wasn't ready to push him in that direction. Wayne, however, was acutely aware that, although the great hockey mind was still there, his body could no longer be counted on to do what it was told.

As the schedule wound down and the Rangers' playoff hopes slipped further and further away, there was increased speculation that this season would be Gretzky's last, even though he was still the Rangers' leading scorer. And whenever he had a chance to play with top-flight talent, his own skills became even more visible. At the All-Star Game two months earlier, he had been named the most valuable player.

With five days left in the season, the speculation ended. Larry Brooks and I—in the *New York Post* and *Toronto Sun* respectively—announced that Gretzky would retire after the final game, a Sunday afternoon affair in New York.

Gretzky himself stopped just short of confirming the news because he had promised the Rangers that the official announcement would be made in New York, and the team was on the road. But he did not deny the published stories.

On the Thursday night, the Rangers played in Ottawa, Gretzky's last road game and his last game in Canada. Earlier in the day, we had exchanged a few words, and as so many others had done, I told him I'd be sad to see him go.

"Don't you try to talk me out of it, too," he said with a smile. "I spent two days fighting off Janet and Barney." (Janet is his wife and Barney was his agent, Mike Barnett.)

He said the decision was not based on any animosity toward the Rangers, who had offered him the opportunity to be traded to any team in the league if he preferred to continue his career elsewhere. The wear and tear, however, had become too great. He admitted he was still bothered by the injured C5 vertebra in his neck and was planning to have at least one more steroid injection in the summer because he still had trouble turning his head.

Even so, the Ottawa fans clearly wanted him to reconsider.

"Just one more year, Wayne," read a banner hung on the wall outside the Rangers' hotel.

The Corel Centre staff working the visitors' dressing room had used white tape to affix a simple message to the front of their shirts: "NO."

The rabid pro-Senators crowd recognized that they were witnessing a momentous event and applauded the announcement of Gretzky's name in the starting lineup. They applauded again when he won the opening faceoff, although, as usual, it didn't look as though his opponent, Alexei Yashin, was trying very hard. The fans also cheered when the scoreboard flashed an image of Gretzky sitting on the bench and a recording of Tina Turner's "Simply the Best" was played.

With a little less than five minutes remaining in the game, the fans broke into a chant of "One more year! One more year!" Then, with Carly Simon's "Nobody Does It Better" booming from the speakers, the fans gave Gretzky a thunderous ovation.

After the game ended in a 2–2 tie, Ottawa's Igor Kravchuk skated over and asked Gretzky for his stick—and got it. All the other Ottawa Senators skated over to shake his hand. The crowd clapped and cheered like a concert audience awaiting an encore. Janet was at the game, as were Gretzky's three children—Paulina, Ty and Trevor—and seeing the adulation from the fans, Janet broke into tears. Before long, the boys joined her. Gretzky came out to acknowledge his selection as the game's "only star"—the usual three-star selection was put on hold for the occasion. Then, because the ovation continued, he came back to do another quick turn on the ice in front of the bench.

The crowd was still not content. The ovation continued. Eventually, Gretzky came out for his third curtain call. By this time, he had taken off his skates, so he simply stood on the players' bench and waved to the crowd.

"When I went back out for the third time, I got kind of emotional," he said, "because that was the first time it really hit me. Before that, it was in the back of my mind. Now it was real."

Next came a nationally televised news conference, which followed the usual Gretzky formula. His minders announced that only two more questions would be allowed, but Gretzky kept answering them as long as the media wanted to ask them.

"I didn't expect this kind of response from everyone to say, 'One more year, one more time.' It has been tremendous," he said after the game. "It has been a fun day. I even talked to the prime minister, which was very nice. He encouraged me to come back, too."

Even then, Gretzky didn't make his retirement official. But he came close. "I really feel right about which way I'm leaning," he said. "At this point in time I haven't heard anything that has swayed me a lot. I thought about this for a long time.

"I told Gordie Howe (who played in the NHL at fifty-two) that his records were safe unless a miracle happens in the morning, and I'll probably make it official." He did. The next day, at a press conference in New York, Gretzky summed up the situation in the simplest of terms.

"I'm done," he said.

There was still one game remaining in the Rangers' schedule, the Sunday-afternoon affair against the Pittsburgh Penguins, but after that, Gretzky's remarkable career would be over.

"Probably, that will be the emotional time for me," he speculated, "when I take my skates off. Up to this point, I've been pretty calm. I've been encouraging people to smile and to be upbeat, people around me, my teammates. But that will be the tough part."

In essence, the decision to retire was a gut reaction. He always had an uncanny ability to sense the moment on the ice, and with that same prescience, he sensed that this was the moment to end his career.

We will never know if he was right or wrong. We will never know if he could have come back with the Rangers or another team the following season, had a 100-point season and won a Stanley Cup. On the other hand, what if he had come back and suffered a serious injury? Millions of people would have been asking, "Why did he do it? Why didn't he quit when he was ahead? He stayed around too long!"

The fans might not have known the answer to this conundrum, but Gretzky did. "My heart is telling me this is the right time," he said. "I don't think there's ever going to be a day that goes by that you don't love the sport and love the game. And as I said to Janet yesterday, a year from now, I could be in the exact same situation with everyone saying, 'Just go one more year. You can still play.'

"I'm at peace of mind. It's the right decision. This is the right time. This was not something that was decided in a week."

And although he would never say it on the record, there's no doubt that he wasn't terribly happy about winding down his career playing for a team that couldn't capitalize on his remaining skills. During the season, the Rangers had tried to acquire Pavel Bure but couldn't pull off the deal. Had they done so, Gretzky would almost certainly have played another year. There were even times when his natural ebullience had seemed to be fading, something that had never happened in his younger days.

The losses mounted, as did the number of hits he had to absorb. The game had become more of a grind for him. Every summer, he had to work harder to get ready for training camp. In the previous few years, a personal trainer had kept him in shape during the off-season, and while his dedication to the game never wavered, he found it increasingly difficult to return to the level of conditioning he had exhibited the previous season.

So after some pensive, solitary moments in darkened hotel rooms and some quiet discussions with friends who were sworn to secrecy, he made the decision to retire.

We were reminiscing on the day he announced his retirement, and he said, "I wanted to leave the game with everyone saying, 'He could have played one more year.' I know I could have played one more year."

There were some sad moments. The loss in the Nagano Olympics had hit him hard, and he had been sure he would earn another Stanley Cup ring when the Los Angeles Kings appeared to be in control of the final series against the Montreal Canadiens in 1993.

But most of his memories were happy ones, a reflection of a long, productive career that is unmatched in hockey history.

He laughed about playing in the World Hockey Association in a Minnesota rink that had transparent glass boards that made life miserable for goalies who often lost sight of incoming shots.

He remembered the old Calgary Corral, where the Flames played when they moved north from Atlanta. It had a two-tier bench, the rear one about four feet higher than the front one. One time, he had just returned to the bench when Dave Semenko, on the upper bench, yelled, "Hey Gretz, come up here quick." Gretzky climbed up and said, "What is it, Sammy?"

"Nothing," said Semenko. "I just wanted you to have to make this climb for once." Because Gretzky was so often double-shifted, he had never been on the upper bench.

His greatest goal, he thought, was the one he scored to win an over-time game against the Calgary Flames in the 1988 playoffs, a few weeks before Edmonton Oilers owner Peter Pocklington sold him to the Kings.

But the greatest goal didn't come in what he considers to be his greatest game. In his greatest game, he didn't score at all.

"That was the second game of the 1987 Canada Cup series," he said. "That was the best game I ever played in my life."

With his final NHL game being an afternoon start, the team's usual morning skate was forsaken. But there was still a regular practice on Saturday, and it turned out to be one more emotional moment in a highly emotional week.

He got to the Rangers' suburban practice rink earlier than usual, two hours before the 11 a.m. practice. He always enjoyed everything about the game, even the practices, and for his last one, he wanted extra time to savour the moment.

He participated enthusiastically, as always, but when it was over, Muckler suggested he hadn't worked hard enough. The coach told every-body else on the team they could leave the ice, but ordered Gretzky to do some extra skating—red line to blue line, red line to red line, then red line to blue line again.

Gretzky just laughed. "Screw you, Muck," he said. "I retire."

Then the players gathered on the ice for a team picture. An on-ice photograph was a tradition started by the Edmonton Oilers when Gretzky led them to their first Stanley Cup in 1984. On-ice team shots of non-playoff teams were far from the norm.

"We're going to do it again tomorrow after the game," Gretzky chuckled later. "It might be the only time a team gets its team picture taken on the ice without a Stanley Cup in the middle of it."

Up to that point, Gretzky's final practice had been everything he had hoped it would be. But then, the mood became a bit more sombre.

"I was good when I woke up," Gretzky said. "I was fine. But in the room, after the practice, Brian Leetch gave a great speech. It was pretty emotional. I was overwhelmed. When Brian gave that speech, that's when I kind of caved."

"Caved" was a euphemism for saying the battle to hold back the tears was finally lost.

"It was such an emotional speech," Gretzky said, "that I had to slip back to the trainers' room."

When he returned, his teammates presented him with a "Steinbrenner chair"—a large overstuffed leather armchair in the shape of a baseball glove. (There had been a good deal of publicity in New York when Yankees owner George Steinbrenner had got such a chair, and Gretzky had mentioned he would like one. His teammates took him at his word.) The trainers made a contribution as well, giving him a gold-plated lifetime pass for two to any major-league baseball game.

"It was surprising," Gretzky said. "I didn't expect any gifts. I had a great day, but it was really emotional."

After that, he did a series of interviews, mostly for television, and met with various team officials to discuss the retirement ceremonies. By the time he was able to leave the rink, it was after 4 p.m. That made it a seven-hour practice.

The retirement game itself did not amount to much. With the Rangers already eliminated from the playoffs, the fans just wanted to get the game finished and say goodbye to Gretzky.

Gretzky himself felt uncomfortable. The Penguins wanted a win that could improve their playoff position, but they knew it was Gretzky's day. Out of respect, they didn't want to hit him or even hinder him more than was absolutely necessary. He, in turn, was aware of what they were doing, but he wanted to play well for his fans without taking advantage of the Penguins' generosity.

He got an assist on the Rangers' only goal of the afternoon, but Pittsburgh's Jaromir Jagr scored the winner in overtime. Jagr, who also had a sense of occasion, embraced Gretzky and said, "I didn't mean to do that."

Gretzky laughed and told him, "That's what I used to say."

As Gretzky did lap after lap around the rink, the crowd cheered lustily. Photographs of those victory laps are still among the most coveted souvenirs of his career.

"My dad uses that picture for more charity events than any other picture," said Gretzky in 2012. "They get five hundred to eight hundred dollars at tournaments and stuff for that picture autographed." Naturally, he still signs as many copies as his dad wants.

With the post-game celebrations, his speech to his teammates, and some television interviews, it was more than an hour after the game ended when Gretzky, still wearing his Rangers jersey, held his final media conference as an NHL player. He admitted he had found it difficult to play the game, but managed to keep his emotions under control until well into the final minute of regulation time, when Muckler called a time-out.

"He's got a daughter who was about to give birth in Edmonton," Gretzky said. "I came over, and he said, 'I want to tell you something.'

"I said, 'What?'

"He said, 'I just had a grandson today and you've got to get the winner.'

"Maybe when I was younger, I might have got that winner for him. I didn't get it today, and I know it's the right time to retire."

Even so, he admitted, "It's going to kill me not to play. But time does something to you, and it's time. I feel really confident about my decision. I haven't wavered once in seven days."

Much later—in 2008, to be exact—Gretzky revealed that the day of his retirement was his greatest day in hockey. My friend Scott Morrison was writing a book in which players talked about their greatest days in hockey, and Gretzky was making a business swing through southern Ontario. One of the stops was at a golf course that was hosting the tournament he sponsored, and he suggested Morrison and I meet him for lunch.

With just the three of us sitting at an outdoor table on a beautiful Ontario day, we tried to get him to blow off the afternoon and come golfing with us—for the comedy value if nothing else. He was tempted, but as usual, he stuck to his commitments. When Morrison asked him about his greatest day in hockey, we were surprised at the response. We had expected that he would talk about some of his great games or some of his great achievements, but he didn't.

"I would say my last game in New York was my greatest day in hockey," he said. "I knew that would stump a few people, but I thought about it a lot. Everything you enjoy about the sport of hockey as a kid— driving to the practice with Mom and Dad, driving to the game with Mom and Dad, looking in the stands and seeing your mom and your dad and your friends—that all came together in that last game in New York.

"My dad and I hadn't driven to a rink in years and years, but we drove to the rink together that morning. It was sort of the same conversation on the way to that game as it was when I was eight years old. Make sure you work hard. Make sure you backcheck. I'm sitting there going, 'Wow.'

"It was an emotional day for me to be able to look up into the stands and see my mom and my dad, my family and friends. As an emotional day, that was the greatest day of my life. It put the ribbon on my career, pulled it all together. I knew then there was no difference between playing as an eight-year-old and going to a game and being a professional hockey player at thirty-eight and playing your last game. The feeling was still the same. The excitement was still the same. The relationship with your family was still the same. The game itself was the same. The only difference is I wasn't quite as good as I used to be. That's what I remember the most.

"I had no second thoughts that day about retiring. I wasn't scared of retiring from the game of hockey and the practices and everything that goes with hockey.

"What I knew was that I was completely done with preparing for a season—three or four hours a day of getting ready to be physically ready to go in September. I knew I wasn't mentally ready to do that any more, and that's why I never had any second thoughts.

"The last thing my dad said to me when we got to the rink—I think his exact words were, 'You know, I'd really like to watch you play one more year.' And I was, 'Whoa!' That was the most pressure I felt. You know, because he was a fan like everyone else and he was a big fan of mine, he didn't want me to retire, and I think it hurt him more than anyone else.

"But I was ready. I got nine goals that year. That was it. Nine goals. That's what I got the last year.

"On the drive home, my dad was pretty down about it, so he didn't press it again, but I knew it was time and, like I said, I had no regrets. I remember sitting on the bench with thirty seconds left in regulation, and John Muckler called a time-out. I'm thinking, 'I've got thirty seconds to go.' But that day just brought it full circle for me."

CHAPTER THREE

Late one night in 1995, after a Los Angeles Kings home game, Wayne and I were wandering through his garage, on the way into his Encino house for a post-game beer or two, when I spotted a trophy on a shelf alongside some household tools and cardboard boxes. It was a neat little thing, about six inches high and clearly a quality object and a replica of a larger trophy.

"What's that?" I asked.

"Oh, that's the Campbell Conference Trophy," said Gretzky. "They give you one of those if you get to the Stanley Cup final."

I suggested that the garage was a strange place to keep a championship trophy.

"It's a second-place trophy," said Gretzky. "It means we didn't win the Cup. That's why it's in the garage."

Second place has never meant much to Wayne Gretzky, even if you're talking about second place in the best hockey league in the world. He hides it well behind a calm demeanour, but when it comes to hockey, he has always been driven.

If you ask him about his superstar skills, he'll usually say that he wasn't born with them. He'll say that those skills were learned, not inherited. That's his modesty coming through. But if pressed a bit, he will admit that his father, Walter, had a different view. "I can remember my dad telling me that the Good Lord had blessed me with something special," he said. And we all know that, deep down, Wayne Gretzky very rarely disagrees with the opinions of Walter Gretzky.

So which is it? Was Wayne born with God-given skills that made his hockey stardom a matter of predestination? Or was he just an ordinary kid who tried a game and loved it so much that he became its best player in history?

It would be nice to be able to answer those questions with certainty, but there is no clear answer.

Even though Walter at times leaned towards the God-given theory, he also recognized the impact of teaching. "My dad always said that kids can be taught how to anticipate what's going to happen on the ice," Wayne said. "And he always said that kids can be taught to handle pressure.

"He says that he really believes that I learned it all. He doesn't believe that I had it handed to me on a silver platter."

In other words, even Walter Gretzky, the world's leading authority on the talents of Wayne Gretzky, espouses different theories at different times.

Wayne himself concedes that he always loved to skate, but he was not one of those people who felt gifted the first time he was exposed to his sport. When he was learning to skate, he fell down as often as every other child who finds himself in that situation. But after each fall, he'd get up and go back at it, determined not to fall again—which, inevitably, he did. Still, he never gave up. He says it was this dedicated approach that took him to the top.

Yet the more you look at Gretzky's phenomenal achievements over the years, the more it becomes evident that the reason for his greatness goes beyond mere determination. There's no doubt that Wayne worked hard and spent a lot of time on the fabled backyard rink that Walter built for him in Brantford—Wally's Coliseum, as the family called it. "The guy who had the yard behind us had about six hundred pucks in his back yard from shots that I missed," recollected Gretzky with a laugh.

But lots of kids work hard, and they don't do what Gretzky did.

In a sport where a fifty-goal season is considered excellent, he had a fifty-goal weekend. Granted, it was a long weekend and he was in a hockey tournament, but even so, fifty goals in four days is an astonishing achievement.

He was thirty months old when he started skating, and he played on his first organized team when he was six. It was a team of ten-year-olds, and Gretzky made the cut as a five-year-old. But when the organizers learned he was only five, they told him he was ineligible. They did, however, let him play the next year.

That was his first season in organized hockey. He got one goal. In his second year, he got 27. In his third year, he got 104 goals and 63 assists in 62 games. In his fourth year, he got 196 goals and 120 assists in 76 games. In his fifth year, he got 378 goals and 120 assists in 72 games.

If you're going from one goal to 378 in the space of five seasons, you're doing it with a lot more than just hard work. If mere hard work were the answer, every one of the NHL's six Sutter brothers would have scored 300 goals every year he was in the league.

It should also be noted that throughout the developmental phase of his hockey career, Gretzky was always playing against kids who were older than him—up to six years older. Most NHL players have birthdays in the early months of the year because, when they were growing up and being selected for rep teams, an extra few months often made a significant difference in development. Gretzky has the ideal hockey birth month—January—but having a few extra months on his side made no difference. He was giving away *years*.

As most people know, that's why he tucked in one corner of his sweater. The rest of the kids on the team were always bigger, so to avoid having his sweater around his ankles, he would tuck in one corner.

Years later, when Nike paid vast amounts of money to have NHL teams use their sweaters, they were horrified to learn that the side of the jersey that featured their trademark swoosh was the side that Gretzky tucked into his pants. They redesigned the sweaters and moved the swoosh.

Like many youngsters, Gretzky worked to develop his hockey skills, but it appears to be his mental approach to the game that set him apart. First of all, at every stage of his life, he was determined to succeed in his chosen field. But he also had an intuitive sense about the game, an awareness that can't be taught.

Coach Mike Keenan saw it firsthand during the 1987 Canada Cup when his team was playing against the United States.

"Wayne was just so incredible," he said. "It was in Hamilton and the building is full and everybody is cheering and he was coming down the ice in the neutral zone on the far side from our bench. He was going down the boards as fast as he can, and all of a sudden, he just makes a ninety-degree turn at the red line to the referee and says, 'They've got too many men on the ice.'

"Sure enough, they did. There wasn't one person in the whole building who knew it, but he did. I got the sense that he knew where all his friends were sitting in the building as well. That was scary, but that's how perceptive he was."

Gretzky's good friend and longtime teammate Paul Coffey had no doubt Keenan's recollection was accurate.

"I saw him do that umpteen times during games with Edmonton," he said long after both of them had retired. "He'd be skating down the ice and yelling at the ref, and I'd say, 'What the hell is he yelling about?'

"He'd be going down the ice with the puck, yelling, 'Too many men on the ice. Too many men on the ice.'"

That was the factual part. Then Coffey started laughing and added the bit that has become part of the standard embellishment as the story grew over the years. "He'd say, 'I've just gone around five guys. I'm going around my sixth . . .'" Gretzky and I talked about that faculty during a chat in 2013, and I mentioned his ability to both evaluate players and recall all the aspects of every game. "I could pick that up pretty quickly," he agreed. "I was like Scott Bowman. I could remember every player in the game."

Then he laughed and said, "Now I can't remember anything in life, but I can still remember everything that happened in a hockey game. My wife tells me that I'm supposed to pick up some milk on the way home and I forget, but I can remember everything about hockey."

His uncanny ability not only to know where everyone was on the ice, but to be able to recall it has often been demonstrated. When he started with the Oilers, videotape equipment was expensive, so the Oilers didn't have any. Most games weren't televised, so the team couldn't get a tape from the broadcaster.

If the Oilers' coaching staff was mulling over a botched play from the night before, coach Glen Sather would go to Gretzky and get him to describe where everyone had been on the ice at the time things went wrong.

"If you ever stop and talk to him about a game, he can recall every play," Sather said. "He could tell me not only where everybody on our team was on the ice at any time, he could tell you where everybody on the other team was on the ice. He always knew. He was like a human video-tape machine."

Gretzky laughed when I mentioned Sather's observations to him. "It was fear," he said. "I was always the smallest kid on the ice. I wanted to know where everyone was so that I could stay away from them. People say I've got great peripheral vision. It's just awareness. I was always so much smaller than everyone else, I had to be alert."

Let's face it, hockey—more so then than now—is riddled with headhunters. As long as Gretzky played, there was never any shortage of opponents who were quite willing to take him out using illegal tactics.

Whether we like it or not, physical violence is part of hockey's heritage, even at the highest level. Bobby Clarke's premeditated slash that broke Valeri Kharlamov's ankle in the 1972 Summit Series is a prime example.

During the 1994 NHL lockout, there were whispers that some players might break union ranks and play for replacement teams. "They can do it if they want," said NHL Players' Association vice-president Ken Baumgartner, who had been a teammate of Gretzky's, "but the rest of us will be back someday and they should remember that hockey is a game which lends itself well to retribution."

Anyone who understands hockey accepts that intimidation is part of the game. Hockey is a physical sport, and to many of us, that is one of its attractions. But unfortunately, the level of violence often exceeds reasonable bounds, and that is why Gretzky had to stay alert. It is not an exaggeration to say that if he had not done so, he would never have made it to the NHL. The injuries would have taken too great a toll.

Steve Ludzik saw it first-hand. With the exception of Gretzky's immediate family, there are few people who had more direct involvement with Gretzky's hockey development than Ludzik. He too was born in 1961. They were ten when they first faced each other, playing with mostly twelve-year-olds, and two years later, they participated in the same Quebec Pee-Wee Tournament, although their teams didn't play each other. Both graduated to the NHL, where, during his six years with the Chicago Blackhawks, Ludzik was usually assigned the job of trying to keep Gretzky under control.

"We first played against each other on March 17, 1971," recalled Ludzik. "It was a hockey tournament in Brockville, and I played for a team called Jack's Pack. We were the cream of the crop in Toronto and lost just one game in two years. We had heard of this kid from Brantford who had scored three hundred goals or something, but that was before the internet or videotape, so we figured it was just some kid playing against really weak teams and getting inflated numbers—if it was even true.

"We thought this had to be a bunch of BS about this guy scoring all these goals. I was looking forward to it because I always liked to compete, and I thought I could give him a good go because we were a good team, and I was sure I could skate as fast as him."

Gretzky was playing for the Nadrofsky Steelers, and in those days, he wore number 9 because it was the number worn by his hero, Gordie Howe. He also wore white gloves and used four wraps of white tape on his Koho stick. He didn't use any tape around the butt end, which was unusual, but Gretzky had played a lot of lacrosse and was accustomed to a stick with no tape on the shaft.

Even though Gretzky was only ten, he had already developed a following and the arena was packed.

"I remember he got hit by a guy on our team named Bob Patterson," recalled Ludzik. "He blasted Gretzky right at centre ice. I don't know if he lost any teeth or not, but he shook himself off, got the puck, and he had this look of determination about him.

"He zigzagged through the whole team, and to put emphasis on it, he went by Bob Patterson twice until he fell down. He went around him once, then came back around and beat him again. He went in and out, and put so many moves on our goalie—east-west, north-south and head fakes—that the poor goalie wound up in the corner of the rink and Gretzky just slid the puck in. He had an empty net by the time he finished with everybody.

"People don't understand that Gretzky would play forward, then when he got tired, he'd go back and play defence. If you look at programs from that year, Gretzky is listed as a defenceman. . . . He'd play the entire sixty minutes."

Jack's Pack beat the Steelers 4–3. Gretzky scored all three of his team's goals.

"I tell people he was emotional after the game," said Ludzik, "but the real story is he was crying because he had never lost that year. They were unbeatable. He was really upset, and people were sticking microphones and TV cameras in his face, and flashbulbs were going off.

"I wanted to go over to him and say, 'Man, you're game.' There were three thousand people in that building watching a ten-year-old kid play against twelve-year-olds and we were a better team. That's why we won. We were from Toronto and he was from the little town of Brantford. He put on an unbelievable display. I can remember it like it was yesterday. I just stood there and said, 'Wow.'

"I remember jumping on the ice with my teammates when we won the game. I really wanted to go back to touch Gretzky and tap him on the pads and say, 'You're the real thing,' but I didn't do it because, being a ten-year-old kid, that wasn't cool.

"I always regret not having done that. I remember coming home, and my dad had cut out a picture of him that had been in the paper, and my dad said, 'That's the greatest player that's ever going to play. You watch. This kid is going to be great.'"

The next time Ludzik encountered Gretzky, they were in the 1973 Quebec Pee-Wee Tournament. By that time, Ludzik had made a uniform adjustment.

"I was a smaller guy as well," he said, "and I used to tuck my sweater in, too, because I didn't want anybody grabbing on to my sweater, but once I saw that Gretzky was doing it, I said, 'I can't tuck my sweater in now.' That's how kids think."

Even though he kept it to himself, Ludzik was enthralled by Gretzky and, while they were in Quebec, watched him play as much as he could. Once again, he was in awe. "At one point, he killed an entire two-minute penalty by himself," recalled Ludzik, "just zigging and zagging and weaving back and forth. For some reason, the crowd booed.

"One game he played against a team from Dallas, Texas. I think the score was 20–1 and Gretzky scored, I've got to say, fifteen goals. After the game, he had to motor to get off the Quebec Colisée ice because people were trying to pull his stick out of his hand and pull his gloves off his hands."

In fact, all the sticks Gretzky had taken to that tournament got stolen by souvenir hunters—even the one that was entrusted to a security guard while Gretzky did an interview—and Walter had to go out and buy some more.

"He ate in the mess hall with a thousand of us," said Ludzik, "but he couldn't even get his supper down because he spent so much time signing autographs."

When Ludzik got to the NHL, he had to treat Gretzky like any other opponent. "I checked him all the time, and I tried to get under his skin," Ludzik said. "It was fun to play against him. I'd try to pin him against the boards and he'd say something like, 'You've got the wrong guy, meathead.'

"When we played in Edmonton I'd take that train that goes from near the hotel and get out to the arena early for the Oilers' morning skate because I was just mesmerized by Gretzky's skills. I used to just love to watch him.

"All along, people had been saying, 'He's too skinny . . . he's scared . . . he can't skate . . . he can't shoot.' I always say he's the greatest player ever because he wasn't strong. As a matter of fact, he was kind of weak. He wasn't fast. He was just an average skater. His shot wasn't that great. He wasn't quick. There was no one thing you could point at and say, 'That's what makes him great.' But he could put it all together like nobody else ever could. He had the heart of a lion."

Gretzky will admit that, away from hockey, he's not a particularly competitive person. But for as long as he can remember, he knew he would never be satisfied with merely getting to the NHL. He wanted more. Much more.

"I've always had this feeling that I didn't want to be known as just a hockey player," he told me when he was only twenty-two. "I never wanted to be known as just a guy who played hockey and you read in the papers that he scored a goal last night or got an assist or got into a fight. It had to be more than that.

"A lot of hockey players have had the opportunity that I've had. Some of them have carried it through like Gordie Howe did, but there have been other people who have said, 'Hey, this is great. Tomorrow I don't have to practise.'

"What happens is that when they start losing their hockey skills and they're not playing well, they lose the other part, the fringe benefits, the fun of travel, the meeting people. When you forget that, you're in big trouble.

"I'm not stupid. I don't get invited to go on TV shows and do charity work because I'm a nice guy. I get invited because of my name in hockey and what I've done the last three or four years. When I stop doing that, I probably won't get all those invitations.

"Not everybody forgets, but a lot of people do. It's a cruel world out there."

Wayne's father, Walter, was—and still is—his idol. Alan Thicke, another Canadian who had made a name for himself in American entertainment circles, was also a mentor to the young Gretzky. These two helped give him the proper grounding in life.

"Alan and my father have made me aware that the reason I get to meet all these people and the reason that I'm fortunate enough to live the life that I live and travel to the places I travel to, is because of what I do on the ice," he said.

"If I stop performing on the ice, all that stuff is going to slip away."

At that point, he was three years into his NHL career, but his hockey career had existed for most of his life. He did his first newspaper interview when he was nine, and the headline on the story was "Hull, Richard, Howe and Gretzky." It sounds like a reasonable quartet today, but at the time, three of those names belonged to hockey legends and the fourth was a nine-year-old kid.

By the time he was thirteen, he was a poised teenager doing a half-hour interview with Peter Gzowski on the CBC.

He arrived in Edmonton to join the Oilers when the team was still in the World Hockey Association and he was too young to be allowed to play in the NHL. Dick Chubey and Jim Matheson, the hockey beat writers for the two Edmonton daily newspapers, interviewed him at the airport, and Chubey was astonished by the poise and eloquence of this skinny teenager. At the end of interview, he congratulated Gretzky on the way he had handled it.

"Well you've got to remember," said the seventeen-year-old, "I've been doing it for almost ten years."

Gretzky could have played professional hockey when he was fifteen. "My first offer was from Jack Kelley with the New England Whalers," he told me in 2013. "He offered me a $25,000 signing bonus, then $50,000 a year for three years, and then $150,000 a year for four years. He said he couldn't justify paying me more than $50,000 the first three years because I could still be playing junior and making $20 a week."

More offers were to come. "I played in the world junior tournament in Montreal when I was sixteen," he said. "I was really lucky because somebody got injured so they put me on the team. On Christmas Day, when we played the Czechs, I had three goals and three assists. The next day, John Bassett was in Montreal and offered me a two-year deal at $80,000 a year to play in Birmingham right then and there."

Bassett was the owner of a World Hockey Association franchise that had been the Toronto Toros. He moved the team to Birmingham, Alabama, where it became the Bulls, and later, perhaps expanding on the idea that had its nucleus with the Gretzky offer, built a team that became known as the Baby Bulls. It featured a number of players who were too young to play in the NHL, including Michel Goulet, Craig Hartsburg, Rob Ramage and Rick Vaive.

Gretzky was enthralled with the offer. "I would have signed right then and there," he said, "but my old man said, 'You're going back to school.'"

The next year, he went to the Indianapolis Racers. "Nelson Skalbania came along and the offer was $250,000 to sign and then $100,000. Then $175,000 a year for three years, and then a four-year option at $200,000 a year. We never got to that. The $250,000 was the big selling point."

Being only seventeen, Gretzky needed his father to handle the money, and Walter kept everything in perspective. After agreeing to the $250,000 signing bonus, a veritable fortune for a teenager in 1978,

Wayne told Walter he wanted to buy a car. Walter gave Wayne a cheque for $5,000. "You can go and get whatever you want," said Walter.

"That's $5,000," said Wayne. "Where's the other $245,000?"

"In the bank and that's where it's going to stay."

Wayne didn't want his father to think he was extravagant and bought a used Pontiac Trans-Am for $3,800. When he got to the NHL and started shattering records, his approach to life didn't waver.

"The big concern was if the league folded," said Gretzky in 2013. "If it folded, where was I going to play? The NHL was so against young players, and was I good enough to play in the NHL? I couldn't go back to junior, so my dad really wanted to make sure I was financially taken care of, just in case after one year, I had nowhere to play. It would have been a problem. I would have had to go to Europe and play in Sweden or Switzerland for two years.

"After I signed, I asked him to lend me some money because I had no money in my pocket. He said, 'Here's a hundred. I know you're good for it now.'"

"Walter Gretzky helped Wayne," said Ludzik. "There's no question about that. There's no question that he taught him certain things and helped him deal with things that came up. But hockey players like Gretzky, Gordie Howe, Bobby Orr, that's a God-given talent that comes along about once every fifty years.

"He makes you proud that you were a hockey player, and he makes you proud you played in his era. He was the man. He was Mickey Mantle. He was Joe DiMaggio. He was Babe Ruth. He was everything rolled into one. I enjoyed playing against him, and I felt honoured just to talk to him."

CHAPTER FOUR

On January 26, 1982, Gretzky was finally able to go into an American bar for a post-game beer. Being as concerned about his reputation as he was, he would never have taken a chance by entering a bar underage, but this was his twenty-first birthday.

By then, he was in his third NHL season, shattering records night after night, and well on his way to setting an NHL mark for most points in a season (212, a record that fell four years later when he racked up 215).

A few weeks earlier, he had just finished scoring fifty goals in the first thirty-nine games of the season. The previous record for the fastest fifty goals, held by Maurice Richard and Mike Bossy, was fifty games.

By the end of the month, Gretzky was almost certain to surpass the NHL record of most goals in a season—seventy-six, by Phil Esposito in 1970–71—and in fact finished the season with ninety-two.

But when the media brought the Gretzky birthday to the nation's attention, the reaction to his brilliance was astonishingly negative. In Brazil, Pele had been declared a national treasure by virtue of his brilliance on the soccer field. In Canada, hockey fans, many of whom were in the media, tried to outdo each other in pointing out Gretzky's shortcomings. Being a national treasure was nowhere in the picture.

Granted, some of the criticism came from the United States. Stan Fischler, an American hockey writer who had christened himself the "Hockey Maven," insisted in *The Hockey News* (a Canadian publication) that until Gretzky had been smashed into the boards a few times by defencemen in the mould of the legendary Black Jack Stewart, his records were suspect, and he could not be considered to be a great player.

Stewart was certainly a tough player in his day. But since he couldn't skate backwards, it was not likely he would have managed to come within ten feet of Gretzky. It's hard to crunch anyone into the boards from ten feet away. It was an astonishingly stupid remark, but certainly not unique.

Many Canadians, of course, were upset that Gretzky was highly paid. Canadians rarely like to see anyone get a lot of money, especially other Canadians. The problem with that line of thought was that it overlooked a major point: Gretzky was highly paid because wherever he went, buildings sold out. That meant the owners of those teams pulled in a great deal of money—much more than Gretzky was getting. But the fans tended to focus only on Gretzky.

Gretzky was also criticized because he hadn't singlehandedly defeated the Soviets in the 1981 Canada Cup. The Canadians lost the final game of that series 8–1, and only eight more goals from Gretzky could have changed the outcome. How could he be called great if he couldn't even contribute that much?

Two criticisms of Gretzky were even sillier than those already mentioned. Nevertheless, they were repeated relentlessly in the media and wherever hockey fans congregated.

The first was that he was shattering records because the league was so watered down.

Why anyone would consider the league to be watered down at that point was never made sufficiently clear. The World Hockey Association had been absorbed into the NHL three years earlier, so the competition for NHL jobs was tougher than ever. Talented Europeans were starting to come into the league and even Americans were fighting for NHL spots.

But even if one were gullible enough to accept the watered-down theory, why wasn't the league diluted for other stars, like Bossy, Peter Stastny and Marcel Dionne? Why weren't they, as veterans, destroying all the long-established records the same way that this twenty-one-year-old was?

Furthermore, when the WHA teams were absorbed, they were allowed to protect only two skaters and two goalies. The rest were either reclaimed by the NHL teams that held their rights or went into a dispersal draft. As a result, the Oilers as a team were not particularly strong.

When Phil Esposito set his scoring record, he had the likes of Bobby Orr, Ken Hodge and John Bucyk to contribute to his cause. Bossy had Bryan Trottier, Denis Potvin and Clark Gillies. Guy Lafleur had Steve Shutt and Jacques Lemaire, not to mention a host of other players who made up what was the most dominant team in NHL history.

And Gretzky? It's true that Glenn Anderson, Paul Coffey and Mark Messier were on that 1981–82 team, but they were still a long way from their peak years. In fact, they rounded out the top four in Edmonton Oilers' scoring that year, but Gretzky outpaced them by 107, 123 and 124 points respectively.

And if the league was so watered down, why was Gretzky sixty-five points ahead of Bossy, the second-leading scorer, when the season ended? In all the years that the NHL had been in existence, the biggest margin between the scoring champion and the runner-up had been twenty-three points. Gretzky almost tripled that.

But an even sillier suggestion, one that I had to dispute regularly on the call-in radio show I hosted around that time, was that there was a secret league edict forbidding any checking of Gretzky.

Astonishingly, that theory exists to this day. It defies all logic, and its adherents are on a par with those who believe that the earth is flat, that Elvis Presley is still alive or that the end of the world is imminent. But those people existed in 1982 and they exist now.

Their argument is that the NHL wanted to get more attention, and to do so, it needed someone to dominate scoring and break all the meaningful records. Gretzky was deemed to be the man, and in order to facilitate his quest, the league commanded all its players to leave him alone.

Well, that would definitely do the job, wouldn't it? After all, no NHL player has ever ignored a league edict about violence.

There's also the matter of the coaching fraternity, not a group known for shouldering the blame if it can be shunted somewhere else. Isn't it a stretch to believe that a coach who just lost a playoff series—and perhaps his job—because Gretzky ran rampant would not mention in the post-game press conference that his team would have done better if they'd been allowed to check Gretzky?

Thousands of players came and went in the NHL during the course of Gretzky's career. The likelihood of such a major secret being kept by so many people for so long, particularly when it was no longer in their interest to do so, simply defies belief.

In the later stages of his career, Gretzky was one of the league's elder statesmen, and he had established himself as a player who did not run opponents, did not use his stick as a weapon, did not take cheap shots and did not fight. By that time, no one took a run at him. Similarly, they did not take a run at Steve Yzerman, Joe Sakic, Ron Francis, Adam Oates, Mike Modano and a host of others. But it had nothing to do with any secret edict. It was simply an adherence to the accepted code of conduct in the NHL.

In the earlier stages of his career, before Gretzky became an elder statesman, opponents did not take a run at him for two reasons. One was Dave Semenko; the other was Marty McSorley.

Because of those two players, the league definitely had a no-hit edict for Gretzky, but it certainly wasn't secret, and the punishment wouldn't come from the NHL head office.

"At the first sign that anybody might be thinking of going after him," said McSorley, "I'd skate over in front of their bench and say, 'Guys, that's not going to happen tonight. If anybody thinks it is, come on over right now and we'll talk about it.'

"That usually put an end to it," said McSorley, "but I always let them know that I didn't care about suspensions. I'd tell them, 'You go after Gretz and you're going to get hurt. You may get hurt so bad that I'll get suspended, but I don't care. You should, though.'"

Semenko didn't talk as much as McSorley. He preferred a stony— and scary—glare to get the message across, but he had the same mindset. When it came to hitting Gretzky, there was to be zero tolerance.

"I don't take any credit for any of Gretz's records," said McSorley. "He set them all, and he's the greatest player the game has ever seen. But I like to think that I helped to make sure that he was able to show everybody what he could do.

"I didn't do anything to set all those records. I just made sure he was left alone to set them."

Another one of Gretzky's teammates in Los Angeles, Ken Baumgartner, offered the memorable observation, mentioned earlier, that "hockey is a game which lends itself very well to retribution." That was the way the tough guys on Gretzky's teams thought in those earlier years. Those who hit Gretzky, or even indicated that they might be planning to hit Gretzky, were subject to the NHL's own particular brand of retribution.

It had nothing to do with a secret no-hit edict.

CHAPTER FIVE

For some reason, perhaps because of the notoriety the concept gained in the Soviet Union, hockey general managers like to build their strategies along the lines of five-year plans. Ask any incoming general manager about his hopes for the team that he has just taken over, and he'll almost certainly say that he envisions a Stanley Cup within five years.

But history shows that it's a Herculean task, and even more so when you start as a "merger team." That's why the achievement of the young Gretzky-led Oilers cannot be underestimated. The Oilers' road to their first Stanley Cup had its potholes and even some washouts. To go from being a "merger team" with a skeletal roster to Stanley Cup champion in five years was nothing short of magnificent.

For those fortunate enough to be unfamiliar with the idiosyncrasies of the National Hockey League governors and the legal battalion that guides their actions, a merger team was basically an expansion team—but with even less chance of success.

When the NHL merged with the World Hockey Association in time for the 1979–80 season, four WHA teams—Quebec Nordiques, New England Whalers, Winnipeg Jets and Edmonton Oilers—entered the NHL.

The NHL wanted to eliminate the competition from the WHA without getting hammered with an antitrust suit—which, in the United States, pays triple damages to the wronged party. To reach its goal, the NHL had to "expand." The arrangement was basically a merger, but the lawyers, being lawyers, didn't allow it to be called that. By the time the merger was effected, the WHA had shrunk from twelve franchises to six. Four of them were sucked into the black hole of NHL expansion, and the other two were left out in the cold.

But teams coming in from the WHA weren't allowed to simply bring along their WHA rosters. They were permitted to protect only two skaters and two goaltenders. The rest were reclaimed by the NHL teams that held their rights—if they wanted them—or tossed into a pool to be picked off at random, not only by the four incoming teams, but also by the seventeen existing NHL teams.

Naturally enough, the Oilers protected Wayne Gretzky. They missed out on their second priority selection of Bengt-Ake Gustafsson because the Washington Capitals claimed he belonged to them, and NHL president John Ziegler, to no one's surprise, ruled in their favour. The Oilers kept goaltenders Dave Dryden (the less-talented brother of the illustrious Ken) and Eddie Mio, whose obscurity was such that one NHL GM, upon reading the typewritten protected list, remarked about his curious surname, which he read as M 10.

Those three players were the base upon which the Oilers were to be built. From that point on, they were on their own.

It was a delightful turn of events for Gretzky, despite the fact that when he signed with the WHA's Indianapolis Racers at the age of seventeen, he had given up any thought of ever playing in the NHL. "I was fine with the WHA," he said years later. "When I signed, I never thought I was going to play in the NHL. I fully anticipated playing my whole career in the WHA."

At the time, his only real interest was the playing side of hockey, not the politics behind the game. Had he been the keen student of the sport that he later (but not much later) became, he would have realized that the future of the WHA, with its shaky financial base, its second-rate arenas, its shifting franchises and its inability to capture major markets, was extremely limited.

But his agent at the time, Gus Badali, recognized the value of the NHL over the WHA. When Nelson Skalbania, the Racers' cash-strapped owner (those who remember the WHA will recognize the redundancy of that description) decided to sell Gretzky, Badali chose Edmonton over Winnipeg because he knew that Edmonton had a new arena and there-fore had the better chance of getting an NHL franchise.

To make life even more difficult for the incoming WHA teams, the NHL governors decided to reverse the protocol for the entry draft. Instead of following the procedure used in all the other expansions that had occurred as the league grew from six to seventeen teams over the previous twelve years, this time the new teams would draft last. That meant that the teams coming in from the WHA could select no earlier than eighteenth.

As it happened, by the luck of the draw, the Oilers were last. With the twenty-first pick overall, they chose Kevin Lowe. With the forty-eighth pick, they chose Mark Messier. With the sixty-ninth pick, they chose Glenn Anderson. Not a bad start.

The next year, they drafted Paul Coffey, and the year after that, Grant Fuhr. The building blocks of the dynasty were in place.

At first, it didn't look much like a dynasty. With the exception of a couple of grizzled veterans, the team looked more like a bunch of kids on a school outing. The pre-game ritual was road hockey—or as near to it as they could come. While fans were streaming into their high-priced seats in anticipation of a battle of hockey's best professionals, the Oilers were running around in their underwear under the stands using a "puck" made from a rolled-up sock wrapped in hockey tape and trying to score on the backup nets that NHL arenas keep near the Zamboni entrance.

Instead of yelling "Car!" when their scrimmage had to be interrupted, they yelled, "Game!"—and went into the dressing room, put on their skates and uniforms, and went out onto the ice for the pre-game warmup.

Gretzky was an immediate success in the NHL. In his first season, he tied Marcel Dionne of the Los Angeles Kings for the scoring championship, but since Dionne had more goals, he was declared the winner of the Art Ross Trophy, and Gretzky the runner-up.

However, knowledgeable hockey people contend that a video review of the 1979–80 season would produce a considerably different tally— that Gretzky would outscore Dionne by ten or more points. Playing in Los Angeles in front of the league's lowest attendance, Dionne is believed to have been awarded assists that he did not deserve, whereas Gretzky, playing most of his games in Canada, got only the points he had legitimately earned. Neither team had many games televised in those days, so there aren't sufficient videotapes to prove either point. Whether Gretzky did or did not deserve the 1980 Art Ross Trophy will never be known.

At the time, Gretzky's many fans were upset, but he wasn't. "That one never bothered me," he said long after he retired. "The only thing I ever questioned was that I thought that they should change the rule so that it doesn't happen again. There will be times again when two guys are tied and they should both get their name on the trophy.

"It didn't bother me. I got ten others. I got my share. But it might be a guy who never gets a chance again."

Gretzky's 137 points gave him the single-season record for a first-year player, but in a decision that was typical of the lunacy that came out of the NHL head office in those days (yes, even more so than today), it was determined that since he had played in the WHA as a seventeen-year-old, he was not an NHL rookie—even though he was ineligible to play in the NHL during his WHA tenure. NHL rules require a player to be eighteen.

The league did concede that Gretzky's fifty-one-goal debut season made him the youngest player to crack the fifty-goal barrier, but it did not give him the rookie record. Similarly, Gretzky's eighty-six assists represent the highest total ever for a first-year player, but the NHL record for a rookie—the definition of which is, of course, a first-year player—is shared by two players who had seventy assists: Peter Stastny (who was twenty-five at the time and had played professionally in Europe) and Joe Juneau.

The official NHL record for most points by a rookie is 132, held by Teemu Selanne, who came to the NHL after fulfilling his military commitments in Finland and was twenty-two.

Today's NHL governors could overturn those earlier rulings if they wanted to. After all, it's just a matter of a change in the record book—a change that would compensate for the lack of common sense on the part of their predecessors.

It was a monumentally stupid decision to make an eighteen-year-old first-year player ineligible for rookie awards, but the NHL has always taken a cavalier approach to its record book. That's why there are never any asterisks, even though, thanks to Commissioner Gary Bettman's propensity for locking out the players on a regular basis, the circumstances under which records are set are in a constant state of flux.

Gretzky didn't let the NHL's idiosyncrasies inhibit his assault on the record book. Two years after becoming the most dominant rookie in league history—no matter what the league's definition of "rookie" might be—he set a record that may never be broken, the one that he now looks upon most fondly. He scored fifty goals in the first thirty-nine games of the season.

"People often ask me about my favourite record," Gretzky said in 2013, "and I tell them that that's the one. I know that records are made to be broken, and that's one of the attractions of sport, but I think that one will be the hardest to break."

Gretzky was already the dominant player in the game by the time of that accomplishment, even though he was only twenty. He had tied (at least) for one scoring title, run away with a second, and was off to another hot start. Going into the December 30, 1981, game against the Philadelphia Flyers, he had forty-five goals in thirty-eight games and already, the coveted fifty-goal target was in his sights.

"I felt sure that I was going to get fifty in fifty," he said, "but I didn't think I was going to get to fifty that night. You don't go into a game thinking you're going to get five, but I did feel that if I got an early goal, I could get two or three and then be really close to fifty."

At that time, the Flyers were a strong defensive team, and their goalie, Pete Peeters, was one of the league's best. Although the Edmonton fans were always optimistic about Gretzky's chances, it seemed likely that he'd have to wait until 1982 to break the record.

"I did get an early goal, and it was kind of fluky," Gretzky recalled in 2006, the twenty-fifth anniversary of the feat. "The puck took a strange bounce off the boards and came right to me. Pete Peeters hadn't expected it, and all I had to do was put it on the net. The strange thing is that if I'd been really sharp, I could probably have had eight or nine goals that night. After I got the fourth and was at forty-nine, I had about three or four really great chances, and each time, I thought I was going to get the fiftieth, but Peeters made great saves.

"Once I got the fourth, I was sure I was going to hit fifty that night, but then, as the game went on, I was starting to wonder."

Despite all the attention being paid to Gretzky and his record, there was still a game going on. In the last minute, the Oilers led 6–5 and, naturally, the Flyers pulled Peeters for an extra attacker. The Oilers were in their own end when the puck came to Gretzky on the right side. With the Flyers pressing for a goal, they were using a forward, Bill Barber, on the left point. A defenceman might have been able to stop Gretzky, but Barber had no chance.

Gretzky gathered up the puck and roared into the middle of the ice as Barber tried to keep up and block him, but to no avail. Gretzky gained the blue line with Barber still unable to get in front of him and slid the puck into the empty net. Fifty goals in thirty-nine games!

Maurice Richard had been the first to score fifty goals in a season when he did it in fifty games in 1944–45, but with so many NHL stars serving with the Canadian forces in the Second World War, the level of competition was not what it might have been.

The only other player who had scored fifty goals in fifty games was Mike Bossy of the New York Islanders. He did it in 1979 on a powerful team that in the subsequent season started its run of four consecutive Stanley Cups.

But Gretzky scored fifty goals in thirty-nine games on a team that was in only its third year in the NHL and was stocked with kids and cast-offs. Furthermore, although few people realize it now, the ice in the Northlands Coliseum, where Gretzky played half his games, was horrible. Later on, to make sure that his stars could exhibit their skills fully, Sather got the ice upgraded, but in the early years, in an attempt to save money, the Northlands management insisted that the old, inferior system remain in place. Gretzky and his mates were forever fighting bouncing pucks.

The hockey world duly took notice of Gretzky's fast fifty, but by that time, his amazing performances were becoming almost common-place. In his second year in the league, he had broken the single-season point record that had been held by Phil Esposito. He also broke Bobby Orr's single-season assist record. He was clearly on his way to breaking Esposito's record of seventy-six goals in a season. As it happened, he ended up with ninety-two and added 120 assists, thereby becoming the first NHL player to crack the two-hundred-point barrier in a season.

Over the course of his career, Gretzky had four seasons with more than two hundred points. No other player has ever reached two hundred.

Gretzky's phenomenal achievements instilled confidence in his teammates—perhaps too much confidence. The Oilers gained a reputation as a brash, cocky team. In many ways, they deserved that reputation. Gretzky himself was never arrogant or cocksure. He worked hard not to appear to belittle his opponents, but not everyone followed his example.

It was understandable. The old veterans who had made up much of the original expansion team had been replaced. Now the team was composed mostly of youngsters who, partly because of their NHL status and partly because of their intimate association with Gretzky's feats, were idolized wherever they went. Swelled heads were inevitable.

How many of us can say that, at that age, in that situation, we would be any different?

Coach Glen Sather did an excellent job of keeping the young players more or less in line. He developed a close association with the Edmonton police department so that misdemeanours that might embarrass the team could be cleared up and hidden from the media. He also developed a tame media corps so that if a reporter did stumble upon a story, he could probably be convinced to keep it to himself.

It must be made clear that in this area, Gretzky, who was always meticulous about maintaining an immaculate reputation, gave Sather no trouble. There were no hidden stories involving Gretzky's misbehaviour because there was no Gretzky misbehaviour.

Most of the time, he ate dinner at home—often with Mark Messier, who, for four years, lived in the same apartment building. When Gretzky went out for dinner and had a drink, he never drove. Whenever he was out in public, he always made sure there was someone around who could corroborate his side of the story, should there be an accusation that he had done something wrong. From the beginning, he has been acutely aware that he is always in the public eye and therefore in the media spotlight. He also knows that if the media latch on to a story that becomes a case of one person's word against another, the allegation never goes away, even if it is later proved to be unfounded.

In trying to keep his young team under control, Sather was always walking a tightrope. On the one hand, he wanted to convince them that they could take no opponent lightly, but at the same time, he was trying to instill a swagger that gave them enough confidence to win the Stanley Cup. In sports, when the matchup involves boys against men, the boys rarely win.

After all, while Gretzky's records were admirable and the players were having a great time running up big scores, the Stanley Cup was still the goal.

After only three seasons of existence, the Oilers finished second in the regular-season standings and appeared to be well on their way to that coveted Cup. The much-heralded five-year concept appeared to have been a far too pessimistic projection.

But the road to the Stanley Cup is not a freeway. It is a bumpy, grinding, demanding track. The Oilers had learned a lot of lessons about regular-season play, but as Gretzky pointed out much later in life, "I always say that there are four NHL seasons every year. First, there's the exhibition season. Next comes the regular season, which is a lot tougher. Then there's the playoffs, which are played at a whole different level. Then comes the finals, and that's another thing altogether."

In 1982, Gretzky hadn't learned that lesson. He was about to.

By the time the playoffs opened that year, the Oilers had emerged as Canada's team. The Toronto Maple Leafs and Montreal Canadiens still had fervent followers from coast to coast, but the Oilers were the darlings of fans whose allegiances weren't as deeply ingrained, a whole new wave of followers.

There was no official survey to prove this point, but those of us who bounced around the country covering hockey in all its venues couldn't help but notice that in the shopping centres, in the schoolyards and on the streets, there were more of the blue-orange-and-white Oilers sweaters than any other kind.

The country was going through difficult economic times in 1982, and for adults, the Oilers provided a brief escape from reality. For youngsters, the Oilers were a team with dash and flair—the new kids on the block to whom the next generation could relate.

Much of this, of course, had to do with Gretzky. The Oilers were led by a born-and-bred, truly Canadian superstar whose image was squeaky clean and whose record-shattering performances were so remarkable that they almost appeared to be the stuff of fiction.

The rest of the Oilers, for the most part, were a group of kids who not only played the game with speed and grace, but clearly were delighting themselves in the process. They roared around the arenas of the National Hockey League scoring more than five goals a night on average and showing such exuberance that there was no doubt that they were having great fun.

They hadn't been in the league long enough to get involved in the peripheral issues. Fans heard only about the Edmonton players, not their agents, their lawyers or their accountants.

There was no hint of dissension, and often Sather's biggest problem at practice was that the players were fooling around too much. They did their usual hockey drills but also liked to stage contests amongst themselves. Who could shoot a puck that would knock a rolling puck off the dasher board? Who could shoot from centre ice and hit the crossbar? Who could balance a stick vertically on his nose the longest?

By virtue of their second-place finish, the Oilers were to open the playoffs at home with a best-of-five series against the fifteenth-place Los Angeles Kings. The Oilers had lost five games at home all season. The Kings had won only five road games.

The Oilers were thirty-one games over .500. The Kings were seventeen games under. The Oilers had earned 111 points, the Kings sixty-three.

The series started off exactly as expected. The Kings tried to intimidate the Oilers, a strategy which resulted in their being down 4–1 before the game was ten minutes old. To that point, the Oilers had made the Kings pay for their transgressions and remained poised.

Suddenly, that poise and discipline disappeared. Although the Oilers could hardly have foreseen it at the time, that was the high point of the series for them. Sather made tactical errors; the players ignored the game plan; the confidence that had served the team so well in the regular season and made them believe they could score enough goals to compensate for mistakes backfired. Even Gretzky had a bad series.

Not long after the Oilers built that early lead, Dave Semenko made an awful play, and Sather benched him. Sitting down your toughest player in a game where the opponents have clearly shown an inclination towards intimidation is a questionable strategy. "That was the best thing he could have done for us," chuckled star forward Charlie Simmer of the Kings afterwards.

Over the course of the game, Los Angeles scored four power-play goals and was up 9–8 late in the third period. It was not exactly a demonstration of the tight playoff hockey for which the NHL is known. Then Gretzky caught the contagion of ineptitude. He had a clean breakaway with ninety seconds left but flubbed the shot, dribbling the puck towards goaltender Mario Lessard. An empty-netter made the final score 10–8.

In Game Two, the Oilers gave every indication that they had learned their lesson. This time, they did everything a playoff team should do. The intensity was there. The goaltending was sound. The discipline was unparalleled. Even though the Kings were playing inspired hockey, Gretzky gave the Oilers a 3–2 victory in overtime.

The series moved to Los Angeles, where the Oilers went right for the jugular and rolled to a 5–0 lead after two periods. Kings owner Dr. Jerry Buss went home claiming he didn't feel well.

Los Angeles forward Dave Taylor didn't blame him. "I wouldn't feel too well, either, if my team was down 5–0 after two periods," he said.

But Buss missed the team's greatest moment under his ownership: the famed Miracle on Manchester, named after the street on which the Fabulous Forum was located.

Even L.A. coach Don Perry hadn't expected what was to come. "I just told them to go out and play like it was 0–0," he said. "Play a good period and maybe it would carry over to the next game. I never thought we could win. I've never seen anything like this in all my years of hockey."

What he saw was a five-goal outburst by the Kings, the fifth coming with five seconds left in regulation time after Gretzky, of all people, lost control of the puck deep in his own end. Then, in the overtime, the Kings needed only 2:35 to win it on a goal by Daryl Evans.

Gretzky scored twice and added two assists in the 6–5 loss but saw himself as one of the culprits. "It was stupid hockey," he said. "Wasn't it bad enough that we killed so many penalties in the first two periods without being stupid enough to take more? We were stupid enough to think it wouldn't catch up to us. It did.

"This series should be over now. We blew a 4–1 lead in Game One and a 5–0 lead tonight. We should be catching the plane home now instead of going into Game Four with our backs against the wall.

"Now there are five or six of us who are a game away from having to go to Europe [to play for Team Canada in the world championships] instead of being two series away from the Stanley Cup final."

For all their flash and glitz, the Oilers had not learned to deal with playoff hockey. Even today, the referees tend to be lenient in the post-season, but at that time, the lone referee ignored incidents that would have earned penalties in February. In playoff overtime, nothing short of an axe murder would earn a penalty.

The Kings were clearly trying to intimidate the Oilers, but instead of shrugging off the infractions and waiting for power plays that would inevitably come—although perhaps not as often as they might have liked—the Oilers retaliated.

Of the five goals the Kings scored in that fateful third period, two were scored while the teams were playing four on four and two were on the power play.

Gretzky, unused to such treatment, had fallen prey to the tactic like everyone else. He had taken thirteen minors in the entire eighty-game season, but had four in the three playoff games.

The Los Angeles players were trash talking. They told him he was gutless because he wouldn't get involved in the many scrums. They told him he was a crybaby. They told him he was spoiled. Jay Wells, the Kings defence-man designated to neutralize Gretzky, was especially caustic. "He thinks he's too good to do anything but score," he told the media after one game.

When the jostling started, the Forum fans tended to join in with their chant of "Kill Gretzky! Kill Gretzky!"

But Gretzky was doing what Sather had demanded. On one occasion in Game Three, nine players charged into a melee. All were given penalties ranging from five minutes to the duration of the game. Gretzky stayed out and was not penalized.

When I asked Gretzky if he wanted to respond to Wells, he said he didn't. "Jay Wells is a nobody," he said, which seemed a pretty good response from somebody who wasn't responding. "I just go out and do my job on the ice, and hopefully, he'll do his job, whatever his job is."

The Oilers won the fourth game, but they were no longer the confident, swaggering kids who had steamrolled the NHL in the regular season. They were playing desperate hockey, a concept that, prior to the playoffs, had been foreign territory. Instead of being loose, they were tight. Instead of playing with confidence, they were playing scared, getting rattled, and, as a result, taking stupid penalties.

They took an ill-advised penalty early in the deciding game, and the Kings went in front. The Oilers came back but took yet another stupid penalty, and the Kings scored again. This time, they stayed in front, and the Oilers, the prohibitive favourites, the darlings of Canadian hockey, were out of the playoffs. Gretzky and a few of his teammates were heading to Europe.

The only bright side was that valuable lessons had been learned. After three years, the Oilers had started to progress down the four-stage path to the Stanley Cup that Gretzky had spelled out: exhibition hockey, regular-season hockey, playoff hockey and Cup final hockey.

The exhibition season didn't really matter, although throughout his career, Gretzky played in every game because he knew that fans had paid to see him, even if it was the preseason.

When I asked him about that in 2013, he chortled. "Strach, every year I played fourteen exhibition games," he said. Players of Gretzky's calibre usually play no more than six exhibition games. "One year, we went to the Stanley Cup finals—we beat Philly that year in seven games. I played in the Canada Cup—beat the Russians in three games, and Slats gave us four days off, and then I played in twelve exhibition games. Then we went to the Stanley Cup finals again that year and beat Boston."

"Slats was really good about it," Gretzky continued. "It was a choice of staying after the morning skate and staying for an hour or playing in the game that night. I'd rather play.

"Mess and I were the same way. We'd play every game. We didn't care. We just played. That's what we do. It didn't bother us at all.

"The Oilers would go into places like Dallas and Tampa Bay and Miami and Atlanta—places that didn't have teams in those days. They just wanted to make money, and we didn't care. We enjoyed it. What else are you going to do? You might as well play.

"The crazy thing was that Slats would play those games like they were playoff games. He'd double-shift guys and have you killing penalties and be out on the power play. It wasn't like he was rolling four lines. He always played to win. He wouldn't know how to not do that.

"I remember we were playing an exhibition game in Dallas in September when they didn't have an NHL team, and Mess and I were double-shifting!"

Sather had played for the Montreal Canadiens when Sam Pollock was the general manager and had picked up one of Pollock's commandments: When you've got the sweater on, you always play to win, no matter what the stakes might be.

The 1982–83 Oilers clearly knew how to win in the regular season, and after the Los Angeles humiliation of the previous spring, they knew through bitter experience the kind of hockey that was needed to win in the playoffs.

The next test would be to see if they knew how to win in the Stanley Cup final, a test the New York Islanders would willingly provide.

As far as that Oilers team was concerned, the regular season presented only one serious question: When they got to the Stanley Cup final, would they be good enough to win?

Everyone agreed that the Oilers would be in the playoffs with a high seeding. In their first and second years in the league, they had barely managed to squeak in. In the third year, they finished second overall. This time, even though they wouldn't say it publicly, they intended to gear down a little in the regular season to make sure they'd be fresh for the playoffs.

This prompted a new round of criticism for Gretzky to handle. In accordance with the plan, he logged less ice time, but then the same people who had said that his slew of records came only because he spent so much time on the ice started criticizing him for not matching the previous season's record-setting pace.

"I think last year was a special year," explained a healthy Gretzky with still a month to go before the playoffs. "Everybody on the team worked so that I could get my records. I double-shifted a lot more than I am this year.

"I know my responsibility is to score goals, to put the puck in the net, but we were criticized last year for tiring Wayne Gretzky out for the play-offs. Last year, Glen gave everybody a chance to go after individual awards and individual achievements and then, at the end of the year, we were criticized for not worrying about the team and for forgetting about the hockey club. I don't feel I was tired. Glen doesn't feel I was tired. But this year, that can't be an excuse."

It wasn't. The Oilers reached stage three of the four-part "Gretzky season," when they cruised through the regular schedule and survived the opening stages of the playoffs. Now they had to learn how to win a Stanley Cup final.

Their opponent, the New York Islanders, who were on a run of three consecutive Stanley Cups, had also eased off a bit in the regular season and had settled for a fifth-place finish overall. As they closed in on what they hoped would be a fourth Cup, they faced a major problem: How could they do what no one else in the NHL had done? How could they stop Wayne Gretzky?

Trying to find a way to stop Gretzky was not a new challenge for anyone in hockey. Coaches had been working on it since Gretzky was seven years old. And no one had found an answer yet. You could reduce his impact, but you couldn't stop him.

Nevertheless, it was a fundamental question, not only for that particular playoff season but for every team that encountered Gretzky during his entire career. As such, it deserves an in-depth examination.

First of all, it must be conceded that no single-faceted approach ever worked. Gretzky was such a genius on the ice that he was able to quickly work out what strategy the opponents were utilizing and devise a counter-strategy.

For instance, there were those who tried to shadow him with a forward. He would respond by positioning himself near a defenceman. "When teams have a guy on me, which a lot of teams do," he said, "it's very difficult for me to get in the open. It's really tough with all the hooking and holding that goes on behind the play.

"So basically, what I do is go and stand beside one of their defencemen and eliminate two people." Now two opposition players would be sticking with Gretzky while his remaining teammates enjoyed a man-power advantage.

Furthermore, you can never legally cover a man so well that he can't make a pass. You can stop him roaming, but you can't stop him passing— and Gretzky was as dangerous setting up goals as he was scoring them.

When the Montreal Canadiens assigned super-checker Doug Jarvis to cover Gretzky in the opening game of the 1982 playoffs, Gretzky didn't get a single shot on goal. However, he did get five assists, an NHL record at the time.

Physical intimidation didn't work, either. For one thing, Gretzky was extremely adept at avoiding checks. For another, until he reached the respected-veteran status accorded to long-time NHL players who don't fight, he always had someone on his team who could make sure no liberties were taken.

A further relevant point is that although Gretzky couldn't do more than two chin-ups, he had phenomenal hockey stamina, as he showed in the 1987 Canada Cup.

If you assigned a single checker to watch him, you had to find someone who could match his ice time, and there weren't many who qualified.

The Toronto Maple Leafs, a team on which Gretzky routinely feasted, instituted a policy of trying to keep the puck away from him. But to do that, you had to keep the puck away from the entire Oilers team. Otherwise, as soon as they got possession, they'd feed Gretzky. No wonder Gretzky loved playing in Maple Leaf Gardens.

The Vancouver Canucks sometimes designated six checkers on the premise that no one person could do it—a whole line was needed—but since Gretzky was on the ice so much, two lines had to be assigned rather than one.

The drawback to that approach is that it cripples your offence. Of course, you could simply let Gretzky do what he wanted and battle offence with offence. But since the Oilers were routinely averaging more than five goals a game in those days and had Grant Fuhr in the net, that strategy wasn't such a good idea, either.

So usually, after examining all these options, coaches decided that they couldn't stop Gretzky, but they'd try to minimize his impact by assigning a quality player to watch him as closely as possible. Next question: Which player?

Some teams used a defenceman. Some used a centre. Some simply selected the best checking forward and juggled accordingly. In those early Edmonton years, it appeared that the best tactic was to assign a right winger despite the fact that Gretzky played centre.

The reasoning had its merit. Gretzky was a great skater, even though he never agreed with that assessment. After his retirement, he told me that he felt his eldest son, Ty, had a lot more natural skating ability than he did. "If I could have skated like Ty, I would really have been something," he said.

Gretzky had the ability to change direction on a dime, and to most of us, it didn't matter which way he turned. But to the trained eye of the professional hockey observer, he seemed to be more effective moving to his left than to his right. Therefore, the idea was that until Gretzky got the puck, the checking right winger would keep parallel with him as much as possible. Once Gretzky got possession, the winger would move directly at him, forcing him to move to his right, not the more dangerous left.

At this point, the hockey strategist is thinking, "Well, who is watching Gretzky's left winger, the guy who would normally be the responsibility of the winger who has now decided to attach himself to Gretzky?"

That job has to fall to the right defenceman, and that's where the strategy encounters difficulty. There aren't many defencemen in the world who are good enough to make those split-second coverage decisions and then carry them out effectively.

This, then, was the problem the New York Islanders faced as they entered the 1983 Stanley Cup final against the Oilers.

The Islanders were coached by Al Arbour, a superb strategist in his own right. Furthermore, Arbour was extremely close to Scott Bowman, probably the best strategist in the history of hockey. In theory, coaches never help each other out. In the real world of the National Hockey League, they do. Arbour's strategy was a combination of the best points of the options mentioned above.

First of all, the Islanders not only forced Gretzky to his right, they forced all the Oilers' big gunners—Mark Messier, Paul Coffey and Glenn Anderson—to the right because they all shot left and would be forced to use their backhand.

They used a physical approach on Gretzky as much as possible. They kept mostly within the bounds of legality, but players like John Tonelli, Butch Goring, Bob Bourne and Bob Nystrom were veteran checkers who knew how to take away Gretzky's time and space.

To counter the problem of finding a single checker who could match Gretzky's thirty-five to forty minutes, the Islanders used a defenceman. A good defenceman can log that much ice time, and that approach would leave the Islanders' forwards free to focus on the offensive side of the game.

The key to all this, of course, was Denis Potvin. He always played left defence, so when Gretzky was pushed to that side by the Islanders, he had to encounter Potvin. Because the Islanders were so stacked with experienced players, they were able to react accordingly when Gretzky moved elsewhere to pull Potvin out of position.

The Islanders had found the only way to stop Gretzky: they put together a better team. Everybody on the roster had to play at an elite level, not only physically, but mentally. A Hall of Fame defenceman has to be part of the equation as well, not to mention a Hall of Fame coach and a whole whack of Hall of Fame forwards.

The following season, other coaches, having noticed the Islanders' success, tried to follow the formula. But a tactic that works against Gretzky for four games—which was all the Islanders needed to win the Cup—didn't work over a full season because Gretzky made adjustments. Furthermore, the rest of the teams in the league didn't have the kind of talent that had won four consecutive Stanley Cups.

Gretzky often tells the story of leaving the Nassau County Coliseum after Game Four. He dreaded the necessary walk down the hall past the dressing room of the victorious Islanders, expecting to see a bunch of happy, laughing players slapping each other on the back. Instead, he saw players who were bedraggled, bleeding and dog-tired.

At that moment, he realized what he would later enunciate. After the regular season and the playoff season comes the Stanley Cup final season. Each phase is difficult, and each is more demanding than its predecessor.

But Gretzky had faced a lot of challenges in his life, and although he might have failed initially, sooner or later, he invariably came out on top. Therefore, in his mind—and in the minds of the Edmonton Oilers— the 1983–84 season was devoted to getting another crack at the Cup.

The Oilers continued their assault on the record book, led the National Hockey League in attendance and filled the net in one arena after another. They finished first in the standings, generated more revenue than any team in the league and averaged almost six goals a game—446 in eighty games, to be precise, an NHL record that stands to this day.

But whenever you talked to any of the Edmonton players during that season, it became clear that their interest in any of these achievements ranked a distant second to getting another crack at the Islanders. Since the only way to get that second chance was to reach the Stanley Cup final, it was clear where the Oilers' priorities lay.

Nevertheless, it seemed that every year, whatever the team's ultimate target might be, Gretzky would eclipse another long-standing NHL record along the way. This time, he ran up a streak of fifty-one consecutive games in which he got at least one point. In fact, the record was a lot more impressive than that number would indicate, but as has been mentioned before, the NHL often takes a rather curious approach towards its record book. As far as the league was concerned, the record for consecutive games with points belonged to Guy Lafleur with twenty-eight. But Gretzky also had a point in each of the final eleven games of the previous season.

"Those don't count," said league officials. "That was last season."

Yes, but there weren't any games between seasons.

"Doesn't matter. It's a different season."

If you count those earlier eleven games, Gretzky's streak was really sixty-two consecutive games.

"I knew about the record because guys had been asking me about it," said Gretzky, years later, "but it didn't really hit me until I came out for the warmup in the forty-sixth game. It was in the old Chicago Stadium and there was a big sign hanging up there saying, 'The Streak Stops Here.'"

As far as Oilers public relations man Bill Tuele was concerned, there was no reason to keep close track of the numbers. "He'll go all the way," he said after Gretzky broke Lafleur's record. "He'll go the entire eighty-game schedule. Who's going to stop him? A four-point game is just an average night for him." (That was something of an exaggeration. Gretzky's average was closer to 2.5 points a game. Even so, barring injury, Tuele's projection did not seem far-fetched.)

But what few people knew was that Gretzky was indeed injured.

"I probably shouldn't have been playing because my shoulder was really bothering me," he explained afterwards, "but in the NHL, if you sit out a game, the streak ends, so I stayed in. We were winning by a goal late in that forty-sixth game, and I still didn't have a point. Naturally, the Hawks pulled their goalie. The fans booed! They didn't care if they lost as long as I didn't get a point.

"I went out there, and there were only a few seconds left when Troy Murray tried to make a pass that I blocked. I scored into the empty net with two seconds left to keep the streak alive.

"For the next five games, my shoulder was really sore, but I kept playing and kept getting points. Then, in the fifty-second game, against Los Angeles, I didn't get a point. After that, I didn't play for the next six games until my shoulder healed."

Had he stayed in the lineup, he almost certainly would have broken his own record for points in a season, which, at that time, stood at 212. Instead, he had to settle for a measly 205.

In earlier years, he might have stayed in the lineup despite the nagging shoulder injury. Not this time. The priority had changed. Records didn't matter. The goal was the Stanley Cup.

There are many hockey fans who will insist that no one has ever scored a hundred goals in a hockey year. But that year, Gretzky did—if you include the playoffs. He scored eighty-seven in the seventy-four regular-season games he played and added a further thirteen in the playoffs—yet another NHL record.

Even so, the 1984 playoffs were not directly dominated by Gretzky. It was one of the few occasions—probably the only one—that a major achievement of the Gretzky-era Oilers did not depend primarily on his contributions.

He certainly had an impact. He got his goals, and he forced the Islanders to dedicate so much effort towards minimizing his accomplishments that it detracted from their own offence. But this time, the Oilers were what they needed to be: a total team. Glen Sather and his staff knew that, the previous season, they had been beaten by the Islanders because the Islanders were the better team. They were determined that it wouldn't happen again.

After the Oilers swept the Minnesota North Stars to guarantee their place in the final, they had a nine-day break. Sather first acquired the services of the late Roger Neilson, a brilliant defensive coach known as "Captain Video" for his use of videotape.

In 1984, videotape represented the cutting edge of technology. Neilson was a pioneer in analyzing the tapes—finding a team's weaknesses, strengths, and, more important, its tendencies.

In the case of the Islanders, the tendencies far outweighed the other considerations. This was a team that was well coached and stable. It had won four consecutive Stanley Cups. You didn't suddenly break into the Islanders lineup and decide to freewheel or introduce a few of your own innovations. You played Al Arbour hockey. You played Islanders hockey.

The Oilers' assistant coaches took the information that Neilson provided, and by the time the team finished that nine-day hiatus, the players knew more about the Islanders' tendencies than the Islanders did.

When hockey chroniclers look back at the opening game of the series and examine the Oilers' 1–0 victory, they invariably point out the contributions of the grinders. What they don't point out is that, time after time, what appeared to be a blossoming New York attack was thwarted when a perfectly placed Oiler intercepted a pass.

The other thing they don't point out is that the grinders were involved because almost all the play was along the boards. Ever since the Oilers entered the NHL, their attack had been based on an up-the-middle breakout. When in doubt, throw the puck up the middle and Gretzky or somebody would gather it in and take off.

Against the Islanders, every breakout was along the boards. Nothing went up the centre, and the New York defenders, doggedly clogging up the middle as ordered, stood there confused while the Oilers roared down the flanks.

A number of other strategic factors were involved.

The Oilers had always liked to hit the head man with a pass on a breakout. In this series, they started using the head man as a decoy. But the Islanders, accustomed to covering that lead man, invariably stuck with him, thereby leaving a hole for the second man.

Neilson had spotted the tendency of Denis Potvin, who generated a high proportion of the Islanders' attacks, to circle behind his net and then either carry or pass the puck up the middle. When he tried that in this series, he invariably found his path blocked by an Edmonton checker. And so it went.

The Oilers were so well versed in the time-tested—or perhaps timeworn—New York strategy that they were able to effectively counter it.

With no Edmonton passes going up the middle, Gretzky's involvement was reduced. Similarly, he was usually the head man on the breakouts, but now the Oilers were hitting the second man. Furthermore, the Islanders were still blanketing Gretzky as much as possible.

For all these reasons, he was not as visible as usual. But more important to the Oilers and to Gretzky himself, they won the Cup, beating the Islanders in five games. Despite their reputation as a team of defensive incompetents, they allowed a total of only six goals in their four victories.

Before the deciding game, Gretzky made an impassioned plea to his teammates. Essentially, he told them to keep on doing what they were doing, to ignore any individual achievements and to keep producing the team effort that was working so well. He said that while he was happy to rack up all his records, they were not his goal. "I said the only thing that matters is the Stanley Cup," he said. "Nothing else."

And when he finally got to lift it, he nearly dropped it. "I almost fell over backwards," he said a couple of hours later when most of the hangers-on had left and only the players and a few close friends remained in the dressing room. "I was starting to lose my balance, and I was yelling, 'Help! Help!' I didn't realize how heavy it was."

"I didn't realize how light it was," said Dave Semenko with a grin.

"I almost dropped it that time," chuckled Gretzky years later, "but by the fourth time, I was really good at it."

That triumph saw the beginning of what is now a tradition—the players taking turns with the Cup over the course of the summer. "Glen came in the room," recalled Gretzky, "and he said, 'You guys won it. You take it.' It saw all of Edmonton for three days."

The Cup was sweet vindication for Gretzky. As he sat in the room in his champagne-soaked underwear, he said, "All the stories written about us, even the nice ones, have always said, 'But they have never won the Stanley Cup.' Now I won't have to read that again."

But he could read about one of the few successful five-year plans in hockey history. The Oilers had just completed their fifth year of NHL existence.

CHAPTER SIX

Wayne Gretzky was only twenty years old when he first wore a Team Canada sweater at the professional level. The occasion was the 1981 Canada Cup, a tournament orchestrated by Alan Eagleson for the usual two reasons: First, to make money for Alan Eagleson; second, to give Canada an opportunity to claim dominance in international hockey.

It was successful in the former aim, but less so in the latter, and as for being a learning experience for Gretzky, it mostly involved learning mistakes to avoid.

In the years to come, this maturity proved to be beneficial to Canada. By the time the next Canada Cup rolled around, in 1984, Gretzky was far and away the best player in the world, and his views were given serious consideration by management. The longer he stayed in hockey, the more this was the case. His exposure to the pitfalls of international tournaments allowed him to be influential in helping organizers avoid them in the future.

But in 1981, he was just a kid, too young to go into bars in the United States. He was in awe of many of the players on the team and, like most players of any age, scared stiff of Scott Bowman, the coach.

Gretzky quickly learned that when a team represents Canada, politics can never be avoided. The players had to scrap their CCM Team Canada practice jerseys because Quebec law didn't allow any form of advertising that did not include French in larger letters. Since CCM had no Équipe Canada sweaters, the Team Canada sweaters had to go. After all, NHL players wearing unilingual sweaters while they practised could do irreparable damage to the status of the French language in Quebec.

Gretzky also learned that most high-level players hate training camps—and for that matter, tryout camps. Those concepts were to disappear in the years to come, but in 1981, both were firmly entrenched.

The players arrived in Montreal for the camp a full two weeks before the first exhibition game, and on most days, they practised twice. Even for the NHL season, players showed up only four or five days before the first exhibition game. There was no shortage of grumbling.

Furthermore, half the players who sacrificed part of their summer break to come to the camp didn't make the cut. To elite players, many of whom had never failed to make a team in their lives, this was an acute embarrassment, and it subsequently became clear that this process was not the ideal way to form a national team.

But as usual, Gretzky was focused on the positive aspects, and when he learned that Guy Lafleur was going to be his linemate, he was ecstatic. Even though Gordie Howe had always been his biggest hero, Lafleur was high on the list. At the same time, he saw absolutely nothing wrong with the concept of having Steve Shutt as the third member of the line.

Shutt, Lafleur and Jacques Lemaire had been the dominant line in the NHL until Lemaire left for Switzerland two years earlier. Having Gretzky replace Lemaire seemed like an excellent idea.

"We talked about this as far back as May," said Gretzky. "It's quite an honour. I'm going to listen to what the other two have to say, and then we'll go through the process of getting used to each other. I've got to see where each one goes under different circumstances.

"I'd like to let Guy or Steve do most of the puck carrying," he said. "I rarely carry the puck between the blue lines. I let the good puck handlers do that."

Lafleur wasn't sure he agreed with Gretzky's assessment of his own puck-handling abilities, but he had no objection to the strategy.

"Wayne is a specialist once he's inside the blue line," he said. "Once he has control of the puck, they can't get it off him. He just waits and waits until he can see somebody open, then he gets the puck there."

Lafleur also liked the idea of Gretzky taking charge once the line established possession in the offensive zone. "He's always in control," he said. "He's not a mad dog out there. He knows where he's going, and that's very important if the line is going to be successful."

The last time Lafleur and Shutt had played in a meaningful game, they had been victims of Gretzky's wizardry. In what was a stunning upset, the fourteenth-place Oilers, who had barely squeaked into the playoffs, had swept the mighty third-place Montreal Canadiens in the best-of-five first round.

Even before that, Gretzky had opened the eyes of a lot of hockey fans, having won the Hart Trophy as the league's most valuable player in each of his first two seasons. He had just won the scoring title, and there's no doubt that his name was certainly well known. But it was that upset of the Canadiens that made most Canadians aware of his talent. In that era, communication was not what it is today. The Oilers' games were rarely televised in Edmonton, let alone anywhere else. Hockey fans had seen the numbers that Gretzky had been putting up, but most of them had no idea how he did it.

Then, in 1981, as the Oilers faced the Canadiens on *Hockey Night in Canada,* amazed fans saw a player who dominated the game from behind the net, of all places. This wasn't the way hockey was supposed to work. You were supposed to come down your wing and stay in your lane. If you had to go behind the net, you got back out front as quickly as possible.

"Usually, I go into the corners or behind the net," conceded Gretzky. "That's basically my style. But we'll have to work on learning each other's style. If the line is going to be successful, everybody has got to be in there making plays."

Lafleur was willing to give it a try. "I've played with Steve for so many years now that he always knows what I'm going to do," he said. "He knows if I turn this way, I'm going to drop the puck. He knows if I turn that way, I'm going to shoot. I think what Steve and I have to get used to is those plays Wayne makes behind the net. We've never practised that sort of play with the Canadiens and I don't really know whether to stay on the wing or go to the net.

"But we'll work it out, and I'll tell you one thing: it's sure a lot better to play with him than against him."

He almost did neither. Gretzky, who has always been a very cautious driver, relied on others for rides around Montreal during training camp. When Lafleur offered him a ride to the suburban hotel and said he was fine to drive, Gretzky went with him. He idolized Lafleur, and if Lafleur said he was fine, Gretzky wasn't going to argue.

But Lafleur—who nearly killed himself driving home alone later in his career—lost control of his car and spun it on a Montreal expressway. Fortunately for Canada's two greatest stars of the day, not to mention for the hockey world, the pair escaped harm.

"He didn't roll it, but it spun out in a 360," said Gretzky in 2013. "It was wet that night. You know how when you're going up a hill and you give it more gas and the wheels spin? We were driving back to the hotel and it did a full 360 almost twice. My goodness, we were so lucky. It was a busy highway. We were so lucky that no one hit us. I thought we were done. It was only about six or seven at night, so the road was still busy, and I still don't like to think about it. I thought it was over."

Astonishingly, the story never got into the papers. In Quebec, a wayward sneeze by a hockey player is enough to warrant a three-page spread, but this one stayed under wraps.

Clearly, to this point in the Canada Cup tournament, Gretzky's first professional international exposure left something to be desired.

Although he and Lafleur worked well together, Bowman wanted more from the left winger, so he replaced Shutt with Gilbert Perreault. Now, the expected dominance of the line became evident in the exhibition games. In the opening game of the tournament, Gretzky, Lafleur and Perreault racked up a total of ten points, and Canada beat Finland 9–0.

But in the fourth game of the tournament, Perreault, who had already accumulated nine points, broke his ankle. In another blow to Canada, goalie Billy Smith suffered a broken finger. Smith was also at the peak of his game. He had led the New York Islanders to the Stanley Cup three months earlier and, two years afterwards, won the Conn Smythe Trophy as the most outstanding player in the playoffs.

Even so, Canada rolled through to the final game undefeated. But that was just a prologue. Now they were to play the Soviet Union head to head. The winner would get the Canada Cup.

The Soviets had a powerful team. For the most part, this was the team that had embarrassed the NHL all-stars in the 1979 Challenge Cup, winning two of three games and taking the final game 6–0. But it had also suffered the embarrassment of losing to the United States at the 1980 Lake Placid Olympics in the "Miracle on Ice" and was eager to make amends.

The Canadians started well, with almost total territorial domination in the first period. They outshot the Soviets 12–4 but couldn't beat goaltender Vladislav Tretiak, who was nothing short of magnificent. Five days earlier, in a round-robin game that was basically meaningless, Vladimir Myshkin had been the Soviet netminder, and the Canadians put the puck past him seven times. But now Tretiak was in the net, and any confidence the Canadians might have felt quickly evaporated.

The teams traded goals in the second period, but then Ray Bourque— who, like Gretzky, was only two years into his NHL career—bobbled the puck in front of his own net and handed it to Sergei Shepelev. Soviets don't miss chances like that, and the Canadians were on the slippery slope.

By the end of the period, the Soviets led 3–1, partly because they were playing exactly the way they needed to play to be successful. They were atoning for their weaknesses while the Canadians weren't. Marcel Dionne had stepped into the breach to replace the injured Perreault, but the Soviets evaluated the situation and reacted accordingly. They opted for blanket coverage of Lafleur and Gretzky and left Dionne alone. The result was that Dionne had four great chances and missed all four. Gretzky and Lafleur were kept off the scoreboard.

With both teams, the weakness was the defence corps, mostly composed of young players. At the slightest hint of pressure, the Soviet defencemen slammed the puck down the ice or flipped the puck into the stands. In those days, a team was free to pursue either tactic. You could change personnel after an icing and there was no penalty for putting the puck over the glass. The Canadian defencemen tried to be more creative and got burned.

In the third period, Canada unravelled. When they went down by three goals, they clearly saw their fate. The Soviets, never ones to throttle back, kept coming and scored three more goals in the last five minutes. The final score was 8–1.

Canadian goalie Mike Liut was never the same afterwards, but he really hadn't played that badly. He didn't make any sizzling saves, but the blame for the lopsided score should have been shared more than it was.

The nation was outraged. It was asserted that Bowman had been outcoached, even though he had won five Stanley Cups. Liut was vilified. The players were judged to be overrated and lazy. Eagleson muttered something about never staging another Canada Cup.

The next day, the prime minister staged a ceremony to honour the team. After all, they had done their best for Canada, even if they had lost a game. Only two players had the good grace to attend. Gretzky was one of them.

CHAPTER SEVEN

G retzky hardly had time to catch a breath of summer air after winning his first Stanley Cup in 1984 before he was back in the rink—this time in Banff, Alberta.

Alan Eagleson had decreed that it was time for another Canada Cup, another attempt to prove that Canada was at least the equal of the Soviet Union on the hockey rink. Similar quests had come to naught in the 1979 Challenge Cup and the 1981 Canada Cup, but thanks to Gretzky and the Oilers, North American hockey had changed. The Oilers had shown that their primarily Canadian brand of hockey was better than anything the rest of the National Hockey League had to offer. Now, the Oilers' top players, along with some other stars from the rest of the league, hoped to show that the Canadian brand of hockey was even better than anything the rest of the world had to offer.

Glen Sather, the man who managed and coached the Oilers, was selected to do the same for Team Canada. And in a remarkable coincidence, Banff, where Sather had a summer home, was chosen as the site for the initial training camp. Calgary and Edmonton, the two closest NHL cities, were selected as the sites for all the important games.

A little clarification is needed for the claim that Sather was selected as coach and manager. He was selected as coach and one of the members of the managerial team. But it was always clear that he had more clout than others in the group, which included David Poile of the Washington Capitals, Serge Savard of the Montreal Canadiens, Emile Francis of the Hartford Whalers, John Ferguson of the Winnipeg Jets, Harry Sinden of the Boston Bruins and Bill Torrey of the New York Islanders.

When Team Canada got off to a sluggish start, Sather staged a coup. He fired all the other managers, thereby confirming his status as the GM. His position was further confirmed by Eagleson. "Sather has had carte blanche since day one," he said.

Some of the departing GMs were miffed; most accepted their dismissal. Sather was his usual brash self. "What were we supposed to do," he asked, "meet after every game and talk about line changes? Did they seriously think we could run a team by committee?" Apparently, they did. That's why the committee was formed. But after the members gave their input, it was Sather who made the decisions.

"I don't want to make a big thing of this," said John Ferguson. "I want Team Canada to do well. That's why I got involved in the first place. We still see ourselves as part of the team, and I don't want to say or do anything to hurt their chances."

What Sather wanted from his team was clear. He wanted an offence that was built around Gretzky, and he wanted a skating game that would allow Team Canada to beat the Soviets. The former was a foregone conclusion; the latter came as a surprise to many. Ever since the opening minutes of the famous 1972 Summit Series, Canadians had conceded that the Soviets were superior skaters. In subsequent head-to-head battles, Canadian strategy had been built on beating the Soviets in many areas, but not always legally and certainly not in the area of skating.

Sather was convinced that times had changed. The Oilers' high-tempo style, as exhibited not only by Gretzky, but also by Paul Coffey, Mark Messier and Glenn Anderson, had proved to be superior in the NHL. Now, the Edmonton stars were to be complemented by speedsters like Doug Wilson and the core players from the New York Islanders dynasty, including Bob Bourne, another strong, fast skater.

At first, the concept showed every sign of being a dismal failure. Three games into the tournament, the Canadian record stood at 1–1–1. The win was against Germany, hardly a challenging opponent. Next came a tie with the United States, a team that in those days was pretty much on a par with Germany. Then came the loss to Sweden.

In the post-game dressing room, with only one game left in the round-robin stage, Sather delivered a blistering verbal attack on his players, pulling no punches and naming names along the way. Gretzky's was one of them.

"You don't like to hear it," said Gretzky, "but you know he's right. We were awful. It's not just one or two guys, it's all twenty. If we play like this again, we won't make the playoffs."

The problem was a fairly simple one to identify: the team was not playing as a team. Instead of being united for a common cause, three factions were going their separate ways. There was an Islanders group, an Oilers group and an everybody-else group. In any team sport, nothing will be accomplished if there is no sense of common purpose.

After the loss to Sweden and with elimination looming if Canada lost the next game to the Czech Republic, Larry Robinson took charge.

Later, Robinson would become Gretzky's coach in Los Angeles, but at this point, Robinson was just an unhappy player. He had five Stanley Cups to his credit and was two years away from his sixth. Furthermore, he was generally conceded to be the toughest guy in the league. He was universally respected. And he was not the least bit pleased with what he saw.

Accordingly, he stood up at a team meal and, like Sather, named names and pointed fingers. He said he had worked hard to establish his reputation and he had no intention of being part of a team that wound up embarrassing Canada because its players cared more about petty squabbles than national pride.

If Canada failed, he said, fans wouldn't blame it on the Islanders or the

Oilers; they would blame it on the individual players. He wasn't ready to accept that blame, and he didn't want to be on the ice with anyone who did.

The result followed a plotline that Hollywood would love—if Hollywood cared about hockey. Spurred by Robinson's speech, the Islanders and Oilers played together as a unit. To show that he had received the message, Sather started a line composed of Islanders—rather than Gretzky's line, which had started every other game. The Canadians handily defeated the Czechs and then went on to the semifinal against the Soviets, which turned out to be one of the best games ever played.

"It wasn't just the Larry Robinson speech," recalled Gretzky as we reminisced about the series more than two decades later. "That was the big one, but before that, we were going along in our merry way, and as players, especially the Oilers guys, we didn't realize or know there was any kind of friction between the Islanders guys and the Oilers guys. We honestly didn't. We were just playing.

"I don't know individually if players felt that way or not, but just because we weren't winning, it all kind of manifested itself and came to a big head.

"Bob Bourne actually called a private meeting with just the Oilers' players and the Islanders' players, and basically put it on the table. He said, 'Listen, we were tremendous enemies when we played against each other, and that's a good thing because we both want to win the Stanley Cup and that's what makes us great. Now we've got to put our differences aside.'

"He said basically that we all had to get on the same page. Bob Bourne did that privately in the hotel. It was quite the meeting because I didn't think there was tension, but obviously there was, and when you're not winning, something's wrong.

"Then, the next day, Larry stood up and made his speech. It was a great speech. Larry was the most respected guy ever to be a part of Team Canada. He was the kind of guy who didn't say anything. He was friendly with each player. If you were a young guy, he made sure you felt comfortable. He kept everybody loose in the locker room.

"So when he stood up, we were all kind of in shock because Larry never did that. That wasn't his field. And when he did and he made that incredible speech, everybody sort of went, 'Whoa!'"

Buoyed by the easy win over the Czechs, Canada rolled into the next game against the Soviets in a confident mood. It was only a semi-final, but the hockey world perceived it as the final. These were the two clear tournament favourites, the world's two hockey powerhouses, going head to head in a game that would see one of them eliminated.

The game lived up to its billing. Even the staid, detached members of the coaching staff got caught up in the emotion. "I sat up in the press box and kept track of the good scoring chances," said Team Canada assistant coach Tom Watt. "They had the first four of the game, then we had the next four, and that was it for the first period, 4–4. In the second period, we had ten good chances to their two. After that, I was so excited, I couldn't get them all down."

Despite having been the dominant team, Team Canada had trailed 2–1 late in the third period. It was time for Gretzky to go to work.

"We were putting lots of pressure on them," recalled Doug Wilson years later. "We came down, and Gretz had the puck in the far corner. It was one of those ones where we had all sorts of pressure on them for two or three minutes and we just couldn't tie the game. Then, all of a sudden, Bob Bourne went to the front of the net and Gretz got it back to me and I fired it onto the net."

Wilson was known for his blazing shots from the point into the upper corner, but this one was far from typical. It just trickled in.

"Bobby Bourne created all the traffic and was causing all kinds of trouble in front of the net," said Wilson. "I wasn't really at the point. I was at the top of the circle. It was a wrist shot. It hit the goalie and went through the goalie. It dropped into the crease and slid in."

As if the game hadn't been sufficiently exciting already, it now went into sudden-death overtime, where even a routine shot could end it. When the Soviets got a two-on-one break, Canadian hearts sank. The

Canadians had rarely allowed an odd-man break all night because they knew from bitter experience that a short-term manpower disadvantage of that nature usually resulted in a Soviet goal.

The only Canadian back was Paul Coffey, a man much maligned—unfairly—for what were perceived to be defensive liabilities. But on this occasion, Coffey not only broke up the rush, he led the charge the other way and, after a stretch of exerted Canadian pressure, fired the shot from the point that Mike Bossy tipped into the net. Canada had won. And they had done it by outskating the Soviets, not by beating them into submission.

After that, a win over the Swedes in the final was anticlimactic and almost automatic.

The victory in Canada Cup 1984 marked the beginning of a stretch of Canadian dominance in the international game—and of a close friendship between two of its greatest stars, Gretzky and Igor Larionov.

Walter Gretzky, who spoke enough Russian to make himself understood, and his close friend Charlie Henry had managed to help Larionov and another player elude their KGB watchdogs after the semifinal game.

"They snuck down the back elevator, and Charlie Henry picked them up," said Gretzky. "It was a six o'clock game, if I remember rightly, so it was about nine-thirty when we picked them up. Igor kept saying he had to be back by midnight."

Everybody went to Calgary's famed Electric Avenue, which, after the Canadian triumph, was living up to its name.

"There was Igor and another Russian player, and I don't know his name," recalled Gretzky in a 2005 interview. "There were two Russians, and the other one didn't speak any English. He smoked more cigarettes and drank more than any of us. He was an unknown. I think he wore number 31 and he was a right-handed shot. That's all I remember about him."

By this point in his tale, Gretzky was laughing. "Igor got back by midnight. The other guy we lost. I don't know if he ever got back. He might still be living in Calgary, for all I know. It's funny now, but we were worried then."

As for Larionov, "He was standing there talking to me," Gretzky said, "and the whole time I'm thinking, 'This guy is talking to me and whole time we were playing against him, I was thinking he didn't understand a word I was saying.'

"I would talk to our guys and say, 'Coff, you stand there and I'll get the draw to you,' or say to someone else, 'You go over there and I'll throw it to you up the middle.'

"The whole time, Igor knew exactly what I was saying. The first time I knew he spoke English was when we were standing there, having a beer. He started telling me, 'We all want to play in the NHL, and maybe one day it will happen.'

"It was an incredible night because Charlie snuck him out past the KGB. Igor said he would like to defect, but the government wouldn't allow it; but he said, 'One day, we hope we can all play in the NHL.'"

Five years later, he did.

CHAPTER EIGHT

I t can be said of every sport: the truly great players don't just rewrite the record book; they change the way the game is played.

In hockey, Bobby Orr changed the essence of the defenceman's game. Wayne Gretzky changed the essence of the forward's game.

Before Orr, defencemen stuck to defence. They rarely trespassed into the opposition's zone except to join a brawl. Only the most daring—Montreal's Doug Harvey, for example—would rush the puck. Carrying the puck up the ice was the forward's job. A defenceman passed the puck.

Similarly, before Gretzky, a forward stayed in his lane. During one Toronto Maple Leafs training camp in the sixties, lines were even painted on the ice parallel to the boards and ten feet out from them. Wingers were not to cross those lines.

But Gretzky roamed all over the ice; so, naturally, his linemates did the same. With defenceman Paul Coffey utilizing all the offensive innovations that Orr had introduced to the game, the only Edmonton player not likely to be involved in the attack was the goaltender.

But Gretzky was instrumental in an even more significant change in the game. He was the first star to kill penalties on a regular basis and the first to turn a four-on-four situation into an offensive opportunity. Prior to that, the top coaches always sent out defensively oriented players in four-on-four situations. There were checking lines and there were scoring lines.

"It [the game] started to change with Wayne Gretzky," explained Scott Bowman, arguably the greatest coach in the history of the NHL and a devoted student of the game. "I think that was the biggest thing. When Edmonton started to use Gretzky to kill a lot of penalties, they decided that they were going to get those guys playing more."

At that point, in the early eighties, Bryan Trottier had done some penalty killing with the New York Islanders, and Bowman himself had occasionally used Jacques Lemaire in that capacity in Montreal, but those were exceptions.

"Most of the time before that, you had enough guys that were specialty players that you either played offence or killed penalties," Bowman said. "Guys like Jean Beliveau and Bernie Geoffrion never killed penalties."

The new strategy, the brainchild of Glen Sather and his staff, was a crucial factor in the Oilers' post-season successes. For one thing, it allowed Gretzky to get his usual ice time. In that era, the playoffs were often fight-filled and teams could spend a lot of time playing short-handed. At the same time, the playoffs had been steadily expanded (fifteen years earlier, a team needed only eight wins to earn the Stanley Cup) and had become a true marathon, a test of endurance, not only because of the extra games but also because of the extra travel. If you wasted players by leaving them languishing on the bench, you tired out others and flirted with disaster.

There was another way in which using Gretzky in what had formerly been a defensive situation was beneficial. If the opposition relied on a line that got a lot of ice time—the Triple Crown Line in Los Angeles, for example—and you designated one line of your own to check them, some of your players were going to get shortchanged on their ice time.

Again, that could tire out some players and waste others. But by using Gretzky and Jari Kurri to kill penalties or play four on four, ice time could be more balanced.

The biggest factor of all, of course, was that Gretzky and Kurri were so dangerous that they distracted the opponents who were either on a power play or in a four-on-four situation.

One NHL coach of that era, who can't be identified because he would be admitting to a questionable tactic, told me that, one Saturday morning, he paid a youngster to ask Coffey for a stick. In the afternoon, he measured the stick and confirmed his suspicions: it was illegal. If the game was close, he planned to call for a stick measurement in the third period and get a power play.

But before he was able to put that plan into action, the Oilers took a penalty, and Gretzky scored shorthanded. Shortly afterwards, the Oilers took another penalty. This time, Gretzky set up Kurri for a shorthanded goal. The idea of a stick measurement was abandoned.

By the time the 1985 playoffs rolled around, Gretzky and Kurri had elevated the shorthanded attack to an art form. In 1983, the Oilers had set a record of ten shorthanded goals in the post-season, a record that still stands. In the 1983–84 season, Gretzky scored an NHL-record twelve shorthanded goals even though he played only seventy-four games.

The late Bob Johnson, coach of the Calgary Flames in the mid-1980s, wanted his team to be aware of Gretzky's potential in short-handed situations and made the point as forcefully as he could to his players. "A lot of his short-handed goals start when he takes the puck from someone," he told them. "The secret is not to play one on one with him. I don't care who you are or how good you are, don't test him. If you want to test him, make arrangements to go out there and try it in practice. Don't go out there and do it during a game. He'll beat you."

At one point in their 1985 series against the Chicago Blackhawks, the Oilers had scored eleven goals during power plays—six on their own power play and five when the Hawks had the advantage.

"With the type of players we have," explained Sather at the time, "we find that it's better to be on offence than on defence at any point in the game.

"We feel that no matter how many men we've got on the ice, once we get the puck, we should always go on offence. It always seemed kind of strange to me to have guys like Wayne Gretzky and Jari Kurri, who can handle the puck so well, sitting on the bench when we were short-handed, when the kind of guy you want out there is a guy who can handle the puck well.

"You also want someone who can find the open spaces on the ice, and you're never going to get someone who can get into the holes as well as Wayne."

Naturally, the tactic needed some cooperation from the Edmonton defencemen.

"It's not as if we're looking for a goal every time we're out there," explained Coffey. "If a guy is on me when I get the puck, I don't look. I just whack it around the glass as hard as I can. Your main concern is to make sure they don't score.

"But if I have a second, I look for Wayne. Usually, I look right up the middle because as soon as he sees I'm going to get possession, he'll break at full speed and he heads for the opening. The defencemen are most likely to be spread, so he usually has room up the middle.

"Jari plays a bit more defensively. He'll stay back a bit longer, but once he sees the puck going to Wayne, he takes off as well and they'll often trap a defenceman and get a two-on-one."

Gretzky had no problem with the concept. "Coff was a great long passer," he said. "He used to make a pass from behind our net to centre ice like it was a four-foot pass."

Even when the other primary defensive pair of Lee Fogolin and Kevin Lowe came onto the ice, Gretzky continued to be a short-handed threat.

"Fogey and I look for him as well," said Lowe, "but he's usually closer to the boards when we're out there because he knows that we're more apt to bang it off the boards if we get a chance.

"Wayne is an intelligent player. He knows that the puck is more likely to come up the boards, so that's where he goes."

It didn't take long for the Oilers' coaching staff to realize that utilizing Gretzky during an opposition power play provided a number of benefits. If he got the puck, he was liable to get or create a decent scoring chance. Even if the chance was thwarted, he—and/or Kurri—had killed valuable seconds off the power play. Also, Gretzky's presence allowed the Edmonton defencemen to become more involved in the attack.

"If he's got the puck in their zone, you can afford to step up a couple of feet," explained Lowe, "because you know that he's not going to give the puck away and get you trapped. Fogey and I have killed penalties for a couple of years, and we're confident when Wayne is out there. We know that it's safe to move in and get a good shot."

That was another key. On some teams, an offensive chance might occasionally be created on a short-handed situation, and the players would try to make the best of it. But with the Oilers, those breaks were part of the game plan. Every player knew how to respond.

"We know what we have to do in our own zone," said Gretzky. "We play a very aggressive box. We like to close in on the puck in a hurry, and then, when we get the puck, we don't like to just fire it down the ice.

"One of the major problems when you're on the power play—and we're guilty of this too sometimes—is that you get lackadaisical. You figure you've got the extra man, so you don't have to work as hard. But really, when you're on the power play, you have to work harder."

And because the short-handed attack was part of the game plan, it had variations depending on who was on the ice, even if Mark Messier's line was out. It's no coincidence that the top three scorers of short-handed goals in NHL history are Messier, Gretzky and Kurri.

"When Coff is out there, I try to go up the middle," said Gretzky. "He makes those long passes crisply and accurately, and as soon as I see the puck going over to him, I just take off. With the other guys, I go to the boards and come around from behind."

While this was going on, Kurri would also be reading the play. "I break as soon as Wayne does," he said, "but we both try to make a quick turn.

That throws their guys off a bit, and it often means that one of their defencemen gets caught so we get a two-on-one.

"Usually I end up going down the left side because I can get a better shot from the left side. There's more area for me to get the shot off. Wayne often slows down a bit because he knows I'm coming later, and then, if we've got a two-on-one, I just wait for one of those nice passes he makes."

Coffey agreed with Gretzky's approach. "On the power play, you have to work twice as hard," he said. "There's a tendency to let up because you've got the extra man. That's Wayne's philosophy. Sometimes you're going to catch the other team sleeping.

"It's not great to get a short-handed goal scored against you. I don't know if it's the most demoralizing thing that can happen, but it sure doesn't help. And the thing to remember is that it reflects on all five guys on the ice. It's not just one guy."

The Oilers' short-handed feats got the most attention because the league kept separate statistics only for short-handed goals, not four on four. But when Edmonton played four on four, they used what was primarily the same approach—springing the forwards, especially Gretzky and Kurri, up the middle.

In many ways, the Oilers caused even more damage in four-on-four situations than they did short-handed. On the ice, there was nothing the other general managers could do about the Oilers' short-handed game. Off the ice, they found a way. They changed the rules.

Until the end of the 1984–85 season, coincidental minor penalties produced a four-on-four situation. At their subsequent summer meeting, the GMs cited consistency as a reason for instituting a rule change, saying that since coincidental fighting majors did not make each team short-handed for five minutes, minors should not leave each team a man short for two minutes.

It was a rationalization, as everyone knew. Sather was livid. "It's ridiculous," he said. "You're taking away a great and exciting part of the game." The GMs' decision still needed approval from the governors.

Posing for his portrait in his Hespeler minor novice team uniform, in 1974.

Playing for the Sault Ste. Marie Greyhounds in 1978.

Aged 17, with the Indianapolis Racers in the World Hockey Association. Gretzky was still too young to play in the NHL.

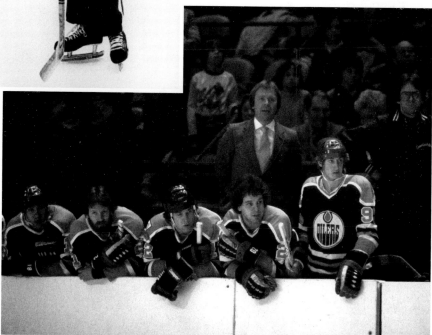

Gretzky gets ready to go back over the sign-free boards in 1980 as coach Glen "Slats" Sather watches the play.

Gretzky vs. Vladislav Tretiak: In the final game of the 1981 Canada Cup, the Canadians started well but couldn't beat Tretiak, whose play was magnificent. The Canadians lost to the Soviets 8–1.

Fifty goals in thirty-nine games! Gretzky sets what he says is his favourite record of the 61 he held when he retired. Philadelphia winger Bill Barber, playing defence on this occasion, makes a futile dive to stop Gretzky putting the puck into an empty net.

1984 Stanley Cup finals. The Oilers' Glenn Anderson hopes to start a break-out past New York Islanders Hall of Fame defenceman Denis Potvin.

Islanders forward Bob Nystrom moves in too late to stop a shot from Gretzky in the 1984 Stanley Cup final.

*The Islanders are in disarray as Gretzky scores to help the Oilers move
towards their first Stanley Cup. Goalie Billy Smith is down and out; Denis
Potvin is leaning on the crossbar; and Bryan Trottier is arriving too late.*

Before the deciding game of the 1984 Stanley Cup finals, Gretzky said that while he was happy to rack up records, they were not his goal. "I said the only thing that matters is the Stanley Cup. Nothing else." The Cup was sweet vindication for Gretzky. The Oilers had just completed their fifth year in the NHL.

"Hopefully, they will look at it from the point of view of the overall good of the league," Sather said.

They didn't.

"I think the NHL is making a big mistake," said Gretzky. "I think the NHL should be more concerned with butt-ending, spearing and three-hour hockey games than getting rid of four-on-four situations."

In 1993, when the Edmonton dynasty had ended and the Gretzky-Kurri threat was no longer the scourge of the league, the rule was rescinded. Sheer coincidence, no doubt.

But in the 1985 playoffs, the Oilers were still able to capitalize on their innovative approach, and Gretzky led them to their second successive Stanley Cup. He had thirty assists, an NHL record until he broke it three years later, and seventeen goals; and he won the Conn Smythe Trophy as the MVP of the playoffs. He had learned his Cup-final lessons against the Islanders. The Philadelphia Flyers, a different style of team altogether, were, like the rest of the hockey world, unable to contain him.

It would seem that Gretzky had nothing left to prove, and really, he didn't. But being Gretzky, he kept on proving it anyway. He was at the peak of his career.

CHAPTER NINE

As far as their supporters were concerned, the Edmonton Oilers of the Gretzky era were confident and self-assured. As far as their detractors were concerned, they were cocky and arrogant. It was hard to make a strong case against either stance because the Oilers always walked that line. Whichever point of view you espoused, there was plenty of evidence to prove your point.

Over the years, Sather and co-coach John Muckler shared the task of keeping the Oilers' ebullience under control, of focusing the talent without letting the cockiness breed complacency. The more success the Oilers had, the more difficult that task became, and once the team had won back-to-back Stanley Cups, it bordered on the impossible.

In that era, it was the great misfortune of the Calgary Flames to be stuck in the Smythe Division with the Oilers. Throughout the Edmonton dynasty, the Flames were the second-best team in the west and, on occasion, the second-best team in the entire National Hockey League. But because of the 1980s playoff format, only one of them could get past the second round, and it tended not to be the Flames.

In 1986, the two teams renewed their annual rivalry. As usual, the Oilers were expected to be the survivor. There was ample precedent.

The Flames opened the series with a 4–1 road win, but there was little concern on the part of the Edmonton players, even though Gretzky had been banged around all night. Jari Kurri suffered a similar fate. Every whistle seemed to prompt a minor scrum—sometimes a major scrum—with lots of pushing, threatening and face-washing. For impartial viewers, it was terminally tedious, but for Jim Peplinski, Neil Sheehy and Tim Hunter, it was a trip to the Promised Land. They were the three main perpetrators of the scrums, and they were merely following the explicit orders of Calgary coach Bob Johnson.

Distasteful as it might have seemed to Oilers fans—and to purists, for that matter—it was the best possible strategy for the Flames to use. There was no sense in getting into an end-to-end battle with the explosive Oilers. Instead, they aimed to distract them, to take them off their game, to bang them around, to inhibit their movement through hooking and holding, and to slow down the proceedings.

Today, that set of tactics probably wouldn't work. Officiating standards have changed. But in that era, with only one referee and the traditional approach that all rules were relaxed in the post-season, it was effective.

It was clear that if the Oilers were to advance in the playoffs, they'd have to forsake the style they loved and play a much grittier game. They bore down and did enough to win Game Two in overtime, but lost Game Three. Gretzky was easily the Oilers' best player, but few, if any, of his teammates were playing up to his level. He had taken a six-stitch cut under the chin from a Calgary stick, but it was considered to be just a part of playoff hockey. "This series is a long way from over, believe me," he said. "When you're playing for the Stanley Cup, you're playing for an awful lot. We're not going to roll over and give someone the Stanley Cup. They're going to have to take it away from us."

At that point, there was every indication that the Flames were poised to do just that.

The Edmonton players remained confident—or cocky, if you prefer—but the coaches didn't share their conviction. "We're not playing the way we're capable of playing," said Sather. "We're not pressing, and we're not getting into the holes. Whether the problem is with the players' not getting into the holes or whether it's Calgary interfering with us so much we can't get there, I don't know. Only the individual player can tell you whether he's giving the second effort or whether he's letting a guy hold him up so he can't get there." Translation: "My guys aren't trying hard enough."

Assistant coach Bob McCammon added, "They're physically intimidating us. I don't mean that they're physically beating up on us. They're just playing a strong physical game and we're allowing it. Out of nine periods, they've won eight."

The Oilers' coaches knew what needed to be done. The problem was that the players weren't doing it. To make their point, Sather and his two assistants ignored the next practice. The players were on the ice by themselves. The message was clear: if you're not going to listen to us anyway, you might as well do whatever it is you want to do.

As the series progressed, the Oilers sporadically followed the game plan the coaches laid out for them. Gretzky continued to be consistently outstanding, but Kurri seemed to be bothered by the Flames' physical play. Messier was nursing a groin injury, and Coffey was going through one of his occasional slumps. Of the six core players, therefore, only Gretzky, Glenn Anderson and Grant Fuhr were playing up to their normal standards.

When the Flames opened a 3–2 series lead, Sather, clearly worried, made a desperate move. For the first time in five years, he split up Kurri and Gretzky, putting Kurri on Messier's line and Anderson with Gretzky.

"It was a gutsy move," said Gretzky. "The line changes were a good shake-up. Mess likes to go to the net. That gave Jari some room. Andy likes to go to the net, and that gave me some room."

Whether the moves made a big difference or not was unclear. But the Oilers did win. After six games, the series was tied.

Game Seven was memorable, but for a reason that Oilers defenceman Steve Smith would prefer to forget.

With the score tied early in the third period, Fuhr left the puck for Smith behind the net. When Smith tried to make a pass up ice, he fired the puck off the back of Fuhr's leg, and it bounced off it and trickled into the net.

The Oilers' season was over.

The cockiness that had often stood the Oilers in such good stead had killed them. Throughout the series, the coaches tried to instil a game plan. Again and again, the players ignored it.

Defenceman Kevin Lowe knew what had happened. "We kept wanting to revert to our normal style," he said, "but over the past couple of years, we've really won the championship by grinding it out. In the games that we won in Calgary in this series, we did it by grinding it out."

Sather was aware of it as well. "We lost as a team," he said. "We had lots of time to come back. We kept dipping and diving at the blue line and twisting and turning. We told them from the beginning that they should dump it in and use the points.

"I guess this team still has some growing up to do. There are still some people who believe that the ones who are running the team don't know what they're doing." In hindsight, it turned out to be a good lesson. And as the adage says, experience is the best teacher. What the adage doesn't say is that experience tends to come at a very high price. In this case, the price was a Stanley Cup that, given what was to follow, would have made the Oilers one of only two teams in NHL history to win five consecutive Stanley Cups.

In sports, as in life, success breeds imitation, so the following season, when the Oilers faced the Philadelphia Flyers in the Stanley Cup final, they knew what to expect. The Flyers would do everything the Flames had done—and more. When the Flames decided to use a host of skill-neutralizing tactics, they were wading into relatively uncharted waters. But this was the way the Flyers played every day, and the approach had lifted them to second place in the overall NHL standings behind the Oilers.

The Flyers were masters at physical intimidation—some of it "accidental," such as Ron Sutter slamming into a goalie with astonishing regularity; some of it downright vicious, such as the stick-swinging of goalie Ron Hextall. On top of that, the Flyers not only held players, they held sticks. They were nowhere near as bad as their famous predecessors in Philadelphia, the Broad Street Bullies of the 1970s, but they did adhere to exactly the same principle: the referee won't call everything because the game would become a travesty, so just keep committing the infractions because you'll get away with most of them.

Had the Oilers been the same team as the year before, the Flyers would have come out on top. But to their credit, the Oilers had not only learned their lesson, they were coming in with a different approach. For the first time in their existence, they were heading down the mountain. Throughout their first four years, they had been climbing the mountain. Then they got to the summit and stayed there for two years. Then they got knocked off. This time, they were facing the choice of battling their way back to the top, or continuing their slide and giving their critics all the ammunition they wanted. For the first time in their hockey lives, there was a fear of failure.

"We changed a lot of people over the year," said Sather on the eve of the series, "but I think that handle was a misrepresentation of our hockey club. I think sometimes they got uptight, and it was perceived in a different way. I've seen these guys on occasion play in a certain way, and you wonder what happened.

"Guys will say, 'Oh, it's a lackadaisical attitude on their part,' but it's not. They've got nerves the same as a lot of other people do."

The series against Philadelphia was a tough one, as tough as any the Oilers faced in their run. And it took them seven games. But finally, with Gretzky leading the way with thirty-four points in twenty-one games, the Oilers persevered.

They had won their third Stanley Cup in four years, and they were back on top of the hockey world.

———

For those first three Stanley Cups that Gretzky won, the story line had been essentially the same.

The Edmonton gang, their young players now aware of the rigours of the playoffs, cruised through a regular season that was all sweetness and light. No morale problems. No injuries. No defections. Then, in the playoffs, with only hockey on their minds and being the heavy favourites, they called upon the tactics that had served them so well, cranked up the defence a bit, and won the Cup.

In the case of their 1988 Cup, only the last three words of that story line were true.

Until the playoffs started, it was a horrible year for the Oilers. The rift between the team and penny-pinching owner Peter Pocklington was growing ever wider. Messier skipped training camp to support his demands for a better contract. Coffey took it a giant step further: he held out so long that the acrimony reached the breaking point. Coffey announced that he was so sick of dealing with Pocklington that he would never again play for the Oilers. He was traded to Pittsburgh.

Even Gretzky, who usually managed to rise above the internal conflicts, got caught up in this one. Like the rest of the team, he was despondent during the early stages of the season. From a hockey point of view, these guys had grown up together. They were like a family, and now Coffey was gone.

The mood in the dressing room, which had always been full of outgoing, fun-loving guys, was noticeably muted. It wasn't funereal, but it certainly wasn't anything like what it had been.

"I was a big part of it," admitted Gretzky years later, "because I was close to Coff, and I couldn't understand why Slats had traded him, why they couldn't have worked out their differences. I was probably as down as anybody—more down than anybody."

Coffey wasn't an original NHL Oiler. Only Gretzky, protected at the time of the WHA merger, was. But the guys who were subsequently drafted or had been there for the first Cup were viewed within the team as originals. Andy Moog and Randy Gregg were both in that category, and they too were absent that season.

Moog, like Coffey, was unable to come to contract terms and left. Gregg, a doctor, wanted to practise medicine while playing hockey and forsook the Oilers for Canada's national team in the upcoming Calgary Olympics.

A couple of other players who were not originals but who had been around for the 1987 Cup run, Kent Nilsson and Reijo Ruotsalainen, had gone back to Europe.

Then, to make matters worse, Gretzky suffered the first serious injury of his career and missed sixteen games in mid-season.

The cumulative toll of these setbacks was that, for the first time in seven years, the Oilers didn't finish first in the Smythe Division. For the first time in seven years, they didn't earn 100 points. Even Gretzky's streak ended. Ever since his first season, when he had the same number of points as Marcel Dionne, he had run away with the scoring title. This time, he finished second to Mario Lemieux.

By the end of the regular season, the Oilers appeared to be a team in total disarray. The accepted wisdom, throughout the league, the media and hockey's fan base, was that the Edmonton dynasty was over.

As the playoffs opened, there was certainly no evident reason to challenge that view. The Flames had not only finished ahead of the Oilers but had become even stronger at the trading deadline with the addition of two excellent defencemen, Rob Ramage and Brad McCrimmon. Adding those two to the best power-play point tandem in the league—Al MacInnis and Gary Suter—appeared to make the Flames invincible.

They certainly seemed that way to Calgary's media and fans (two groups that often overlapped).

Both the Flames and Oilers survived the first playoff round, and on the morning of the next series opener, I wandered into the lobby of the downtown Calgary hotel where the Oilers were staying. "Have you seen this?" asked Muckler, brandishing that morning's *Calgary Sun*. "And all this," he continued, waving his arm at the array of Flames banners hanging all over the lobby. "It makes me wonder why we bothered to come. We don't have a chance."

Two weeks earlier, even Muckler might have believed that. But since then, the Oilers had twice bounced back from three-goal deficits to dispatch the Winnipeg Jets, and in the process, the old Oilers had been resuscitated. Suddenly, the team's lifers accepted the guys who were new to the team. Just as suddenly, the new Oilers felt that they were a part of the squad, not just interlopers. Because players don't get paid in the playoffs, the recurring gripes over salaries had become irrelevant. They just wanted to go out and prove that, no matter what anyone else might think, the dynasty was still very much alive.

"Against Winnipeg, we noticed it right away," said Kevin Lowe, one of the originals. "There was a considerable difference in the way the guys reacted. There was camaraderie."

But the Flames were not the Jets. They were a powerful team that relied heavily on their power play. Justifiably so: its success rate in the regular season was a whopping 29.5 per cent. But in the opening game, they scored only once in nineteen minutes of power-play time, and that lone goal was something of a fluke. The Oilers won 4–3.

Suddenly, there was concern in Calgary. But it was early. A loss in the opener could be overcome.

Gretzky had a different scenario in mind. "The rivalry at that point between Calgary and Edmonton got so intense, it got out of control," he said. "Not just with the players; the cities got into it. I remember going to Calgary thinking, 'We're in for a dogfight because they have home-ice advantage.'

"We were down 3–1 in Game One. We ended up coming back and winning."

Gretzky remembered the reaction of Calgary coach Terry Crisp. "He said, 'I don't know what happened. We outplayed them. We dominated them. Gretzky and Kurri were nonexistent, and they ended up getting the tying goal and the winner and we lose 4–3.' He was right. I remember thinking, 'We had a bad game and we won.'

"Now I'm thinking if we can win Game Two, we're going to beat Calgary. And we really felt that Calgary was the only team in the NHL that could beat us. Teams could beat us once in a while, but over seven games, there was no way.

"That was when I was engaged to Janet, and it was about four o'clock in the afternoon of Game Two. She said, 'You'll never guess what happened.'

"I said, 'What?'

"She said, 'I'm pregnant.'

"We'd sort of planned it that, once we got engaged, that would happen. I went to the rink and I was on a high."

Once again, the Flames had a late lead—4–3 this time with four minutes left—but the Oilers, using the play that had been such a staple over the years, went to the attack with a long pass up the middle. It's a play that coaches abhor, a play that can get a kid sent back to the minors. When you use that play, to quote songwriter Jim Steinman, you're living in a powder keg and giving off sparks. But in this case, the passer was Gretzky and the puck was right on target. Mike Krushelnyski, standing at the red line to conform to the offside rules of the era, didn't even stop the puck. He just put his stick on the ice and redirected it to a streaking Kurri. That was all the Oilers needed. The game was tied.

The old Oilers were back—in more ways than one. In the intermission prior to overtime, Sather told his troops, "Go out and play to win. Play to your strengths. Don't lay back worrying about stopping them from scoring."

Back to river hockey. Back to original Oiler hockey. Someone—no one remembers who—piped up, "Even short-handed, Glen?"

"Even short-handed," said Sather.

The Oilers were so determined to attack that Messier, trying to get a scoring chance, hauled down Joey Mullen beside the Calgary net. Now the Flames, with their vaunted power play, had an opportunity to pull this one out.

For the first forty-six seconds, Sather used his defensively oriented penalty-killing forwards. Then he sent out Gretzky and Kurri. Sather's message was still ringing in their ears. Attack. Even short-handed.

Immediately, Gretzky pounced on a loose puck, started a rush down the left side and set up a scoring chance, but Mike Vernon made the save. Seconds later, Gretzky was at it again, but this time, he came down the left side alone. He stepped over the blue line and, only about six feet from the boards, blasted a shot. It was a blur. It was also in the net.

"I went to the rink on a high after finding out Janet was pregnant," he recalled decades later. "The next thing I know, it's 4–4 and it's overtime and I'm coming down the wing and I'm thinking, 'There's no way I'm missing this.'

"That's as hard as I can hit it. No question. I can't hit it any harder.

"That was the greatest goal of my career."

He remembers the moment with great pride—and a little bit of shame. It may be the only time in his career that he gloated.

"When I scored," he recalled. "I remember turning the corner, and at that time, the Zamboni was right there. I'm yelling, 'Take the ice out.'

"The guy said, 'What?'

"I said, 'You don't have to worry. We're not coming back. You can take the ice out.'

"I knew once we got back to Edmonton, we weren't going to lose. Had it been 2–0 for us at home, it still could have been a series, but I knew that once we won that second game in Calgary, they weren't going to beat us."

They didn't. As Gretzky predicted, the series did not go back to Calgary. It was an Oilers sweep.

The Detroit Red Wings were next in the Campbell Conference final and didn't give the Oilers much trouble, thanks to one of the many astute coaching moves that Sather and Muckler made over the years.

This time, they unveiled a new power-play formation. Instead of using the two defencemen as quarterbacks, they let Gretzky do the job from an area at the hash marks near the boards.

"When you've got five on four, somebody's always got to be open," he said with eloquent simplicity. "The key to success on the power play is to hit that open man."

And who better to do that than the best passer the game has ever seen?

On the ice, Gretzky was once again starting to feel invincible. Off the ice, he was coming in for criticism. Even Pocklington, who should have been supportive of his superstar, joined the chorus. He suggested publicly that Gretzky's impending marriage was hampering his performance on the ice.

"That's unfair," said Gretzky. "I've got enough pressure on me, and I've got the owner of the hockey team saying this. Whether he's trying to buffalo the press or whatever, I don't need the extra pressure, and Janet doesn't need it, either. It's unfair and it's uncalled for."

I suggested in a lighthearted fashion that perhaps they should elope.

"We thought about it," he said, "but we've both got families, and we want to enjoy the wedding and let our families enjoy it."

The announcement had set off a media feeding frenzy in Canada, with many observers suggesting it was the country's version of a royal wedding.

"Baloney," Gretzky said. "Nowhere near it. That's unfair, too. We're just two normal people, a Canadian and an American, getting married."

Even Gretzky, who hadn't been out of the public eye since he was a child, was shocked by the media reaction to the impending nuptials. "I guess it's what you come to expect," he said. "I guess it comes with the territory, but I never really had that much attention paid to my personal life until I was engaged to Janet.

"There's no question she has rejuvenated my life," he said. "She has been a big influence on my career.

"This is the first year I faced any kind of adversity, and it could have been a tough year for me mentally. But she made it positive. She was there telling me it was the best thing that could have happened to me."

It made Pocklington's assertions all the more curious. Gretzky was convinced that the arrival of Janet in his life made him a better hockey player, but Pocklington didn't agree. It was a spectacularly stupid thing to say, especially since Gretzky was leading the Oilers to another Stanley Cup and was on his way to his second Conn Smythe Trophy.

After cruising past the Red Wings, the Oilers had little trouble with the Boston Bruins, winning in four and a half games.

Game Four had to be cancelled midway through because of a power failure in the decrepit Boston Garden, so it was replayed in Edmonton, and the Oilers completed the sweep.

But an explanation for Pocklington's remarks was not far away. He was in the process of trading Gretzky and hoping to minimize the negative fallout. It didn't work.

That power-failure makeup game was the last one Gretzky ever played as an Oiler. It was also the last Stanley Cup he would ever win.

CHAPTER TEN

Wayne Gretzky always says that the best game he ever played was the second game of the 1987 Canada Cup final. As far as the rest of us are concerned, the first and third weren't too bad, either.

His father, Walter, originally disagreed with the popular assessment of Wayne's contribution to Game One. But the fact remains that, in that series, Canadians saw not only some of the greatest hockey ever played, but also some of the greatest hockey Wayne Gretzky ever played.

The tournament marked a changing of the guard in Canadian international hockey. The Team Canada coach was to be a first-timer, a thirty-eight-year-old with no NHL playing experience and only four years' coaching experience: Mike Keenan. A promising kid by the name of Mario Lemieux was trying out for the team and seemed highly likely to make the cut. The New York Islanders' involvement, like the team's dynasty, was mostly a memory. Nevertheless, the nation's mood was optimistic, as was always the case at the beginning of these tournaments.

It was far from hockey weather when the thirty-five hopefuls showed up in Montreal on August 4. Montreal is not known for its heat waves, but when they come, they are lengthy and steamy, and this one was no exception.

Gretzky, as he often did in these circumstances, spent a good part of the evening prior to the opening practice hanging around the hotel lobby, chatting with fans, media and the usual assortment of hangers-on. But when the training camp officially opened the next day, he was all business. He had a clear message to send.

As soon as Keenan blew his first whistle—the universal command for the troops to assemble around him—Gretzky, who had been designated captain, skated over to Keenan's side. Mark Messier took a position on Keenan's other flank.

Keenan remembers Gretzky's actions well. "He couldn't get any closer than he was," he said two decades later. "His shoulder was up against me while I was giving some instructions. It was his affirmation of me as a coach. He was telling the rest of them, 'We have to listen to what we're doing here. Everybody has got to be on board.' The very first whistle! The very first practice!"

When I mentioned Keenan's interpretation to Gretzky, he agreed. "Yeah, I did that," he said, "because he was a young guy and nobody knew what to expect of Mike at that time.

"I really thought that Mike, as a young guy, was nervous. I went and stood beside him, and I had Mess go to the other side."

Keenan admitted that he was indeed nervous—until Gretzky's actions affirmed his status. He says he'll never forget that moment.

Even so, he was still "Iron Mike," the nickname he had earned during his years as coach of the Philadelphia Flyers. His was not one of those ironic British-style nicknames where a bald man is called Curly or a giant is called Tiny. They didn't call him Iron Mike because they couldn't think of anything else to call him. This was to be no holiday camp.

Once again, to help fill the coffers of Alan Eagleson, the NHL's best players were forfeiting a major chunk of their short summer, a sacrifice that should not be taken lightly. Once the NHL season is under way, days off are rare. The players either play, practise or travel almost every day for seven months. Many of them then continue the season for up to two more months depending on how well they do in the playoffs.

Yet here were the best players in the game, guys who certainly weren't doing it for the pittance they were to be paid, on August 4 kicking off a tournament that would run until September 15.

Eagleson, in his role as executive director of the NHL Players' Association, said he was representing his charges by giving so many of them a chance to make the team. Coincidentally, this approach also allowed for extra intra-squad games, exhibition games, a longer tournament and a best-of-three final, all of which increased the profit.

Iron Mike put the candidates to work right away with some gruelling high-tempo practices, so much so that, before long, there was discontent. The players knew they would need to be at their best to beat the Soviet Union, the team they all saw as the inevitable opponent in the final, but with those games being so far away, they felt a more leisurely approach might be warranted.

Accordingly, a delegation was sent to confront Keenan. As captain and alternate captain, Gretzky and Messier went. Also present, representing the popular view in the matter, was Raymond Bourque.

Keenan still remembers that incident as much as he remembers the opening practice, but he chuckles when telling this story.

"They came up to me and they said, 'Gee, this is structured, we're working awfully hard,' and so on.

"I said, 'We're playing the best team we ever faced and we have to win this thing, but if that's what you want, I've got no problem backing off you guys.'

"Then I said to Wayne, 'Wayne, what are the expectations of the Canadian public? Of course, it's to win the gold medal. I'm not putting any demands on you guys with the exception of the on-ice practices, none whatsoever, but if you want to back off, we can.

"One thing, though: Am I supposed to tell—or are you going to tell—the Canadian public we're going to back off a little bit because we've got too much work to do here and you want to take it kind of easy?'

"Wayne said, 'Mike, forget this meeting ever existed.'

"The whole meeting took about two minutes. Wayne said, 'Mike, you're absolutely right. I'm embarrassed I'm here. I'm sorry. See you tomorrow.'

"It flashed on him in about ten seconds. What are we doing here? The practices had a lot of tempo, but we never practised more than an hour. We're playing the best team we ever faced and we have to win this thing."

I asked Gretzky if Keenan's recollections correctly represented the way the meeting went.

"That's pretty accurate," he said. "We all said the same thing."

Also accurate was Keenan's evaluation of the opposition. This was near the end of the era in which the Soviet Union made it a priority to dominate sports for the propaganda value, and these matches were seen as a battle of culture versus culture.

The Cold War was still very much in existence. The Iron Curtain was still in place. There were no Soviet players in the NHL. Being an international athlete in the Soviet Union meant that you trained at least ten months a year—eleven or more if you didn't win a world championship—and you trained hard with the full support and pressure of the state behind you.

The team the Soviet Union sent to the 1987 Canada Cup was indisputably the best hockey team that nation had ever assembled, and unless Canada could prove differently, it would also be the best team the world had ever seen.

Gretzky, as keen a student of the international hockey scene as he was of the NHL scene, said it was important to note that the basic Soviet style hadn't changed since the famous 1972 Summit Series. Canada's style had evolved—an evolution that had been forced upon North American players by Soviet domination.

"We're at the point now," he said, "that the European, NHL and Soviet styles have become so similar. In the past, you associated the NHL with tight checking, but now it's tight checking with speed. Every team moves the puck quickly. Puck movement and forechecking are a big part of success in the NHL. That's going to make it a lot easier for us to play the Soviets."

Not easy, but easier. In earlier meetings, the Soviet forwards, with their nifty stickhandling and passing, had moved the puck up the middle and created opportunity after opportunity. But Canadian hockey had evolved to the point that, by 1987, that tactic was no longer effective. Now, the Soviets were going to have to play on the periphery, and it was Canada's intention to own the area along the boards and behind the net. If you wanted to go there, you were going to pay a price.

There would be no goon show. Keenan had banned fighting in training camp, saying that anyone who tried to win a position by fighting would instead lose it. But he still wanted rugged hockey—clean, but rugged.

People like Gretzky and Lemieux—both of whom surprised no one by making the cut—were not expected to throw bodychecks, but the others were to apply what Keenan referred to as "controlled, disciplined aggression."

As Team Canada took shape during the weeks leading up to the key games, so did Gretzky's moulding of Mario Lemieux into a great player.

Only a minimal portion of the information concerning that development comes from Gretzky himself. It is not his nature to make pronouncements on such an issue. Furthermore, it involved a confrontation, something with which Gretzky is never comfortable. Nevertheless, there were plenty of people in that camp who saw it happen and recognized it for what it was.

They say that, had it not been for Gretzky, Lemieux would never have evolved into the dominant player that he became. Obviously, Lemieux had superb talent and, just as obviously, he would have been a prolific scorer. But Gretzky pushed him to go beyond that, to become the best player in the world.

I asked Keenan where Lemieux went when Gretzky stood beside his coach at the opening of training camp. "He was standing in the background," he laughed. "He was in awe."

At that point, Lemieux had never even played in an NHL post-season, let alone a world-level professional tournament. Gretzky was a veteran with Stanley Cup and Canada Cup victories to his credit, not to mention a closet full of NHL trophies.

"Wayne was at that point in his career where he was the best," recalled Keenan, "but I think he needed someone to keep pushing him.

"His attitude was, 'Okay Mario, I'm going to teach you everything I know about this for two reasons. And two good reasons. One, if I can teach you and accelerate your ability in six weeks, it's good for Canada, good for the NHL and good for this team. And two, you're going to make me a better player because now I'm going to be thinking, "Where's Mario?" for the next ten years.'

"He basically said, 'Even though I'm going to teach you everything I know, you're still not going to be as good as me. I'm just going to drive my game up.'

"Wayne never verbalized it, but I saw it unfold in front of my eyes," Keenan said. "He was challenging himself. It was unbelievable. It was great to watch."

It was clear that Lemieux had tremendous talent. He had racked up 351 points during his three years in the NHL despite missing thirty-one games due to injury. Gretzky knew, as did Messier and other Edmonton stars, that Lemieux represented the future of Canadian hockey. Strangely enough, much of the credit for that has to go to Glen Sather.

As coach and GM of the Oilers in their dynasty days, Sather always impressed upon his charges the need to look at the larger picture—the game's heritage and its future. Sather had played for the Montreal Canadiens and seen the impact of tradition and the necessity of passing the torch. In their formative years, the young Oilers stars heard him stress this message and took it to heart.

Now it was time to start passing the torch to Lemieux, and they did so. "Mario was just a kid," recalled Keenan, "and they brought him along. Maybe because of '84 and the internal squabbles, and what they had gone through, there was no delineation, no separation. They were a team.

"They were guiding Mario and bringing him along. He learned quickly, but they had him on the fast track. He was in awe of them when he got there, but he was coming along quickly. You could see it, and his skill set was always so high."

In fact, it was clear to Gretzky that in some areas, Lemieux's skills were superior to his own. Accordingly, once the tournament got under way and a detrimental tendency began to appear, Gretzky felt the need to lay down the law. Although he and Lemieux weren't always on the ice at the same time, they played together often enough that an understanding was necessary. On one occasion, they had generated a break and as they closed in, Gretzky set up Lemieux. Lemieux passed the puck back to Gretzky.

Afterwards, Gretzky announced the future strategy: he would make the passes; Lemieux would take the shots.

Gretzky tries to avoid confirming that he told Lemieux how to play. At first, he put it this way: "All I ever said was, 'Just watch Mess and me. Be the first guy to practice. Practise hard.' It was not so much what we told him. We just said, 'Watch.'

"If Mike said, 'We're going to do twenty-five minutes of skating,' we'd say, 'All right. Let's go.' Don't say, 'Aww, jeez.'"

Gretzky says the message was "Watch." But the implicit message was "Watch, learn and copy."

Others involved in the tournament say that, as the camp progressed, Gretzky became increasingly unhappy with Lemieux's behaviour. The team's home base was Montreal, and Lemieux, on familiar turf and away from the rigours of league play, was enjoying himself— perhaps a bit too much.

Finally, at practice one day, Gretzky exploded.

He told Lemieux he had too much talent to be wasting it this way. He told him that he was letting everyone down—the coaches, his fans, his family and his teammates. He told him that together, they could form an unbeatable tandem, but they could do it only if Lemieux dedicated himself to the game.

That story circulated for some time without corroboration, but finally, more than a decade later, Keenan confirmed it. "I saw that happen on the ice," he said. "I saw Wayne give it to him. . . . That's when Mario became a player."

It was in the following season that Lemieux, for the first time, showed the domination that everyone knew had been lurking in the background and won his first scoring title.

As expected, the Canadians and the Soviets met in the finals. There were some missteps for Canada along the way, including a 9–4 loss to the Soviets in a pre-tournament exhibition game, but by the time the final rolled around, no one really cared about the run-up. When Canada and the Soviets had met in the round robin, the hockey was delightful and the result was a 3–3 tie. A spectacular best-of-three final series was widely anticipated by the fans, and that's exactly what they got.

The opener was played in Montreal, and although the Canadians fell behind 4–1 in the second period, they stormed back and Gretzky scored to give Canada a 5–4 lead with less than three minutes remaining in regulation time.

But Andrei Khomutov brought the Soviets back thirty-two seconds later, and then, 5:33 into overtime, Alexander Semak took a shot that banked off Gretzky's skate and careened past Grant Fuhr to give the Soviet Union the win.

Merely reciting the scoring plays doesn't come close to recreating the drama and the excitement. The entire game was played at breakneck speed, yet there were still crunching checks and glorious defensive plays that matched the calibre of the offensive play.

"That was probably the last of the Russian dynasty," said Bourque. "It was the best hockey I've ever been a part of. The pace was incredible."

Even in overtime—what there was of it—neither team withdrew into a defensive shell, and, as had been the case in regulation time, Keenan was using Gretzky as much as possible.

Walter Gretzky had no problem with how many times his son went on the ice in that game. But he was less happy about how many times he came off. "My dad was really mad at me," said Gretzky years later, when we were reminiscing about that game. "He said, 'Don't you ever do that again!'

"That's really something, when you've just lost a game, and your dad is blaming you for it. He said I had stayed on the ice too long in overtime, and I was on the ice when they scored the winner.

"I'll never forget it. I had asked Mike if my dad could go on the charter from Montreal to Hamilton, and Mike said, 'Sure.'

"So we're getting onto the bus and my dad says, 'How are you feeling?'

"'I'm a little tired,' I said.

"He said, 'No. I mean how are you feeling?'

"I said, 'What do you mean?'

"This is what his exact words were. He said, 'You lost the game.' That's what he told me.

"I said, 'What?'

"He said, 'You stayed on the ice too long on the fifth goal, the one to tie it. You shouldn't have been out there.'

"I'm thinking, 'Oh yeah. This is going to be a nice flight.'

"I said, 'I've just got you a ride on the charter and you're telling me that?'"

Wayne always took his father's criticisms to heart. There's no doubt that he was determined that his father would have no cause for complaint after Game Two. The result was, by his own estimation, "the greatest game I ever played in my life."

He had other great games, but they weren't a patch on this one. "Second is not even close," he said.

There could hardly be a better time to produce it. The Canadians had already lost one game in the best-of-three series, and they were facing what was indisputably one of the greatest teams in the history of the sport.

"I think at that time, the Russian team was the best team in the world," said Gretzky years later. "The level they were at, they could have beaten any NHL team. You always go against the level of the team you're playing against, and that was twenty great players. I didn't get a goal, but that was the best game I ever played."

No, he didn't get a goal. He did, however, get five assists.

Canada came out blazing and had no fewer than fourteen clear-cut scoring chances in the first period. Many NHL games don't produce fourteen scoring chances, even if you combine the efforts of both teams. But the Soviet team was no NHL team. It had the ability to weather the storm and fight back to create chances of its own. Once again, regulation time ended in a 5–5 tie, and once again, the two teams had put on a magnificent display of hockey.

In overtime, the end-to-end play and the glorious scoring opportunities kept coming, but the goalies were equal to the task, and halfway through the second overtime, the score still stood at 5–5.

Gretzky was rarely off the ice. Keenan kept sending him out, and Gretzky, ever obedient to a coach's desires, kept going over the boards. Years later, he told me he was so dog-tired that he was sitting on the bench and no longer had the strength to control his bladder. He started to urinate. "I didn't have enough energy to stop," he said.

"Mike kept going, 'Gretz, are you ready?' I said, 'Mike, I just sat down.'"

But Keenan was ruthless. He kept sending Gretzky out, and finally, at 10:06 of the second overtime, the now-established strategy came into play. Gretzky could shoot or he could pass to Lemieux. He passed. Lemieux shot. Game over.

It was Gretzky's fifth assist of the night and Lemieux's third goal.

Clearly, barring a disaster in Game Three, this was destined to be a series for the ages. Gretzky was exhausted, and after the game, he sank back into the passenger seat of his dad's car. He was going to spend the night in his boyhood home in nearby Brantford.

"We were driving home and my dad says, 'What time do you want to get up?' and it dawned on me. I said, 'I can't believe it. I've got to go to practice in the morning. Mike is having us practise.' My dad says, 'I'm going to call him.'"

As a father, Walter wanted to shelter his son. But as a hockey coach and the man who had instilled so many admirable qualities into that son, he knew the response. Wayne told him to do no such thing.

"Getting up for practice after a game like that was unusual back then," he recalled. "But Mike was ahead of his time. Nowadays, the way we analyze sports, it's better for you to get up and just go and do a light workout. You'll feel better the next day than if you sleep in and lie around all day."

It seemed that the entire country was caught up in the excitement surrounding Game Three. This was fifteen years after the famous Summit Series and a whole new generation of hockey fans had grown up listening to stories of the "greatest series ever." Now it appeared that accolade was to be passed on.

The players were as ebullient as the fans. "The energy in the room was incredible," said Keenan decades later. "I've never felt it before or since in any team I've ever coached. The Stanley Cup team that I had in New York in 1994 was a special team, but with that Team Canada in 1987, you're talking about the elite of the elite, and the energy in the room was unbelievable.

"It was kind of like you couldn't walk on the floor almost. You were above it. But they were very quiet, very serious. They had this rhythm going, this energy getting ready."

Keenan paused, then smiled. "Then we came out and we were getting smoked." Eight minutes into the game, the Soviets were up 3–0.

Looking back, Keenan was able to take that development lightly. But he certainly didn't take it lightly at the time.

Was it to be a repeat of the Challenge Cup embarrassment, when the two teams split the first two games, and then the Soviets won the third 6–0? Was it to be a repeat of the 1981 Canada Cup embarrassment, when the Soviets beat Canada 8–1 in the final game?

This game had hardly started, but already, Keenan had been double-shifting Gretzky. He was exhausted. "He said, 'I need a break.' I could see it anyway," said Keenan. "He was gaunt. He had played his best hockey and it was a super-exhilarating pace, and he said, 'I need a break.'

"I said, 'You've got it.' That's why I changed it up a bit."

Instead of going to his finesse players when the team needed a lift, he went elsewhere, sending out Rick Tocchet, Brent Sutter and Dale Hawerchuk. "I said, 'You guys go out and change this whole game plan because these Soviets are used to finesse and skill. They aren't used to people hammering them and grinding them.' That's when the grinders went out."

They did their job. Tocchet, at the end of a long shift, scored, and Canada was back in it.

Gretzky remembered Keenan's change in tactics well. "We were down 3–0 and I looked at him," he said, "and he sat us down a little bit and played a whole bunch of different guys. That was what made that team great. Rick Tocchet scored. Brent Sutter scored. Those guys got us back in the game.

"People forget we were out of it. I was sitting on the bench thinking, 'We came all the way back in that game two nights ago and now we're going to lose like this?'

"Grant Fuhr shut the door. Brian Propp was playing great. He scored, too. All of a sudden, we're back in the game again and away we went."

The grinders did more than score. They set the tone. The end-to-end hockey was still there, but now it was being punctuated by Soviets being plastered against the glass or flattened against the boards. In the crucial area behind the net, the Canadian forwards were especially effective, and the longer the game went, the more that region was ceded to Team Canada. In fact, of the five goals Canada scored that night on the way towards the apparently mandatory 5–5 tie in the late stages, four started behind the Soviet goal. "It was fierce, the infighting in that trench area," recalled Keenan. "That's where they won those battles to come out and stuff the puck into the net. They weren't pretty, but it didn't matter."

Now the stage was set for more heroics. The clock was ticking down, and with less than two minutes to play, the Canadians set up for a potentially dangerous faceoff in their own end. "The little bit of a surprise," recalled Keenan, "was that everybody thought I was going to send out Mess to take the faceoff because it was in our zone."

Instead, he sent out Hawerchuk.

Keenan liked to go with the hot hand. Hawerchuk was having a good night, and Keenan knew his capabilities well. He had coached him in junior hockey. The other two on the line? Who else but Gretzky and Lemieux?

"I was sitting at the cottage back in July," said Keenan. "I was thinking even then that this would be the matchup in the finals.

"I thought, 'We've got to have something ready for this team we're going to be playing in the finals, and the thing I thought about was the combination of Wayne and Mario with Mario playing right wing for Wayne, but I wouldn't show it until the end of the tournament because I didn't want anybody to pre-scout us before that and get an idea of what was coming. We had only a few things that would make a difference, and that was one of them."

Then came The Goal. With the exception of Paul Henderson's famous goal in the 1972 series, probably no goal has ever been shown so often on Canadian television.

Hawerchuk justified Keenan's hunch by pushing the puck ahead as Lemieux moved into the circle. "Mario came across with the big reach and tipped it," said Keenan, "and away they went."

Lemieux squeezed between two Soviet forwards to get the puck, and as they lunged, they knocked each other down. Before they could get up, Lemieux lured another Soviet out of position by chipping the puck past the pinching defenceman.

Now the puck was out over the blue line and the Canadians were flying towards the Soviet end in possession of the puck. To be specific, Gretzky was in possession of the puck, having picked it up when Lemieux chipped it.

Somehow, defenceman Larry Murphy was in front of both of them, spearheading the attack. When Gretzky crossed the blue line, Murphy went to the net, pulling the Soviet defenceman with him, but he was still open for a pass.

Gretzky knew what he had taught Lemieux: I pass; you shoot.

Lemieux took the perfect pass in the high slot, cruised a few feet and snapped a wrist shot that goalie Sergei Mylnikov waved at but had no hope of catching. Canada was up 6–5 with only 1:26 remaining.

"Mario did what Gretz had told him," said Keenan. "He had told Mario, 'Don't pass it back to me. You bury it.' Murph was a good decoy, and Mario buried it."

Many years later, Gretzky confirmed what he wouldn't admit at the time, but many people knew. He had indeed told Mario the tactical approach he wanted from him.

"You know what I remember most?" Gretzky asked as we reminisced about that tournament. "We were playing the Czechs, and Mario and I had a two-on-one. You know me. I made the pass, and Mario passed it back to me and I missed.

"So we go to the bench, and I looked at Mario and I said, 'Mario, don't take this the wrong way.' I said, 'I know I have more goals than you, but you're a better goal scorer than I am. You're a natural goal scorer. When I give you the puck, just shoot it. That's why I'm giving it to you. You're stronger. You're bigger. You just shoot it. I'm going to give it to you at the last second to make the play.'

"He said, 'Okay.'

"That's what I remember about that last goal. We got the puck. Larry Murphy might as well have been my dad. He was never going to see the puck. But in fairness to Larry Murphy, not everyone would have done what he did.

"He went to the net. How many times in practice do you say, 'First guy go to the net'? If he doesn't go to the net, there's no play.

"So Larry Murphy, he does exactly what he needs to do. He goes to the net. I give it to Mario and I'm thinking, 'Shoot it. Don't give it back to me.' And actually, when I passed it to him, I went like this." Gretzky pulled his hands up towards his chest. "Like I don't have a stick. I don't want it back, because I know Mario can shoot the puck better than anybody in hockey. He put it in the perfect spot."

"I was doing my part," laughed Murphy when we spoke at his 2005 induction into the Hockey Hall of Fame. "I was a decoy. That's what they get for worrying about me. Mario made them pay."

The Canadians hung on for the final eighty-six seconds, and the 1987 Canada Cup was theirs.

It was a magnificent series, not only for Canada but for hockey lovers everywhere. The skill level was astonishing, the action was relentless, and big leads came and went.

But it was an especially sweet moment for a new generation of Canadian fans, coming fifteen years after the Summit Series. Perhaps there's something to that number. The next seminal moment in Canadian hockey was to come a further fifteen years later, when Gretzky, by then an executive, built the team that won the gold medal at the 2002 Olympics.

But as a player, 1987 was his finest hour. He was named the most valuable player. He led the tournament with eighteen assists—Sergei Makarov was second with eight. The goal-scoring leader was Mario Lemieux with eleven.

During Lemieux's career, there were often suggestions that he and Gretzky were not close. Those suggestions invariably came from people who knew neither man.

When Gretzky retired in 1999, his final game was against Lemieux's Pittsburgh Penguins. "I almost cried a couple of times," said Lemieux. "I caught myself, but I remembered the way I felt in Pittsburgh when I skated around and thanked the fans and everybody that had been a part of my career.

"To see Wayne on the ice and to see him cry the way he did, it was very emotional. But I was very happy for him, that he's doing what he's doing."

Lemieux was both gracious and lavish in his praise of Gretzky. "He's such a great ambassador," he said. "He has been a great gentleman for as long as I can remember."

He went on to speak of that fateful 1987 Canada Cup series, when Gretzky pushed him to become better, and confirmed Gretzky's impact on his development. "I think that in 1987, playing with him in the Canada Cup and having a chance to play and practise with him for six weeks, was a great thing," Lemieux said. "He really showed me how to be a winner, how hard you have to work to become the number-one player in the world. It certainly doesn't come easy.

"Not too many people can say that they had that much time to spend with the greatest player in the world. I'll cherish those moments until the day I die."

Keenan remembered it fondly as well. "Mario was still a boy," he said. "He was only twenty-one. He couldn't believe how much he learned about winning. And Wayne said it was the best hockey he ever played."

On that subject, there is no greater authority.

CHAPTER ELEVEN

Wayne Gretzky was enjoying one love affair when another one ended.

On August 9, 1988, he and his new wife, Janet, were three weeks into their marriage and staying at Alan Thicke's house in Los Angeles when he found out that his ten-year love affair with the Edmonton Oilers was over. He had been traded to the Los Angeles Kings.

The trade didn't come as a great shock to Gretzky. As soon as it became apparent that it was coming, he took part in the negotiations, but the timing of the announcement had been in some doubt. It was called a trade because a number of players were involved. Gretzky, Marty McSorley and Mike Krushelnyski were going to Los Angeles. In return, the Oilers got Jimmy Carson, Craig Redmond, Martin Gelinas, three first-round draft picks over a five-year span and fifteen million dollars. But really, it was much more of a sale than a trade, a way for Oilers owner Peter Pocklington to line his pockets.

The trade was initially presented to the public as a deal that Gretzky had requested. But as the facts gradually emerged, it became apparent that the deal had been made by Pocklington. Even general manager Glen

Sather did not have a hand in the proceedings until Pocklington's decision to move Gretzky had become irrevocable.

Only when it became obvious that he was going to be traded, whether he liked it or not, did Gretzky request the move to Los Angeles. The events did not unfold the way Pocklington presented them, with Gretzky approaching him and asking to be traded to Los Angeles.

There were a number of reasons for Gretzky's choice. Janet had a home in Los Angeles, and Gretzky got along well with Kings owner Bruce McNall. Furthermore, as always, he was considering the good of the game he loved so much. He knew that if he went to Detroit—another team that had been making overtures to Pocklington—he would be stabilizing one of the league's traditional markets, but nothing more. The Red Wings are an Original Six team. The Vancouver Canucks were also interested, but at that point Gretzky didn't want to go there either, although he changed his mind later in his career.

Los Angeles was a different story. Gretzky knew that if he could make hockey popular in southern California—and, judging by the response of Kings fans when he had played there for the Oilers, that was almost certain—he would give the NHL a tremendous popularity boost in the United States.

In that era, the NHL couldn't get the television exposure it coveted because it had too many "black holes," too many markets without a nearby team for potential viewers to support. A popular team in Los Angeles could start to change that because Americans, like people of most nationalities, are chauvinistic.

Wayne Gretzky playing in Edmonton wouldn't interest anyone in Florida. But Wayne Gretzky playing in Hollywood for one of their own teams? To an American, that was different. It was the same thinking that led Major League Soccer to bring in David Beckham to play for the L.A. Galaxy. Beckham, like Gretzky, was known worldwide in his sport, and by playing in Los Angeles, he could deliver credibility to an entire league.

The hockey world had seen a similar tactic a quarter of a century earlier when the World Hockey Association tried to establish credibility by luring Bobby Hull away from the NHL.

Even though Gretzky did not make the move to change the face of the NHL, he was fully aware of the potential impact. He might not have foreseen the NHL that exists today, with one-third of its teams in the southern part of the United States, but he certainly realized that he could at least change hockey's status in California and the Pacific Coast region.

At the press conference to announce the trade, he said, "The Los Angeles Kings are important to the NHL and this division. We need Los Angeles and Seattle, and we need San Francisco. Hockey is strong in Canada, and it will always be our number-one sport. We need to create that atmosphere in the United States. Hopefully, I can be a part of that."

The Gretzky trade generated shock waves across Canada—and even across much of the United States. Most Canadians were outraged that a national hero like Gretzky was going to leave a Canadian team to play in the United States. There were overtures in Parliament to have the trade blocked by statute. In Edmonton, Pocklington was burned in effigy. The remaining Oilers players even threatened to stage a strike in the hope of forcing Pocklington to sell the team.

For days, the debate raged. Charges and counter-charges flew. The blame game was popular. Was it all Pocklington's fault? What about Janet? What about Wayne himself? How much did the small-town image of Edmonton have to do with it? Was the depressed Canadian dollar a factor? What about the swashbuckling Kings owner Bruce McNall? Was it all a result of the classic Canadian inferiority complex? Was there complicity on the part of the NHL?

In many ways, the debate got silly. But behind it all, for those who really wanted to strip away all the emotions and look at the facts, it was clear that although Gretzky didn't help his case by trying to do Pocklington a favour at the time of the initial press conference, he acted with his usual class and grace afterwards.

Pocklington, naturally, didn't want to be portrayed as a traitorous villain who had sold Canada's best-loved athlete to the Americans, so he asked Gretzky to take the blame for the trade and pretend that he had initiated it.

To make sure that he presented himself in the best possible light, Pocklington hired Jeff Goodman, a former speechwriter for Pierre Trudeau, to prepare his speech for the press conference. One was written for Gretzky as well, but he refused to read it. He threw it away.

But he wouldn't correct the clear implication in Pocklington's statement that "I truly understood when Wayne approached me and asked to be traded to the Los Angeles Kings." Pocklington opened with "It is not my intention to mislead the public" before he waded into an attempt to mislead the public.

Gretzky, for his part, agreed that he had approached Pocklington. "For the benefit of Wayne Gretzky, my new wife and our expected child in the new year," he said, "it would be for the benefit of everyone involved to let me play for the Los Angeles Kings."

At that time, Gretzky never contradicted Pocklington's implication that the trade had been forced upon him by Gretzky and was therefore in need of a quick response. It was nothing of the sort. It was years in the making and partly Gretzky's own fault because he assumed that Pocklington could be trusted and would deal with him fairly. Neither was true. Here is what happened:

When Gretzky first joined the Oilers, Pocklington realized even then that having Wayne Gretzky at your beck and call could be a very valuable asset, so he did not sign him to the standard NHL player's contract. That document, formatted by the league, spells out the terms of the deal, the compensation involved and the responsibilities of both parties. Instead, Pocklington got Gretzky to sign a personal-services contract. In other words, Gretzky's obligation wasn't to the Oilers, it was to Pocklington.

Today, every NHL player must sign a standard league contract, but in those days, with John Ziegler at the helm as president, the NHL head office took a much more cavalier approach to every aspect of the business.

In the summer of 1987, an older and wiser Gretzky, who was fully aware of the financial difficulties that Pocklington was starting to encounter, approached Pocklington to replace the personal-services contract with a player's contract. With an agent, Mike Barnett, and a financial advisor, Ian Berrigan, working for him, Gretzky emerged with a five-year deal. Because he had heard the rumours that Pocklington might trade him, Gretzky got a clause inserted that gave him the right to opt out of the final two years and retire. If he played the five years, he would become a free agent.

Pocklington agreed to the terms, but the existence of the opt-out/ free-agency clause worried him. With every day that passed, Gretzky got closer to his release dates and, as a result, his value decreased.

There was, of course, an easy way out of this dilemma. Pocklington could offer Gretzky a long-term contract at a suitable salary. But that option wasn't even a consideration for Pocklington, who paid Gretzky such a relatively low salary that he didn't crack the list of the top 100 best-paid athletes in North America. There were times, even when Gretzky was head and shoulders above everyone else in the sporting world, that he wasn't the best-paid player in the NHL.

So, having dispatched the option of paying Gretzky what he was worth, Pocklington took the alternate course. It soon became apparent to hockey insiders that Gretzky was on the block, and offers started to come in.

At the press conference, in his usual attempt at self-aggrandizement and to indicate that he wasn't being as mercenary as he was, Pocklington said, "A few months ago, the Vancouver Canucks, through a Vancouver businessman, offered to pay more than we are receiving from the Kings. The deal was refused."

The reference was to a deal being brokered by Pocklington's old friend Nelson Skalbania, who sold him Gretzky's rights in the first place back when the two owned teams in the World Hockey Association. The idea was that Skalbania would be the middleman in a deal that would see Frank Griffiths, who owned the Canucks, and Jim Pattison, who owned a number of businesses in Vancouver, cough up twenty million dollars for Gretzky.

Griffiths would get Gretzky's services as a player and Pattison would get him to shill for his car dealerships, among other things. Griffiths despised Pattison, so Skalbania probably couldn't have pulled off the deal, but that didn't stop Pocklington from alluding to it.

Either way, it made Gretzky aware he was going to be sold. He told Pocklington that if he was to be moved, Los Angeles would be his choice. Knowing that McNall was dying to get Gretzky and extremely liberal with his cash (or anybody else's, as it turned out), Pocklington agreed. And since he was doing Gretzky such a great favour, he said, he expected Gretzky to reciprocate by saying the trade was his idea.

Gretzky went to Los Angeles to resume his honeymoon and, unbeknownst to Pocklington, was in McNall's office when the two owners began discussing the terms of the trade. McNall put the call on speakerphone so Gretzky could hear.

They talked about the players involved, and they talked about the cash. They talked about the timing of the announcement. All aspects seemed to be complete when Gretzky began shaking his head. "Get Marty," he mouthed to McNall.

"I need Marty McSorley to be thrown in as well," said McNall.

"I'm not sure about that," Pocklington replied. "I'll have to talk to Glen Sather about it."

Gretzky started waving his arms frantically. "Hang on a second," said McNall and he placed Pocklington on hold.

"You can't let him talk to Glen," Gretzky said. "Glen will never let Marty go. Tell him you have to have Marty."

McNall reconnected with Pocklington. "No, Peter. We have to get this deal done," he said to Pocklington, "and Marty has to be in it or the whole deal is off."

Pocklington included McSorley in the trade.

The deal was done. Gretzky was a King.

But there was another twist to the story, and this part refers not to what was, but to what might have been.

When Gretzky signed that five-year standard player's contract with its three-year opt-out clause in 1987, it was shipped off to the NHL's head office to be filed. The old personal-services contract was a thing of the past.

But in a rare burst of scrutiny, the league decided that some of the new clauses had to be reworked. The changes were relatively minor, but nevertheless, they had to be made and the contract was shipped back to the Oilers.

However, the changes were not made, and nobody at the league level seemed to worry about it. Gretzky, the best player in the world and by far the biggest draw in the National Hockey League, played the entire 1987–88 season and won a Stanley Cup with the Oilers without a contract!

By that time, Gretzky knew that Pocklington was planning to move him. The day after the Oilers won the Stanley Cup, he went down to the rink for the official team picture and afterwards sat in the sauna with his buddy Jari Kurri.

"Jari, I don't think I'll be back," he said. "I think I'll be somewhere else by next season."

Recalled Kurri, "I said, 'Come on. I can't believe that's going to happen.' But he had that feeling when he talked to me.

"Later that summer, I was teaching at my hockey school when my agent, Don Baizley, called and told me there was a big rumour that Wayne was going to be traded. It wasn't final at that time, but it was soon after. I took my phone off the hook. There was nothing I could say."

Gretzky had a reason for his prophecy. "That was the day when everything started," he said. "We had the phone call from Vancouver. It was a tough situation. We'd just won the Stanley Cup."

He paused for a moment, then laughed. "I thought I'd played pretty well."

That was not a bad assessment. He had just been awarded the Conn Smythe Trophy as the most valuable player in the playoffs.

With the Vancouver call alerting him to the possibility of a trade, Gretzky sought a legal opinion on his contractual situation. Meanwhile, the NHL's board of governors, apparently finally having woken up to the seriousness of the matter, had struck a five-man committee to look into Gretzky's contractual status. Both the governors' committee and Gretzky's lawyer came to the same conclusion: if Gretzky wanted to press the matter, he was almost certainly entitled to declare himself a free agent.

Fortunately for Pocklington and the NHL, it was not Gretzky's nature to dash off to the courts at the first hint of a disagreement. He still wanted to play in Edmonton, but because Pocklington had other ideas, he prepared himself to move on.

"Would you want to go back and play for somebody after you got a phone call [to discuss the acquisition of your services] from another owner?" he asked me rhetorically.

"I could go back and play, and love the city and love the people. But how can I go back and play for a guy that wants to move me? It's as simple as that. I'm not bitter, and by no means am I trying to get into a war of words. For ten years, I had nothing but great things to say about what that team meant to me and what that city did for me.

"But out of the blue, while I was on my honeymoon, I got a phone call from another owner. That's when there was no turning back for me as far as I was concerned. That's when I felt that it was best that I be moved on."

He had played the first year of what, legalities aside, was a five-year deal, and in Pocklington's view, time was of the essence.

"In fairness to the Oilers," said Gretzky, "I had them in a position they didn't like to be in. I had them in the situation that in four years, I was a free agent without compensation—no compensation whatsoever."

Still, anyone who knows Gretzky knows that he would never have simply walked out on a team and a city that had been his life for what would have been fourteen years at that point.

"They got scared," said Gretzky. "They thought I might."

Over the years, Gretzky's animosity softened. In 2013, I asked him if he had ever had any further contact with Pocklington. "I saw him a couple of times," he said. "I said to him, 'Now that I've got into management I can understand why you did what you did.' We get along well now.

"Even when he traded me, he said, 'Look, I'm going to trade you.' He never lied to me."

Pocklington, by the way, eventually saw his financial empire crumble. He sold the Oilers in 1998 and moved to the United States. In 2008, he declared bankruptcy with assets of $2,900 and liabilities of $19.7 million.

In 2009, he was charged with bankruptcy fraud. In May 2010, he pleaded guilty to perjury and was placed on probation until 2013.

CHAPTER TWELVE

T he Los Angeles Kings had always spent their training camps in much the same way that they spent their regular seasons: in virtual obscurity.

Their chosen site was sleepy Victoria, British Columbia, a sedate community so well known for its geriatric population that it was often referred to as "God's Waiting Room," and the Kings' camp fit its surroundings perfectly. It was as devoid of excitement as the city, garnering only the most minimal attention from the media. A Vancouver hockey writer, en route to the Canucks' camp in Duncan, B.C., might make a fleeting appearance. The beat reporters of the two Los Angeles daily newspapers showed up out of a sense of obligation but always with a clear mandate from their editors to produce as little copy as possible. The Los Angeles electronic media stayed home, and for the most part, so did Victoria's hockey fans.

All that changed radically in 1988.

In the tiny Juan de Fuca Community Centre, where the Kings practised, an audience in double figures had been considered a busy day. Not in 1988. Not with a Gretzky sighting available. The place was so packed that management began to worry about safety issues and fans had to be turned away.

The Kings quickly announced that their first scheduled exhibition game—against the Canucks in Duncan—had been sold out. Their first home exhibition game, usually attended only by family and a few bored friends, had also been sold out, even though ticket prices had been doubled over the previous year. And scalpers were selling them at twice the doubled price.

The L.A. beat writers were no longer able to devote their days to tennis, fine dining and hangover-nursing. Now their editors wanted at least one good-sized story every day, and preferably two. Columnists and wire-service reporters from Vancouver settled in for the long haul, as did a horde of electronic media people.

Prime Ticket, which held the Kings' television rights, announced that it had suddenly decided to show sixty-two games that season rather than the originally planned thirty-seven. In that era, this was almost blanket coverage, on a par with what fans of the Maple Leafs and Canadiens could expect from their teams. One of the Prime Ticket producers was dispatched to Victoria to put together some features for the season's telecasts.

David Courtney, who died in 2012, was the team's public-relations man at the time. Few members of the Kings organization felt the changes brought about by Gretzky's arrival more than Courtney.

In the past, he had spent most of his time trying to get people to notice the team. "If someone phoned up and said they wanted the entire team out at sea in their hockey uniforms with fishing rods in their hands, I'd ask what would be a good time to do it," he said with a chuckle.

Now his primary task was keeping the media horde down to a reasonable number and trying to ration Gretzky's time. In the past, there had been no need for media accreditation. Courtney knew the two or three journalists who showed up. This time, there was not only accreditation, it was issued on a daily basis so that attendance could be limited and the credentials could not be passed around among friends.

As for dealing with the numerous requests to interview Gretzky, Courtney sought advice from Bill Tuele, the Oilers' PR man, who had handled that problem for years, and Los Angeles Lakers PR man Josh Rosenfeld, who was in a similar position with Magic Johnson.

It was to be new territory for the personable Courtney. "I guess I'm going to have to learn how to say no to people and make it stick," he said ruefully.

Kings coach Robbie Ftorek had no such problem. He had been saying no to people for a long time.

He said no to those who suggested he follow the NHL tradition of wearing a jacket and tie behind the bench. He opted for sweaters. He said no when asked if he trusted his players to be adults without a curfew. And he said no when asked if he was excited about the acquisition of Gretzky.

"Everybody on this team is equally important," he said. "Everybody makes an important contribution, whether they're players, coaches or the guys who wash towels."

That might be true if Kings fans were showing up to evaluate the merits of the team's laundry, or if the guy who washed towels could make an insipid power play dangerous. It seemed an exceedingly bizarre attitude for a coach to take, and right then, on the opening day of training camp, it was clear that a blowup was inevitable. It was obvious that, barring a change of Ftorek's attitude, no concessions were to be made for Gretzky, and although Gretzky himself would never ask for special treatment, his contributions were so great that a good coach would recognize the need for special handling.

The relationship between Gretzky and Ftorek bears examining because it reveals a number of Gretzky's immutable traits. In his career, he experienced coaches he liked and coaches he didn't like. And although he would never admit it, he probably has less respect for Ftorek than any of his other coaches. But his attitude never wavered: the coach was the boss and he had the right to run the team in any manner he chose.

The first night of training camp, we went out for a couple of beers in a bar adjacent to the team hotel.

"You're going to have trouble with this guy," I said.

"No, it will all be all right," said Gretzky. "I don't see any problem."

I was not surprised at his answer. In all the years I knew him, Gretzky told me lots of hockey gossip, gave me lots of insight into what was happening with his team—and around the league—and passed along a lot of information that was not widely known, to say the least. But he never once criticized his coach.

Most players, once they get to know you well, unload on their coach at every opportunity. Gretzky never did that. Even when the inevitable confrontation with Ftorek occurred, he wouldn't tell me about it. It had happened in front of the entire team, so I had no problem getting the whole story, but Gretzky wouldn't talk about it until long after his playing career had ended.

With Ftorek off-limits, we talked about lots of other things, and then, just before eleven, Gretzky announced that he had to go. This was a lot earlier than our soirees usually broke up. "Why so early?" I asked.

"Robbie has an eleven o'clock curfew."

"He does? That might be okay for the kids who are trying to make the team, but surely he doesn't expect you to be in by eleven."

"It's a teamwide thing," he said.

"Well, you could always ignore it. What's he going to do, suspend you?"

Gretzky just laughed. The team had a rule, and whether it was idiotic or not, he was going to abide by it. Off he went.

Still, training camp is one thing; the regular season is another. Perhaps once the NHL grind got under way, Ftorek might realize that the Kings were a top-flight professional team, not an American high-school team, and treat them like the former instead of the latter. Then again, he might not.

The Gretzky era in Los Angeles was to last almost eight years—a period that brought about major changes in the National Hockey League and made Gretzky a worldwide star. He had been a magnificent player in Edmonton, and he continued to be a magnificent player in Los Angeles. But now he had the Los Angeles media machine promoting him, and he was playing in the United States. Whether Canadians liked it or not—and they didn't—the inescapable fact was that once Gretzky got to Los Angeles, he was accorded an image that he could never have acquired in Edmonton.

It didn't take him long to start building the mystique. In the season opener, he scored on his first shot on goal. Moments later, he assisted on another goal. By the time the game ended, the Kings were up 8–2 on the Detroit Red Wings, and Gretzky had a goal and four assists. He had already passed eighty-three people on the Los Angeles Kings' all-time scoring list.

Ftorek shrugged off Gretzky's contributions, but Jacques Demers, the shell-shocked Detroit coach, didn't. "You can see what Gretzky does to that team," he said. "I have never seen a Los Angeles team come at us like they did tonight.

"I would say, without exaggeration, that he makes everybody on that team a 20 per cent better hockey player. He's going to make them a much better team. They dominated a good Red Wings team—and this is a good Red Wings team. They came at us with purpose and complete conviction, knowing what was going to happen, and they made it happen."

Unlike Ftorek, the Los Angeles players couldn't contain their praise for Gretzky. "It was a lot of fun," said Luc Robitaille, who had opened his season with a hat trick. "The spirit on this team is unbelievable. You know he's going to work hard on every shift. It was fun to bounce off him. You always get chances when you play with him, so you just go down and get those rebounds."

Bernie Nicholls, who had a goal and three assists, said, "He is a treat, that's for sure. I wish everybody had an opportunity to play with this guy. You're playing with the greatest player in the world. He's such a team player and a team person. You know he's always out there giving his best, so you want to give your best. You don't want to disappoint the guy."

Bobby Carpenter had a goal and two assists. "It feels like you've just won the lottery all by yourself," he said. "No one else had the winning ticket. I've been saying right from the beginning of training camp that we didn't just get three or four new players in that trade, we got twenty new players. That's the effect he has on the team."

When the Kings won their first four games, visions of Stanley Cup parades danced in their heads, but before long, the glitter started to wear off. Larry Playfair, a useful player who was well liked by his teammates and the Los Angeles fans, spoke out. Unless you were either a Ftorek favourite or someone who had played hockey with him at some point in his career, he said, you wouldn't get preferential treatment.

Playfair was immediately shipped out for his indiscretion, but there was no escaping the truth of his observation. The team had awful goaltending, and the culprits didn't seem to get a lot of help from goaltending coach Cap Raeder, who, like Ftorek, was an American. Although he later became a solid member of the coaching staff, at that time, his main qualification seemed to be that he and Ftorek had been in high school together.

Ron Duguay, who had played with Ftorek on the New York Rangers, got almost as much ice time as Gretzky, who had not previously played with Ftorek anywhere. Not only was Gretzky not getting his usual ice time, he wasn't getting quality time, either. Snipers like Nichols and Robitaille were rarely his linemates, and often, he wasn't even sent out for a power play.

On the early-November weekend when the team's internal conflicts started to become public, the Kings were in Winnipeg. Gretzky usually had Carpenter and Bob Kudelski as his linemates, but on this occasion, he was flanked by Hubie McDonough and a defenceman, Marty McSorley. Gretzky scored an unassisted goal, but the Kings lost 8–4 after giving up six third-period goals.

Some disgruntled players, who wanted to remain anonymous in view of what had happened to Playfair, blamed Ftorek. They had intended to relax the day before, a rare Saturday off-day. For a team that travelled as much as the Kings, an off-day was much coveted—especially in this case, because the team was embarking on a twelve-day road trip. Ftorek was unimpressed. He mandated a bowling outing for the entire team. Attendance was not optional.

On Sunday morning, Ftorek was on the ice, snarling at his players and demanding that they work harder during the game-day skate. Little wonder the Jets wore them down in the third period that night.

Of bigger concern to the team than the loss to Winnipeg was the ongoing malaise.

Ftorek's attitude clearly had not changed since training camp. He appeared to feel that if he admitted that one player was better than the others, he would somehow injure the psyche of the lesser players. In American high schools, where Ftorek had learned his hockey, that might have been true. In professional circles, especially circles staffed primarily by men who had battled their way through Canadian major junior hockey, it was not the case. The players knew who was good and who wasn't. They knew who should be on the ice in crucial situations and who should stay on the bench. And since their coach, by his actions, made it clear that he either did not know those things or was in denial of them, it followed that they had no faith in him.

The season was only a month old, but already, one of the recurrent questions in hockey circles was "How long can Robbie Ftorek last as coach of the Kings?"

The stock answer—only partly in jest—was "As long as Wayne Gretzky lets him."

But in reality, that answer was totally wrong. Gretzky had no wish to interfere in the coaching of the team. That was a decision that had to be made by the general manager—who, in name, was Rogatien Vachon, but who, in fact, was Bruce McNall.

The friction between the coach and his team was becoming so obvious that McNall was repeatedly asked how long Ftorek would last. A week after the bowling incident, McNall said that Ftorek would last the season, "unless he dies."

But by the end of November, McNall was ready to go back on his word. There had been a blowup between Gretzky and Ftorek, and as far as McNall was concerned, that meant Ftorek was finished. He could have a job within the Kings organization or he could go back to the New Haven farm team, where he had been before becoming the Kings' coach.

McNall never pulled the trigger, and the person who talked him out of it was Wayne Gretzky.

The flash point had come during a game in Detroit. Gretzky messed up a play that cost a goal, and, wanting to make it clear that it was his fault and not anyone else's, he smashed his stick across the crossbar.

Ftorek benched him for a display of temper. It was one of his rules that players must never lose their composure on the ice.

Gretzky does not handle public humiliation well. He had never before been benched in an NHL game, and according to a number of players, Ftorek took the opportunity between periods to announce his motive.

"It's my job to teach people things," he said. "I'm here to teach."

"If you want to be a teacher, go back to New Haven," snapped Gretzky. "I'm here to win a Stanley Cup."

Twelve years later, those who remembered the stick-smashing incident and Ftorek's insistence that composure must be maintained had cause to be amused. Ftorek, then coach of the New Jersey Devils, disagreed with a non-call by the referee and, in a fit of rage, hurled the players' bench onto the ice. He was ejected from the proceedings and given a one-game suspension—presumably by someone who wanted to teach him something.

Ftorek's self-serving stance angered Gretzky so much that he was still infuriated after the game. When McNall tried to talk to him, he turned and walked away, leaving McNall plaintively shouting, "Wayne, Wayne," as the distance between them increased.

The next day, McNall and Gretzky met face to face and McNall explained that he was going to fire Ftorek and wanted Gretzky to be alerted to the situation before he did so.

However, Gretzky insisted that Ftorek should be left in place. It was not a black-and-white situation, but he felt that for the good of the team, the inevitable instability that follows a coaching change should be avoided.

This illustrated one of the many differences between Gretzky and Ftorek. Clearly, both wanted to win, but Ftorek put his principles ahead of the team. Gretzky wouldn't dream of criticizing or embarrassing Ftorek, but Ftorek had no problem embarrassing and criticizing Gretzky.

Not only would Gretzky not denigrate Ftorek directly, he wouldn't even do it implicitly by sulking, floating, spreading dissent or using any of the other time-honoured tactics that many star players have used to get their way over the years.

Eighteen years after the incident, Gretzky finally discussed it with me.

"Throughout my career," he said, "the one thing I really believed in is that although you might agree or disagree with everything the coach says or does, especially when you're a leader or a captain, your best player has to maintain the coach's philosophy.

"I might not agree, but I would never challenge his authority. I don't believe in that. Robbie Ftorek—I lived or died by what he believed in, so he can never look back and say, 'You challenged the coach,' or, 'You screwed the coach.'"

In Los Angeles, as was the case everywhere else he played, Gretzky conformed to the desires of the coach and the needs of the team.

Ftorek, on the other hand, saw only one way of doing things—his way. Anyone choosing to take another route could expect to be disciplined and made an example of, even if the team's well-being was jeopardized in the process.

Adding to the dilemma was the fact that the Kings weren't playing badly. Certainly, their record could have been better, but on the other hand, it was a lot better than it had been before Gretzky arrived. This was uncharted territory for the Kings, so there was no precedent to consult. Perhaps if Ftorek were axed, his replacement wouldn't do any better.

Ftorek was allowed to stay on by virtue of Gretzky's intervention, but he didn't increase his reliance on Gretzky. For McNall, this was a major concern. He had spent ten million dollars to buy the Kings and a further fifteen million to buy Gretzky—which was a good indication of the value he put on Gretzky's contributions. But he had a coach who did not share that valuation.

It is not necessary for a team to like its coach. Scott Bowman, perhaps the greatest coach in hockey history, was not liked by his players— most of the time. Steve Shutt, an integral part of the Montreal Canadiens dynasty that won four consecutive Stanley Cups under Bowman in the 1970s, put it this way: "We hated him 364 days a year. On the 365th day, we got our Stanley Cup bonuses."

It is, however, necessary that a team respect its coach, and with the Kings under Ftorek, that never happened.

Ftorek instituted fines for any player who was on the ice without his helmet chinstrap fastened, even in practice. Again, this might have been almost understandable in an American high school. It was incomprehensible at the NHL level. There were even four-figure fines for any player who left his sweater on the dressing-room floor. Ftorek was, of course, partial to sweaters.

In February, when the Kings were awarded a rare overtime penalty shot, Ftorek selected Robitaille to take it, not Gretzky. Robitaille was stopped and the game ended in a tie. The incident created ripples throughout the league, so much so that when John Muckler, who was coaching the Campbell Conference in the all-star game, discussed the strategy he intended to use, he said, "You know what? We'll even let Gretz take penalty shots in overtime."

While many observers felt that with another coach, the Kings would have won their division, the team was far from terrible, and the early goaltending problems had been resolved.

Within a few months of selling Gretzky, Pocklington had announced in front of a number of witnesses that he would sell Grant Fuhr to the Kings for five million dollars. He later said it was a practical joke, but McNall thought he was serious and tried to follow up on it. When that didn't work, the Kings traded for Kelly Hrudey and finished with a record of 42–31–7, good enough for second in the Smythe Division and what, for fans, was a dream matchup in the opening round of the playoffs.

The Kings would face the Oilers.

CHAPTER THIRTEEN

I t was often said in those days that anyone who left the Oilers organization did so with knives in his back, and Gretzky was no exception. Now that the Oilers and Kings were about to go head to head, the knives started arriving from the front as well.

Back in November, Gretzky had taped an interview with Prime Ticket in which he said that he didn't always get along with Sather and that when Sather was apportioning blame in the dressing room, it was Paul Coffey, Jari Kurri and Gretzky himself who got the lion's share.

By the time the playoffs opened, none of this was a secret. Gretzky had said the same thing to me, and I had written about it months before. Even so, Sather, always looking for a psychological edge, saw it as a good time to publicly accuse Gretzky of turning his back on friends, breaking confidences and a number of other nefarious activities.

It was typical Sather. He was smart enough to realize that his own players still held Gretzky in awe, and with a best-of-seven-game playoff series looming, he wanted to change that attitude. He had been taking occasional shots at Gretzky all season long, but now he accelerated his attacks. He made reference to Gretzky "sitting by his pool, sipping mint juleps."

He also said, "Over the years, he has developed an aura, a mystique. Much of it is crap, but his teammates believe he can do anything."

Offering his view that the November interview had been given out of spite, Sather asked, "Why would he go through all that trouble to cause aggravation and then go out and play golf with our guys?"

The answer to that one was simple: Gretzky wasn't upset with the Edmonton players; he was upset with Pocklington and Sather.

Gretzky had heard all the innuendoes and said nothing. But when the matter came to a head with Sather's remarks about his desertion of the Oilers and the implication of an oversized ego, he shot back.

He had always tried to let the Oilers off the hook by publicly conceding Pocklington's claim that he was backed into a corner. Not this time.

"They say I had them over a barrel," he said. "That's not true. I wanted to stay in Edmonton. I offered to sign an eight-year deal. All they had to do was agree to a non-trade clause. They wouldn't do it."

Once the series opened in Los Angeles, the war of words abated. Sather was now free to make a more tangible contribution by out-coaching Ftorek, which he did throughout. Gretzky was free to make his contribution by providing stellar play, and he made the most of his opportunity.

From the Kings' point of view, the series started with what the cynics saw as two setbacks. First, a debilitating flu bug attacked a pair of key players, Hrudey and John Tonelli. Second, the flu bug left Ftorek alone.

The loss of Hrudey was especially significant, not only because his backup, Glenn Healy, had a record of 0–4 since Hrudey's arrival in a February 21 trade, but also because the Kings were an offensively minded team and Hrudey was a far better puck handler than Healy.

When Hrudey was in net, the Kings knew that a puck dumped into their zone would be properly handled. (In this era, the goalies were free to play the puck anywhere in their end.) After Ron Hextall, Hrudey was the best puck-handling netminder in the NHL. Like Martin Brodeur after him, Hrudey was excellent at firing the puck up the ice to a breaking forward, thereby starting the attack and trapping the opposition's fore-checkers. Healy's puck-handling was something of an adventure.

Healy played well in the opener, and with Gretzky contributing about twenty minutes of ice time, the Kings built a 3–2 lead after two periods. But then Ftorek decided to limit Gretzky's time, sat him on the bench for a six-minute stretch at one point, and the Oilers rallied to win 4–3. The Oilers got their fourth goal with twenty-six seconds left in the game. Even after that, Ftorek left Gretzky on the bench.

Because the media tend to interview the winners, Gretzky was mostly ignored after that game. But when the Kings evened the series in the next game, Gretzky faced wave after wave of reporters who, in one form or another, asked the same question: How did he feel about having to go to Edmonton to face the Oilers?

Gretzky danced around the question a few times, then finally said what everyone knew was the truth but wanted him to confirm: "The cheering is over. The formalities and the friendships are over. They're the enemy now, and they expect to be the enemy. The guys over there feel the same way."

Strange as it may seem so many years after the fact, Gretzky's admission, while clearly not a revelation, was something Canadians didn't really want to hear. As long as he had continued to chat with his buddies on the Oilers, go golfing with them, and say how much he had loved life in Edmonton, the fact that he had left Canada, probably forever, was somehow diminished in importance. But now the issues could no longer be avoided.

Gretzky could only hope that the situation might work in his favour. "Maybe I'll be a distraction," he said. "Maybe they'll be so busy looking at me they won't be looking where they should be looking, and it will work to our advantage. Who knows?"

It was a nice theory, but it didn't come to pass.

With Ftorek mismanaging the defence, the Kings lost both games in Edmonton, but then, with Doug Crossman back in the lineup, the Kings started to play well defensively and came back.

Crossman had been a regular on the Philadelphia Flyers team that had advanced to the 1986 Stanley Cup final. In 1987, he had been by far Team Canada's best defenceman in the Canada Cup. But in 1988–89, he fell into disfavour with Ftorek because he wasn't a bone crusher. As the season progressed, Ftorek had used him less and less, and then finally scratched him from the lineup on a regular basis.

He did not dress for the first three games against Edmonton and played sparingly in the fourth. But he played the rest of the way as the Kings stunned the Oilers by bouncing back from a 3–1 deficit to win the series.

In the seventh game, Gretzky got the Kings started with a goal only fifty-two seconds into the game, and he continued to rally his team even though the Oilers kept fighting back.

Three times the Kings took the lead. Three times the Oilers tied it. But finally, the Kings went up by two with a pair of power-play goals, and then Gretzky scored short-handed to finish what he had started.

For Gretzky, there was some vindication, but he did not feel any of the ebullience that he had anticipated before the series began. He let it be known that he had been aware of the public statements that Pocklington had made. "Mr. Pocklington said after Game Three that people had told him it was a good trade," he said. "We'll see what they say tomorrow."

But that was all the gloating he did. Before the series, he had envisioned fist-pumping and taunts of "I told you so." But when the opportunity arose, he couldn't even come close to bringing himself to do it. He was delighted that his Kings had come out on top, but he was also saddened by the fact that they had done so at the expense of all his close friends in the Edmonton organization.

"I didn't enjoy the series at all," he said. "It wasn't fun for me. We spent fifteen days or whatever it was in the series. I saw those guys every day and we had no words at all. That's not what life is supposed to be all about. You're supposed to be able to talk to your best friends."

Edmonton defenceman Kevin Lowe was so devastated by the loss that he wouldn't even go back into the dressing room with his teammates.

Still wearing his full uniform, including skates, he slumped down on one knee and leaned against the wall.

Gretzky wasn't surprised to learn that Lowe took the loss badly. "Those guys are champions," he said. "No one takes losing harder than Mess and Lowe. That's why they're champions. But long after hockey is over with, no matter who got the fifteen million dollars, those guys and me will still be buddies."

Gretzky even had some good words for Sather, who, along with co-coach John Muckler and assistant coach Ted Green, had walked out onto the ice after the game and shaken hands with all the Kings.

The barbs that Sather and Gretzky had tossed back and forth were now in the past. "Every time I picked up a paper," Gretzky said, "I read something from Edmonton about Wayne Gretzky, and it got to the point that I had to say something. Glen takes losing as hard as anyone, but he has a lot of class."

Sather too tried to be conciliatory. "In my opinion," he said, "Gretzky is the best player in the world. When any team has that, you can never count them out."

The next series against Calgary was nowhere near as pleasant for the Kings. They lost the opener in overtime, then got soundly defeated in the next game. The score was 8–3, and Crossman, who was by far their best defenceman, managed to come out of the proceedings with a plus-rating despite the lopsided score. So, for Game Three, Ftorek sent him back to the press box.

"It's great for us," said Calgary defenceman Brad McCrimmon, a former teammate of Crossman, in a quote that was unattributed at the time. "I feel bad for Crossman because I know how much he wants to play, but we love it when he's not in the lineup."

As the series progressed, Ftorek started to make desperate moves that didn't work.

In Game Three, for instance, he used Gretzky with no fewer than fifteen line combinations. With five minutes left and the Kings trailing 3–2, he started sending out units of four forwards and one defenceman. That move produced a predictable result. The Kings gave up two more goals.

"Why would he do that?" asked a former NHL coach. "There was about five minutes to play. That's lots of time in a one-goal game, too much time to start that sort of thing."

The Kings lost the series in four games, and not long afterwards, Ftorek was fired. No one was surprised.

By June 1, the Kings had hired Tom Webster to be their new coach, although they went about it in curious fashion.

Webster was probably the best candidate on the open market, but the Kings didn't get him because they used a regimented search-and-evaluate process but because Phil Esposito decided it was a good idea.

Top-flight teams in search of a coach usually approach a number of candidates. Then they bring in the prospective coaches and interview them. That way, they can make an extensive evaluation of each candidate. Perhaps more importantly, they also get to hear what insights he might have, not only with regard to maximizing the talent of the team in question but also with regard to innovative methods of coaching. To put it another way, they pick his brain.

The Kings, on the other hand, approached no one. Colin Campbell, then assistant coach of the Detroit Red Wings, approached them, so they flew him in and talked to him. He said he felt afterwards that they had done so just as a courtesy and that at no time was he under consideration.

Webster, who had been coach of the New York Rangers until an ear ailment prevented him from flying, also approached them and was interviewed. Esposito, the general manager of the Rangers, then called Vachon and not only told him Webster was the man for the job, but also negotiated Webster's contract.

That was it. No secondary interviews. No extensive screening. No background checks. Just a call from the old-boy network and the new coach had been hired.

Had the Kings gone through the normal process, they probably would have ended up with Webster anyway. He left the Rangers only because of a health problem that had since been rectified. He had been a successful junior coach with the Windsor Spitfires and had handled Canada's entry in the most recent world junior championship.

But by interviewing no one else, the Kings missed out on a lot of hockey knowledge that might have been useful—to Webster, if to no one else.

CHAPTER FOURTEEN

C alendar years run from January 1 to December 31. Hockey years run from one Stanley Cup presentation to the next.

Gretzky's 1988–89 hockey year had been a veritable maelstrom of activity. He had skated around the Edmonton ice holding aloft the Stanley Cup, and in the victory, had earned his second Conn Smythe Trophy. He had been traded to Los Angeles. He had got married. He had seen the birth of his first child. He had been benched for the first time in his NHL career. He had seen a seven-foot statue erected in his honour outside Northlands Coliseum, the home of the Oilers. He had instigated hockey fever in Los Angeles and been the driving force in the team's surge from fourth-worst in the NHL to fourth-best. He had led the Kings to a playoff victory over the team that had cast him aside. And all this was done while his own coach was working to mini-mize his efforts.

Almost unnoticed while all these other events were happening was the fact that he was closing in on a major record. When the new "hockey year" began, he was only fourteen points away from becoming the National Hockey League's all-time leading scorer.

Records, like everything else in sport, come in varying degrees of importance. Some have merit. Some don't. Some are well known. Some are obscure.

But there is always one ultimate record that can endure for generations. It may even last forever if the sporting establishment grants it permanent status and begins a whole new era of record-keeping. This is the record that says the man named below was simply the best ever. Whatever the aim of the sport in question might be, this man accomplished it more often or better than anyone else.

In hockey, the aim of the sport is to score. When the 1989–90 season opened, no one in hockey had racked up more points than Gordie Howe— 801 goals and 1,049 assists for 1,850 points in twenty-six NHL seasons.

Gretzky was fourteen points behind that total. He had played ten years.

Howe's last NHL season was Gretzky's first. It was an occasion that marked the end of one era and the beginning of another. The long-held beliefs that wingers should always stay in their lanes, that goalies should never leave their feet and that forwards should never skate backwards, not to mention a host of other tenets of the Howe era, were either starting to be discarded or had already gone.

Before Gretzky, no one had averaged more than 1.4 points per game. As Gretzky closed in on Howe's record, his points-per-game average was 2.37.

Before Gretzky, the record for assists in a season was 102. Gretzky had a season with 163.

Before Gretzky, the record for goals in a season was 76. He got 92 in his third year in the NHL.

Before Gretzky, the record for points in a season was 152. Gretzky had already racked up seasons of 215, 212, 208 and 205.

Now he was nearing the all-time record, but this was new territory even for Gretzky. "Longevity records were something I never really thought about a whole lot," he said. "I just played year to year. I never really thought about getting five hundred goals or a thousand points or the 1,850 figure, but now that it's getting close and everybody is talking about it, I look back on my career and it gives me a chance to realize that I've been pretty consistent."

In the NHL, consistency is a rare trait. With its schedule of eighty games or more from coast to coast, a one-month training camp and then, for the better teams, the rigours of the playoffs, the NHL grind does not lend itself to consistency. Players get worn down. Also, for many of the years in which Gretzky played, there was such a great disparity between the good and bad teams that on many nights, the outcome was all but predetermined, and players performed accordingly.

But Gretzky never floated or produced a lackadaisical performance. Bernie Nicholls, who prior to Gretzky's arrival as a teammate had not been able to make that claim about his own play, was amazed. "You look out there in practices or in games and you see that the best player in the history of the game is always working hard," he said. "You say to yourself, 'If he's working that hard, how can I not work just as hard?'"

Gretzky agreed that he always took a totally dedicated approach. "I think that I do it just for the love of the game," he said. "I love to play. Every time I step on the ice, if I don't have a good shift, I'm disappointed in myself. I feel I've let myself down, the team down and the fans down.

"My dad always told me that people come out to watch me play and they might only see me once. It's like a Broadway play. For me, it happens every night, but for the audience it might only happen once. I owe it to them to give them a good performance."

Gretzky had set more than forty NHL records to that point, but the one he was nearing was going to be special, not only because of its magnitude, but also because of his relationship with Gordie Howe.

As a child, Gretzky had idolized Howe, and most fans have seen the famous picture of Howe jokingly hooking a stick around the eleven-year-old Gretzky's neck. Gretzky doesn't remember a lot from the occasion, but he does remember that Howe told him to practise his backhand. He cherished that advice.

It had always been Gretzky's dream to break some of Howe's records, and over the years, the two had become steadfast friends.

After Gretzky picked up six points in his first three games of the season, McNall, ever the promoter, invited Howe to come to Los Angeles and stay with the team until Gretzky broke the record. Needless to say, McNall would pick up the tab.

Gretzky was absolutely delighted that Howe not only showed no resentment at seeing his all-time mark surpassed, but encouraged Gretzky at every step.

The media were delighted to have Howe on hand and asked him the standard questions. Did he remember the night he set his record? "Sure," said Howe. "I was there." Did he feel bad about losing his record to Gretzky? "If I did, I wouldn't be here."

Those may sound like flip, disdainful responses, but they weren't. They were delivered with a little grin, a twinkle in the eye and an aw-shucks tone.

At one point, a woman told him she'd had a dream about him. "How was I?" he responded with a chuckle. He told me that story, then added, "You know, since I've been around the kid, I'm starting to feel young again."

The kid was just as delighted to have him around. Even though Gretzky had a superb relationship with his own father, and Howe was on equally good terms with his own sons, Howe often referred to Gretzky as his "adopted son."

The two were almost inseparable during that stretch, and Gretzky, who seemed more relaxed than he had been in a year, started sprinkling his conversation with items that began, "Gordie was saying the other day that . . ."

"This is great," said Howe with his ever-present grin after watching Gretzky get three more points in a loss to the New York Islanders. "I saw a good game and got to go out in Los Angeles. It's a paid vacation."

Gretzky and Howe had briefly played against and with each other in the long-defunct World Hockey Association. Gretzky was with the

Indianapolis Racers and then the Oilers. Howe and his two "non-adopted" sons played for the New England Whalers.

Gretzky and Howe were linemates in the 1979 WHA All-Star Game (with Mark Howe as the other forward even though he starred as a defenceman in the NHL) and, as usual, the sweater they gave to the skinny kid wearing number 99 was far too big. Gordie grabbed a needle and thread out of the trainer's box and sewed tucks in the sides to make it fit better.

In a way, they got to play together again during the record chase. The occasion was the filming of a commercial in Culver City. "I played with him and it was a treat," said Howe afterwards. "Those passes come over nice and flat, no wobble, just the right speed."

Howe was one of many people who praised Gretzky for his passes. Over the years, if a teammate told Gretzky he liked a certain type of pass, that's what he got. Europeans like Jari Kurri and Esa Tikkanen wanted hard, crisp passes. Others preferred to have them come more slowly. They all got what they wanted, and many got passes they weren't expecting. Gretzky was a master of the saucer pass—a puck lofted over a defender's stick that landed flat and slid onto the teammate's stick without any further bounces.

Howe said he had no doubt that Gretzky would have been just as successful in his era. "He'd have done real well," he said. "He's too smart not to. In fact, he might have even been better. You only had one-line passes then. That holds down the scores, but it also allowed the better puck handlers to make their mark. He's an excellent puck handler.

"Wayne will get at least three thousand points before he's finished," continued Howe. "When he's through, his record will last for a long time."

Howe was close. Gretzky ended up with 2,857 points, but on two occasions, he missed almost half the season due to injuries, and he retired when he was still a high-level player. Even so, Howe was certainly correct in his prediction that the record will last a long time.

With Gretzky five points away from Howe's record, the Kings headed to Vancouver, where the Canucks were coached by Bob McCammon, who had been an assistant coach with the Oilers for two of the Gretzky years. If anyone knew how to slow down the Gretzky juggernaut, it should have been McCammon.

Or perhaps not. "You know what he's going to do in certain situations and you can tell the players what to expect," said McCammon, "but he is so good and his passes are so accurate that he can still get away with it anyway."

One of the tactics Gretzky used so effectively was to skate towards a defender at full speed, then stop, and, while the defender was still backing up, dish off the puck.

"He always did that to set up Jari Kurri," said McCammon. "Now that he doesn't have a Kurri any more, he goes in deeper and hits Steve Duchesne coming in. It's basically the same play but with Duchesne being a defenceman, he has changed it to fit the circumstances."

Some teams still tried to use a designated checker against Gretzky to shadow him wherever he went but McCammon knew that wouldn't work so he chose to go in the opposite direction. Instead of delegating the job to one man, he preferred to assign it to six.

"You need two lines to check him," he said. "He has such stamina and he can stay out there so long, that no one line can do it."

But McCammon conceded that whatever tactic he or any other coach might use to try to minimize Gretzky's production, the inescapable fact was that the more you tried to check him, the less chance you had of scoring.

"If you're really checking him, you have no offence," said McCammon. "You've got one guy with him, so you've got two forwards going in on two defencemen. Gretzky takes one guy so far out of the play that he takes your offence away."

McCammon and his defensively minded Canucks had some success. They stopped Gretzky from scoring. But they didn't stop the other Kings, and Gretzky assisted on three goals. Now he was going into Edmonton, of all places, needing two points to set the record.

Edmonton goalie Bill Ranford, one of Gretzky's many friends on that team, was determined that Gretzky would have to beat someone else for the record and played a superb game. Going into the final minute, the Oilers were leading 4–3, and Gretzky had been held to a single assist.

But with a faceoff in the Edmonton end, Kings coach Tom Webster pulled goalie Mario Gosselin for an extra attacker. Off the faceoff, the puck went into the corner to Ranford's left. Edmonton's Kevin Lowe pounced on it and tried to lift it out of the zone and down the ice. Unfortunately for Lowe, one of the tallest players in the league, Larry Robinson, was at the point for the Kings. He reached up and batted the puck down with his glove. Duchesne then put it back towards the corner, but before it got there, Dave Taylor picked it up and lofted it across the goalmouth. Although Ranford moved quickly across his crease, Gretzky, stationed on the far side, got it on the short hop and fired it into the net.

Wayne Gretzky had become the greatest scorer in the history of the NHL. Gordie Howe was proud. It was on a backhand.

"I was cheering like hell," said Howe later. "I feel I've gained more than I've lost in this."

There were still fifty-three seconds left to play, but the game was stopped for a presentation to mark the occasion. Howe was given the microphone and said, "I'd like to say in all honesty, after spending the last few days with Wayne, I thought I knew him before, but he has just grown an inch taller than he was in my mind. He's a super young man, a great hockey player who shares everything he does. It's really nice for me to be sharing those honours with Wayne."

With the crowd chanting, "Gretz-ky, Gretz-ky," Howe passed over the microphone and, as always, Gretzky handled the situation perfectly. He pointed out that both the teams that had helped him set the record were in the building, and he thanked them. He thanked the Edmonton fans. He thanked his family and Howe. He even made a special point of saying hello to Joey Moss, the clubhouse attendant with Down syndrome he had long ago brought into the Edmonton organization.

Gretzky said that hockey "is the greatest game in the world, and I owe everything I have in my lifetime to the game of hockey."

After a thirteen-minute ceremony, the game resumed and went into overtime. Rising to a dramatic occasion as usual, Gretzky scored again to give the Kings the win.

He made sure that it was a great night not only for himself but also for a number of charities. The memorabilia from that record-setting occasion was set aside and distributed as follows:

Sticks: He used a different stick every shift. Each one subsequently had a numbered brass plaque attached to verify its authenticity and was then donated to charities that were free to sell them to raise money.

The record-setting stick and puck: They were donated to the Hockey Hall of Fame.

Sweater: That, too, went to the Hall of Fame. There had been thoughts of Gretzky doffing it on the spot, but there was a fear that an unscrupulous dealer might later claim to be selling the sweater Gretzky wore for the rest of the night.

Gloves, skates and pants: They were given to Wayne's dad for the "museum" in his basement. Eventually, they will be donated to the Hall of Fame.

Souvenir photographic prints: There were ninety-nine of them, each numbered and autographed by Gretzky and Howe. The shot was taken when they made their TV commercial in Culver City, and both were in uniform. Gretzky wore his Kings outfit; Howe wore the Detroit Red Wings uniform of the era in which he played. All proceeds went to charity.

Commemorative T-shirts: Under an NHL marketing agreement, Gretzky got half the proceeds, and the NHL got half. Gretzky gave his half to charity. The NHL kept its half.

For much of the weekend, Gretzky had mulled over a request to do an "I'm going to Disneyland" commercial seconds after the record was set. Had the momentous goal come in overtime, he would have done it, but he didn't want to do it while the game was still in progress, so Disneyland got shut out.

There were still many more points and goals to come for Gretzky, but now his name was on the sport's most coveted individual record. It was a remarkable achievement that made him more aware than ever of his greatness. But it also made him aware that the years were flying by.

"Gordie was saying something the other day that is true," he said at the time. "The hardest thing about hockey is that the older you get, the more you love it. I've said that many times. I enjoy it more now than when I was nineteen, when I first came in. I think part of the reason is that you know you're getting closer to the end. I love the game now more than ever."

CHAPTER FIFTEEN

B reaking Gordie Howe's record was Gretzky's last major achievement of the decade. There were many more major achievements
to come, but not in the 1980s.

From a hockey perspective, the decade had been Gretzky first,
Gretzky last and Gretzky in-the-middle. Not only had he dominated
the game, both on and off the ice, but he had changed the face of the
National Hockey League, and, by extension, the face of hockey throughout the world.

When the decade began, the NHL was shrouded in negativism.
Fans were lethargic, driven away from the sport by a number of factors,
not the least of which was its lack of parity. The Philadelphia Flyers
garnered 116 points that season, compared to fifty-one for the Colorado
Rockies and Winnipeg Jets. The Rockies, who had moved from Kansas
City, where they were also unable to mount appreciable fan support, were
two seasons away from leaving Denver for New Jersey.

The best players the North American game had to offer seemed
inept in comparison to their counterparts elsewhere in the world. In the
1979 Challenge Cup, the NHL All-Stars lost two of three games to the
Soviet Union's national team, the third by a 6–0 score.

The lack of stability was another factor that cast a pall over the league. In the seventies, teams had moved and battled bankruptcy—not always successfully—with astonishing regularity.

But in the 1979–80 season, like a knight in shining armour, Wayne Gretzky rode onto the scene. His impact was immediate and, over the course of the next decade, almost incalculable.

There were, as there had been throughout his life, the professional contrarians, the naysayers who insisted, for one convoluted reason or another, that Gretzky wasn't really as special as he appeared to be. They said he couldn't have played in a six-team league (a ridiculous assertion) or that he was feasting off a watered-down league—without explaining why no one else did the same. But in a way, the debate was good for hockey.

Instead of discussing the latest lunacy from the board of governors, or the latest inexplicable decision from the league's disciplinarian, or the latest financial woes of a specific franchise, or the latest set of attendance problems, fans were now discussing hockey. They were discussing Gretzky's place in the game, and as a result, the focus switched to the game's positive aspects—its speed, its grace, its artistry and its offence—all of which were exhibited by Gretzky.

As the decade progressed, the spotlight stayed largely on Gretzky's primary team, the Edmonton Oilers, with their five Stanley Cups, the fifth of which came in 1990.

When Gretzky broke into the NHL, the reigning dynasty was the New York Islanders, with their tight, defence-first system augmented by one powerful scoring line. The burning question in hockey became an obvious one: Could the Oilers, with the kind of swirling, high-tempo, high-offence game that had never before been seen in the NHL, overcome an old-style powerhouse like the Islanders?

It was Gretzky who made this debate possible, and his annual domination of the scoring race was the reason that sports fans were discussing hockey again. The NHL was on the rise.

NHL executives, never slow to copy a formula that seemed successful, saw what was happening in Edmonton. They saw that, on a regular basis, Canadian teams were at the bottom of the NHL's road-attendance figures. They saw that, on a regular basis during the Gretzky era, the Edmonton Oilers were at or near the top of the NHL's road-attendance figures.

This was a language the executives understood. Even though you weren't going to find offensive players of Gretzky's calibre, his was the type of game the fans wanted to see—and more important from the owners' point of view, the type of player fans would buy tickets to see.

The teams of the previous decade had featured one or two big shooters. Any guy who could blast the puck was singled out as a curiosity. By end of the 1980s, the numbers had been reversed. Teams had only one or two guys who didn't have a blazing shot.

In the seventies, it was embarrassingly apparent to North American fans that their players couldn't skate with the Europeans. Head-to-head competitions, especially the Challenge Cup, proved it. But, for the 1984 Canada Cup tournament, Glen Sather built a Team Canada that had heavy representation from his Oilers and a stated objective of beating the Soviets by matching them step for step, stride for stride. The strategy worked. No longer was the NHL seen as a league of plodders.

By the end of the eighties, the international doors had opened. Soviet and other eastern European players were on display in the NHL every night and there was no appreciable difference between their skating skills and those of their North American teammates. They were faster than some, slower than others.

There remained some problems over which Gretzky alone had little control. The players weren't paid enough to give the NHL a major-league aura, and television exposure in the United States was minimal—partly because, in vast areas of the country, there were no NHL teams to support.

But in 1988, when Gretzky was sold to the Los Angeles Kings, the foundation was laid for Gretzky's presence to do a lot to overcome those problems as well.

Kings owner Bruce McNall immediately went to work on the salary factor, giving Gretzky an eight-year, twenty-million-dollar contract. (In 1990, he boosted even that number.) At the time, that meant that Gretzky was getting about fifteen times as much as the average player. With a disparity that wide, it was just a matter of time until the gap narrowed, especially for the elite players.

The problem of exposure throughout the United States, on television and in underdeveloped markets, was also soon to be overcome, and Gretzky would play a major role in the solution. From a marketing point of view, he had become, if not the biggest name in American sport, very close to it. Marketing executives agreed that if you wanted the best possible athlete to endorse your product, you had to have one or all of Gretzky, Michael Jordan and Bo Jackson.

That was an absolutely astonishing development. Even with Gretzky's emergence, hockey was a distant fourth in acceptance after baseball, football and basketball. But to the amazement of the advertising world, Gretzky was in with the best.

The bible of the business was *Advertising Age*. In its August 15, 1988, issue, right after Gretzky's arrival in Los Angeles, a feature article warned Gretzky to beware. "Wayne Gretzky may be the most marketable athlete in the history of Canada," it read, "but he's about to learn the ice-cold realities south of the border. Hockey doesn't sell here."

The author had made the mistake of looking at the present and assuming that it portended the future.

"Mr. Gretzky, widely considered the greatest player ever to put on skates, has netted several long-term endorsement deals and more than $1 million a year in Canada," the article stated. "But he has been unable to score consistently with any U.S. advertiser and doesn't appear in any U.S. ads."

At that time, that was partly true. He could have scored some U.S. ads, but he was being cautious. Either way, a little more than sixteen months later, nothing could have been further from the truth.

By then, it was January 1, 1990, and even *Advertising Age* had changed its tune. Gretzky was part of a Nike commercial with Bo Jackson that the magazine called an "unequivocally magnificent piece of advertising." He had just made the first 3-D commercial in history. It was for Coca-Cola and was to run during the upcoming Super Bowl. He was the key figure in an American Express ad campaign that focused on his pursuit of Gordie Howe's record. He had appeared on the cover of *People* magazine once and twice on the cover of *Sports Illustrated.* He had even been the guest host of *Saturday Night Live.*

A series of ads for Peak anti-freeze that featured Gretzky and former National Football League coach Mike Ditka, which had run regularly on *Monday Night Football,* had been replaced by a new series of ads. This time, the ads were done by Gretzky alone.

Four production companies were making pilot episodes of a show they hoped to sell to ABC to follow Ted Koppel's *Nightline.* Independently of each other, they all approached Gretzky to be a guest on the pilot.

A Coca-Cola billboard campaign across the United States featured a picture of Gretzky with the caption, "Official soft drink of the Great One." It didn't identify Gretzky. He had become so well known, there was no need to do so.

Prime Ticket, the cable-television company that held the rights to the Kings' games, ran a billboard campaign in Los Angeles with a simple message: "No cable, no Gretzky."

Because of the magnetism that Gretzky clearly exhibited, advertisers flocked to his agent, Mike Barnett, to try to get Gretzky to promote their product. But in marketing, as in any other aspect of his life, Gretzky imposed standards that set him apart from the others.

"In the United States, corporations tend to not want to commit to long-term relationships, probably because there are so many celebrities,"

Barnett said. "The general feeling is that there is no need to commit to a long-term spokesperson because you can catch the next one on the way up or an even larger one on the way down. That does not fit with our philosophy whatsoever.

"The word 'relationship' is very important to Wayne Gretzky. As proud as he is of his consistency on the ice over the years, he's also very proud of his long-term relationships with companies."

David Burns was the president of Burns Sports Celebrity Services in Chicago, the pre-eminent company in the United States acting as a middleman between sports figures and corporations.

"If you look at the overall picture of sports in the United States, football and baseball get nearly all the commercial attention," he said. "Basketball is next, and after that is hockey; so hockey is the fourth sport.

"The one exception is Gretzky. There is no number two or number three or number four in the list of hockey celebrities. I'm speaking for the States now. There is only one hockey person that people ask for."

Burns rhymed off the reasons for Gretzky's unique status.

"Number one, he has broken so many records that he is the best player by far in the history of hockey.

"Secondly, he is so well represented that anyone who wants to do business doesn't have to play games when he calls Barnett. He is open to talk to anybody, and so many of the sports representatives are the opposite of that.

"Third, Gretzky is just a total gentleman. He is very polite with the press. He is considerate of the little people. Many of the top stars simply do not have those qualities. He has gone out of his way to remember that he owes something to his fans. Those are the qualities that put him on the same level as the top baseball names and the top football names."

Gretzky's qualities had not escaped the attention of the important people at Coca-Cola. Stone Roberts, an executive with the ad firm that had the Coca-Cola account, said, "There's no question that his innate talent is attractive as an image driver to all people. In addition to his talent, his image is crystal clear.

"His image as a leader and a clean liver has really made the community embrace him, and that's what we find particularly attractive for Coca-Cola. We're in it for the long haul, and he's the perfect marriage for our image and how we position our products for our clients.

"There's no better illustration of his acceptance in the United States than what he has done for the Kings."

By that time, the Kings had sold more authorized products—sweaters, hats, jackets and so on—in Gretzky's first year with them than in all the team's previous years of existence combined.

In the NHL's 1987–88 season, the year before Gretzky arrived, six of the nine smallest crowds turned out to watch the Kings. At an average 77 per cent of capacity on the road, the Kings were last in the NHL's attendance standings. The next season, with Gretzky in the lineup, they became the league's best draw at 98 per cent. It is the only time in NHL history that a team was last in NHL road attendance one season and first the next.

Gretzky's contributions to the NHL and its image during the eighties were monumental. He had changed the face of the league. But there was still more to come in the nineties.

CHAPTER SIXTEEN

To a player like Wayne Gretzky, whose life was hockey, Maple Leaf Gardens was his hallowed hall, his Valhalla.

It was where he had seen his first National Hockey League game. Growing up, he watched *Hockey Night in Canada* every Saturday, and with very few exceptions, those games were played in Maple Leaf Gardens. (There were no regional telecasts in those days and definitely no double-headers.)

In his mind, as a child, the famed backyard rink in Brantford wasn't Wally's Coliseum as much as it was Maple Leaf Gardens. That was where he was scoring all his goals in seventh-game Stanley Cup final overtimes.

Had he been a baseball player, the Gardens would have been Gretzky's Yankee Stadium. Had he been a soccer player, it would have been his Wembley. But he was a hockey player and it was no coincidence that, throughout his career, he invariably put on a show in Maple Leaf Gardens.

His first visit to the place he refers to as "a sacred building" came when he was a transfixed, awestruck six-year-old, sitting in the back row with his grandmother, watching the abysmal Oakland Seals.

"We sat in the last row of the greys," he said. "We got there an hour early and I don't think I moved the whole time. I think the first time I got out of my seat was when they announced the three stars."

Only twelve years later, he was back, not just as a player but as the brightest young star in the game, astounding hockey fans everywhere but especially when he played in Toronto. "The easiest thing in the world is to get up for a hockey game in Maple Leaf Gardens," he said with a laugh.

It had been his lifelong ambition to take part in a playoff series in Maple Leaf Gardens, and it was in that special place in 1993 that the Toronto Maple Leafs and Los Angeles Kings staged the major part of a series that remains memorable to this day.

A Stanley Cup final in Toronto would have been Gretzky's ultimate fantasy come true, but it was impossible at the time because the Leafs and Kings were in the same conference. Playing in Maple Leaf Gardens for a berth in the Stanley Cup final was a close second.

For the Kings, it represented an achievement that wouldn't be matched for almost two decades. In the time between that series and their improbable Stanley Cup victory in 2012, the Kings won just one playoff series.

Leafs fans, on the other hand, usually refer to the 1993 aggregation as their last great team. Granted, some of the subsequent Toronto teams had success. They advanced to the conference final again the following season but never seemed likely to win. "We were all worn down by then," explained general manager Cliff Fletcher. Their other conference final appearances were in 1999, against the Buffalo Sabres, and in 2002 against the Carolina Hurricanes, but those, too, came to naught.

But that 1993 team with Doug Gilmour, Wendel Clark and Felix Potvin captured Leafs fans' imagination more than the others, perhaps because of the heroics along the way.

In the first round, they lost the first two games to the Detroit Red Wings, then won four of the next five—two in overtime—to win the series. The second round was a seven-gamer as well, this time against the

St. Louis Blues. On two occasions, the score was still tied after one period of overtime, and both times, the Leafs won in double overtime.

Now the Kings were all that stood between Toronto and a one-series crack at the Stanley Cup, a trophy they hadn't won since 1967. The Kings' run to the conference final hadn't been as dramatic, but it did have its intriguing moments. Having finished only four games over .500 and third in their six-team division, the Kings were doomed to face teams with better records in every round of the playoffs.

But rookie coach Barry Melrose, a disciple of positive thinker Tony Robbins, had his team believing that they could overcome every obstacle.

After knocking off the Calgary Flames in six games, the Kings next had to face the Vancouver Canucks, not an appetizing prospect.

"Going into that series, we had played Vancouver nine times and lost seven out of those nine times," recalled Gretzky. "Then, we didn't just lose Game One, we were awful. We got outhit. We got outshot. We got out-everything. We only lost 5–2 but that was a flattering score.

"Barry came into the room after the game and talked about all the positives. He went over all the good things again and again. By the time his speech had finished, it seemed like we'd won and we were up one game to nothing instead of being down 1–0."

With Gretzky leading the way, the Kings bounced back, defeated the Canucks in six games and waited for the Leafs and Blues to finish their seven-game series.

"Players always say they don't care who they play," Gretzky said, "but I think that's because it's easier to say that. I think you root for the team that you might have an easier time with. We felt in that particular series that there wasn't much to choose between the two teams.

"The only real difference was Dougie Gilmour who was having a great playoffs. He was exceptional. I had a great deal of respect for Dougie Gilmour. We felt that Toronto was a little bit bigger than the Blues, but St. Louis was a shorter flight, and in the west, you always think about that. Still, there was lots of emotion in that series for different reasons. My favourite arena always was Maple Leaf Gardens."

Against Toronto, the Kings once again got off to a poor start.

"My whole life, I wanted to play at least one series in Maple Leaf Gardens," Gretzky said. "I got an opportunity, and I was really excited about it. Then we lost 4–1 in the opener and I was minus-three. I didn't have a very good game, and I remember talking to Janet about it and she said, 'Sometimes you've got to be careful what you wish for because it might come true.'

"I was pretty depressed."

But the Kings bounced back in the second game to temporarily gain home-ice advantage. It didn't last long. Each team won a game in Los Angeles.

In Game Five, there were more heroics from the Leafs. Once again, they won in overtime and needed only one more win to head to the finals.

"After we split the first four, we knew we were going to have to win one game in Toronto," said Gretzky. "It was going to have to be Game Five or Game Seven. At first, you think you don't want to be in a Game-Seven situation, but when you really think some more about it, you realize that in Game Seven, there's more pressure on the home team.

"If the home team wins, everybody says, 'Well, of course they won. They were at home.' But if they let the visiting team win, everybody gets down on them, so they are under a lot of pressure.

"So, going into Game Six, we just said, 'Don't worry about the next game. Just take care of this game, then we'll worry about Game Seven.'"

Game Six was the one that still brings complaints from Leafs fans. In the second period, Gretzky took a shot from the faceoff circle that was blocked by Jamie Macoun. Just as the shot was released, Gilmour skated in from an angle, hitting Gretzky's stick, which slid up Gilmour's arm and clipped Gilmour under the chin.

When Leafs fans talk about it today, they tend to make it sound like an axe murder committed in front of three blind officials. Referee

Kerry Fraser didn't see Gretzky's stick hit Gilmour. Neither did either of the two senior linesmen handling the game—Kevin Collins and Ron Finn—both of whom had the authority to call a major penalty for high-sticking.

For that matter, neither did *Hockey Night in Canada* announcer Bob Cole. Here's his description: "Gretzky's moving towards the net now. The shot. That's blocked. It hit Gilmour. He blocked the shot. It hurt him. He fell."

Under the rules of that era, Gretzky should have been penalized and ejected from the game. Similarly, in an earlier game in the series, Gilmour should have been ejected for head-butting Marty McSorley.

Hockey has a lot of unwritten rules, and one of them—especially in that era before the league's approach changed following the 2004–05 lockout—required officials to be a lot more lenient in the post-season, particularly if a star player was the culprit.

There were many examples. One of the more notable incidents was Pavel Bure's blind-side flattening of Shane Churla with a vicious elbow in 1994. Churla was knocked unconscious, but no penalty was called. Bure was the star of the Vancouver Canucks; Churla was a workmanlike player for the Dallas Stars.

As Churla said afterwards, "If it was the other way around, I'd be gone for fifteen games at least. People would be calling me the biggest goon in hockey." But in that 1993 Leafs–Kings game, Gretzky went on to be the star, something Churla was never likely to do.

"I can't speculate on what would have been or what would have happened if Kerry had made that call," Gretzky said years later when asked about the incident. "The reality is that if I had gotten the penalty, we still may have won anyway. To hypothesize like that is like me saying we would have won the Stanley Cup had Marty's stick not been caught. [McSorley was assessed an illegal-stick penalty in the subsequent series.] That's probably not true.

"Of course the fans are frustrated at that time, and they wanted it to be a penalty, but I wasn't the referee. And I don't think it was a question of Kerry not wanting to call it. I think he didn't see it.

"I didn't do it on purpose. I didn't even know it had happened. After the game, everybody was showing it to me and telling me, so that's when I knew, but obviously, I didn't do it on purpose."

Once again, the game went into overtime, and Leafs fans were expecting the magic to strike again. It was the sixth overtime of the postseason for the Leafs, and they had won the first five.

When it didn't happen, the Leafs had no one but themselves to blame. In the first minute of overtime, Tomas Sandstrom took a pass from Alexei Zhitnik at his own blue line and went end to end unmolested. With the path to the net blocked, he took the puck into the right corner, and the Leafs finally decided that they should take some action. No fewer than three of them converged on him.

When the puck squirted out to Luc Robitaille, who was standing beside the scrum, there was no one left to stop him coming out of the corner all alone. He looked to the far side of the net, and there was Gretzky, left totally uncovered by Bill Berg, who was watching the play from a distance. Robitaille sent the puck to Gretzky, and Felix Potvin had no chance.

"To me, that was the sweetest game I played in my career," Gretzky said. "I hadn't played that well in the series, and there had been some criticism."

That's putting it mildly. Bob McKenzie of TSN, then a columnist for the *Toronto Star*, wrote that Gretzky had been playing as if he had a piano on his back. McKenzie wasn't the only critic. Many observers had opined that Gretzky could play better, but none had put it quite so forcefully.

Gretzky has always been acutely conscious of his image. "If we had lost that game," he said, "we would have been eliminated in six, and a lot of people would have looked at my career and said, 'Yeah, but they lost to Toronto with a chance to go to the finals, and where was Wayne Gretzky?'

"That goal kept us alive, so even though I accomplished a lot in my career, it was one of the most special goals I ever scored."

As it turned out, there were three more to come in the very near future.

Game Seven created a virtual perfect storm for Gretzky. All the factors fell into line, fed on each other and led to what he admits was "one of my two favourite games that I'll always remember." (The other was an international game, so simple deduction tells us that this was Gretzky's favourite NHL game.)

There was his love of Maple Leaf Gardens and his burning desire to add his own episode to the lore of that fabled building. There was the determination to override the criticism of McKenzie and others who had seen his performance thus far as something less than excellent. There was the desire to get another Stanley Cup to answer Peter Pocklington. Whenever Pocklington was asked about his sale of Gretzky, which was often, his smug response, usually delivered with a smarmy smile, was, "How many Cups has Gretzky won since we traded him?"

And there was another incident that came to light only recently and was told to me by a teammate of Gretzky's. In the warmup, he recognized that Gretzky was upset—and not by the circumstances. The pressure of an important game doesn't get to people like Gretzky. The nervousness is there, but it doesn't affect their game.

The teammate skated over and asked Gretzky what was wrong. Gretzky said he was fine. Gretzky's teammate tried a second time and got the same response. After the third query, Gretzky conceded that his afternoon nap had been interrupted by his wife, who, at the insistence of actor Mike Myers, was calling to ask for tickets to the game.

"So that's it?" said the teammate. "You missed your nap?"

"No, that's not it," said Gretzky. "Look at him."

He pointed to the seat he had acquired. It was occupied by Myers wearing a number 93 Doug Gilmour Toronto Maple Leafs sweater.

"G was so mad at that," said the teammate, "that he got all fired up. He was up for that game to begin with, but this pushed him to the limit."

"I felt real good going into that game," said Gretzky. "It was a Game Seven in Maple Leaf Gardens and we scored first. I gave the puck to

Marty McSorley, and Marty had a good chance, but he made a great play and gave it right back to me. All I had to do was put it into the empty net. Then we got a quick goal, and all of a sudden it was 2–0 and things were looking real good.

"But anything can happen in hockey, and they got a couple to make it 2–2."

Through all the years and through all the glory, Maple Leaf Gardens has probably never been louder than that. The Leafs' fans, so starved of success for so long, saw the Kings reeling, their own team charging, and a Stanley Cup berth heading their way. But Gretzky was not to be denied on this night. He seemed to be always on the ice, always in control and always dangerous. Not long after the Leafs had tied it up, Gretzky scored again, this time with a screaming slapshot that was in the net and back out again before Felix Potvin had a chance to move.

"I think that was a big goal," he said with a smile he was unable to contain. "It stopped their momentum."

The Kings went up 4–2; the Leafs came back to narrow the gap to 4–3. But in a goal reminiscent of the classic that Gilmour had scored against Curtis Joseph to win a game in the series against the St. Louis Blues, Gretzky came out from behind the net to bounce the puck off Toronto defenceman Dave Ellett's skate and past Potvin to complete the hat trick.

"That one turned out to be important as well," he chuckled. It certainly did, because the Leafs had not yet given up. With only forty seconds left, Ellett scored for the Leafs to make the score 5–4. Was another miracle finish in the making?

Melrose wanted to make sure that there wasn't. He called for the line that he felt could put a cap on the proceedings: Pat Conacher, Jari Kurri and Wayne Gretzky.

"It was the only time in my career that I didn't go on when I was asked," said Gretzky. I remember Barry saying, 'Conacher, Kurri, Ninety-nine.'

"I said, 'No, Barry. I can't go. I'm too tired. We've got to win this thing.'

"I didn't want to go out there and make a mistake because I was too tired."

For Gretzky to say this, he must have been absolutely exhausted. The fact that he turned down Melrose's request shows how much he had already put into this game.

Instead, Melrose called on Gary Shuchuk, whom the Kings had picked up as a rare Group VI free agent—a player who had been in the minors so long he had earned his release.

Shuchuk was twenty-five when he joined the Kings that season, but he had scored an overtime goal earlier in the playoffs. Even though the Leafs buzzed all around the Los Angeles end in the final seconds, he did the job and was one of the heroes on the ice when the game ended.

The real hero of the occasion was still on the bench.

CHAPTER SEVENTEEN

No matter how tired he might have been after the Kings' triumph in Toronto, Gretzky was rejuvenated and more than ready for the 1993 Stanley Cup final when it began in Montreal.

During the NHL playoffs, the schedule is such that teams customarily play every other day. But in this case, the league had inserted an extra dark day; so, after defeating the Leafs on a Saturday, the Kings opened the final on the subsequent Tuesday—June 1, to be precise.

In theory, the two teams were fairly evenly matched. The Canadiens could reasonably expect to get slightly better goaltending, since Patrick Roy was at the top of his game, but throughout the post-season, the Kings' Kelly Hrudey had been superb.

Montreal also had more depth. It wouldn't have caused Canadiens coach Jacques Demers any great anguish if he were forced to scratch an entire forward line for non-productivity, whereas Melrose certainly had no such option.

The Canadiens were also the deeper team when it came to defence. Any one of the Montreal defencemen who routinely sat out—Sean Hill, Donald Dufresne and Rob Ramage—would have been regulars in the Kings' lineup.

And for those who believe in such things, it almost seemed as if the Canadiens were predestined to win the 1993 Cup. Anyone looking at the list of unlikely circumstances that had preceded their arrival in the final would almost have to believe that this was to be one of those years when everything was ordained to go in their favour.

For one thing, the Canadiens were by no means the cream of the crop in the Wales Conference that year. Based on regular-season performances, the Boston Bruins, who had eliminated the Canadiens in each of the three previous seasons, were a far better team. The Pittsburgh Penguins were the best team in hockey. But the Canadiens didn't have to face either one. Both were upset by lesser lights.

Even the Quebec Nordiques were better than the Canadiens. But Montreal beat them in the first round when Quebec goalie Ron Hextall allowed goals on some astonishingly soft shots.

The Buffalo Sabres were kind enough to eliminate the Bruins in a major upset. However, the guy who was by far their biggest star, Pat LaFontaine, hurt his ankle so badly that he was totally ineffective in his team's subsequent series against Montreal which the Canadiens swept.

Then the Canadiens got to face the New York Islanders, who had gone toe to toe with the Penguins and had to start the series on the road against a rested Montreal team only thirty-nine hours after finishing Game Seven.

And so it went in a year that marked the Stanley Cup centenary. It almost seemed as if some Supreme Hockey Being had decreed that in such a momentous year, they had to win.

But the Kings had on their roster their own being who tended to be supreme in the hockey world: Wayne Gretzky.

Although the Canadiens had some high-quality forwards, such as Kirk Muller and Vincent Damphousse, they had no one who came remotely close to matching Gretzky's level of excellence. As the Leafs had become painfully aware, Gretzky was fully capable of single-handedly lifting his team and winning a game that, on paper, should have been lost.

In the series opener between Los Angeles and Montreal, it appeared that the Gretzky factor would outweigh all the other considerations. Gretzky scored one goal and assisted on three others as the Kings rolled to a 4–1 victory.

The Kings were every bit as dominant as the score would suggest. They crashed the crease at will, a tactic that did nothing to promote camaraderie between Roy and his defencemen; they finished their checks all over the ice; they used their size to go wherever they wanted; and they set up scoring chance after scoring chance.

It was widely conceded that even though the series was only one game old, the Kings were in charge. If they were able to win Game Two in Montreal and take a 2–0 series lead back to Los Angeles, the Canadiens' march to the Cup would end, hundredth anniversary or no hundredth anniversary.

The Canadiens looked lost. Perhaps because they had cruised through the earlier rounds in fifteen games while the Kings were battling every step of the way, they didn't appear crisp. Prior to the series opener, they had played only nine games in thirty-three days.

But following their lethargy in Game One, they didn't do a lot to help their cause in Game Two. They took no fewer than eight penalties that were either stupid, selfish, unnecessary or all of the above.

With only 1:45 left in the game, they were trailing 2–1. The prospects of a Stanley Cup for Los Angeles had never been brighter.

But then it happened. A moment that will live in infamy. A decision that every hockey fan of that era remembers with stunning clarity.

Demers called for a measurement of Marty McSorley's stick. It was one of the most dramatic coaching decisions in the history of the game. If Demers proved to be wrong in his assessment that the curve on McSorley's blade exceeded the prescribed limit, the Canadiens themselves would get a penalty, and the Kings could be expected to easily kill all the time left on the clock.

"They had to have measured our sticks somewhere," said Melrose in 2012. "You don't just make that kind of call unless you're absolutely sure. They had to have had someone in our dressing room."

When the stick proved to be illegal, the Canadiens not only had a power play, but Demers pulled Roy to give his team six skaters against four. With Kings defenceman Rob Blake frantically trying to dislodge John LeClair, who had both feet firmly planted well inside the crease and was blocking Hrudey's view, defenceman Eric Desjardins scored on a shot from the point to send the game into overtime.

The overtime didn't last long. Only fifty-one seconds in, Desjardins scored again. Was this more predestination? It was a hat trick for Desjardins who, prior to that game, had only two playoff goals in his career.

Instead of heading home with a 2–0 lead, the Kings were deflated and were never able to recover. After that, all the turning points swung in Montreal's favour. In Game Three for instance, the Kings fell behind 3–0, came back to tie the score, and appeared to deserve a penalty shot when the Canadiens' Guy Carbonneau covered the puck in the crease in the dying seconds. But the penalty shot was not awarded—a mistake later admitted to by the referee—and Montreal scored again in over-time. In Game Four, the Canadiens had more good fortune. Overtime again. A shot by LeClair banked off the leg of sliding Kings defenceman Darryl Sydor and into the net. It was the Canadiens' tenth consecutive overtime win.

Heading back home with a 3–1 series lead, the Canadiens had little trouble wrapping up the series and, in the process, becoming the last team to win a Stanley Cup with a roster composed solely of North American players.

That defeat was the most heartbreaking Gretzky ever endured, but he bears no grudges against McSorley. At least, not now.

One of the players on that team told me that Gretzky spent the entire intermission between the third period and overtime shouting at McSorley, but Gretzky won't confirm that, and McSorley denies it.

In 2012, Gretzky spoke about the incident. "We won Game Seven in Toronto, and then we went into Montreal and played unreal in Game One," he said. "Kelly Hrudey was excellent and outplayed Patrick. We went into Montreal that first night and won 4–1 and we were winning 2–1 after the second period in Game Two.

"I turned to Luc [Robitaille] and I turned to Marty and I said, 'I can tell you guys right now, somebody has been in this locker room either yesterday or this afternoon and measured the sticks.'

"It really wasn't that big a secret."

It wouldn't have been a secret to Gretzky because he had spent years in the Edmonton organization where the practice was commonplace. It is the custom in the NHL for the home team to supply the locks for the visitors' dressing room, and Glen Sather, the Oilers' general manager at the time, kept one key for the use of his own trainers. In the afternoons, when the visiting team was back at the hotel having a nap, one of Sather's employees would routinely go into the room and measure the curves of sticks that appeared to be illegal.

"We knew back then in those days which guys on which teams had sticks with illegal curves," Gretzky said in reference to the 1993 incident in Montreal. "Even though somebody was in there measuring, which we all thought was the case, we still talked about it after the second period. Marty happened to be the guy that got picked, but he was one of three or four guys that could have been picked. He happened to be on the ice at that time."

In fact, Robitaille, McSorley and Alexei Zhitnik had no legal sticks at the time. When the game resumed, they continued to use illegal sticks because the NHL rules of the day did not allow a team to call for a stick measurement in overtime.

Gretzky took the view that any error in judgment that McSorley might have made on that night was more than compensated for by his earlier contributions to the cause.

"Had we not had Marty, we would never have beaten Toronto," he explained. "Wendel Clark and Marty McSorley in that series played seven of what may be the most physical, hard-fought games I've ever seen two guys play against each other. If we didn't have Marty in that series, we would never have even got past Toronto, so you live and learn."

Gretzky was not the only one who held that view. Leafs coach Pat Burns was fully aware that McSorley not only negated Clark but also took his star forward, Doug Gilmour, off his game. "Dougie has to understand he's our best hockey player," said Burns in explaining why he had called in Gilmour for a one-on-one discussion after Game Three of the Kings–Leafs series. "He can't be taken off his game by Marty McSorley. That strategy of theirs has worked perfectly to a T."

In most sports, teams tend to be highly secretive. National Basketball Association practices are closed to the media, for instance. In the National Football League, representatives of visiting teams are banned. But hockey tends to be a bit more accommodating. Practices are usually open not only to the media, but also to scouts, agents, friends of management and even members of the opposing team. All manner of people wander in and out of dressing rooms.

"I talked about this many times to our guys," said Gretzky. "Why do we allow guys from the other organizations into our room during the Stanley Cup finals? In those days, every team used to supply a visiting-team locker-room guy. It was our own fault. I remember saying that we don't need anybody. We were travelling with everyone in our organization, including John Candy. We had enough people to look after our own locker room.

"It was our own fault. It was nobody's fault but our entire team and our organization. The Canadiens didn't do anything illegal. They just bent the rules a little bit. In saying all that, I don't want to sound like I'm saying that's why we lost the Stanley Cup. The better team won the Stanley Cup that year. It's as simple as that. Montreal had leadership from Guy Carbonneau, Kirk Muller and Mike Keane.

"Mike Keane didn't play Game One, I believe. He was hurt. He came back in Game Two, and he really gave them a pickup. John LeClair played as well as he ever played. We lost. That's all."

That was as close as Gretzky would ever come to winning another Stanley Cup.

———

Even though the Kings lost in the Stanley Cup final, they had risen to a level that the franchise had never before experienced. But as it turned out, it would be nineteen years—long after Gretzky had gone—before they took the final step.

In his era, the team was never again as dominant on the ice. Off the ice, serious trouble was brewing.

Near the end of the 1993–94 season, Gretzky was asked to drop by the office of his friend Bruce McNall, the owner of the Los Angeles Kings. This was not at all unusual. The two often travelled together. They often dined together. They shared business enterprises, including racehorses and the Toronto Argonauts of the Canadian Football League. They shared speculative purchases, including a rare baseball card.

They even worked together to end the 1992 strike by the NHL Players' Association. They flew back from a round of talks in New York in McNall's plane and went verbally toe to toe about the issues. McNall finally told Gretzky that if he could get the players to make the concessions they had discussed, then he could get the owners to make the concessions Gretzky sought as well. The season, which had appeared to be in jeopardy, was resumed shortly afterwards.

For the six seasons Gretzky had been in L.A., Bruce McNall always seemed the same. He was rotund, cheerful and affable. But on this day, he was different. "Two days before the season was over," recalled Gretzky, "I said, 'How are you doing?' He said, 'Bad. Very bad.'

"He had me come into his office for a whole day. He explained what had happened and what was going to happen. He didn't mislead me at all."

For McNall, it was the beginning of the end of a meteoric rise that had been followed by an equally rapid descent. In Los Angeles, and indeed throughout the hockey world, McNall had become almost as famous as Gretzky himself. He'd so impressed the other owners that they had made him chairman of the NHL's board of governors. No major event in Los Angeles was complete without McNall's presence. Hollywood stars flocked to the Fabulous Forum and dined at his table.

It was, of course, a facade. McNall was never really what he appeared to be, at least financially. That was what he told Gretzky during that day-long meeting. All his assets were either gone or going.

According to documents subsequently filed in United States Bankruptcy Court, McNall owed no less than $244.5 million.

By the spring of 1994, McNall was in full retreat. He had sold 72 per cent of the Kings and had been forced to resign as chairman of the NHL's board. Fraud charges began to be filed against his employees, and a succession of guilty pleas insured the sale of the remaining 28 per cent of the team, as well as McNall's eventual downfall.

"I was never a good businessman," McNall told me. "I never viewed myself as a businessman ever and that's probably why I got myself in all this trouble. A tough, hard businessman doesn't do all the stupid things I did. They're tight with the dollars. They're watching everything. They're not allowing their people to do whatever they want to do without having a firm hand on it all."

He was sentenced to sixty-two months in prison for bank fraud and wire fraud, and it was tough time, most of it spent in maximum-security institutions across the United States, not at all like a Club Fed in Canada.

He did time in solitary confinement. He was shackled and transported around the country chained to a seat in a decrepit, converted school bus with no air conditioning. He was sometimes locked up for twenty-three hours a day, and because of the kind of resentful mentality that exists in prisons, he was occasionally made to suffer because others were jealous.

But wherever he went, he received regular visits from Gretzky. Even those happy moments had their drawbacks.

"To have a friend who shows up when it's not popular is really remarkable," McNall told me after his release. "Wayne Gretzky is clean living itself. His whole life is based on that. For him to maintain the friendship and loyalty that he did, it was just amazing.

"When he came to visit, it was like a zoo, except the guards were all asking for autographs. It was great.

"And I got blamed for it, by the way."

Still, the calls were worth the aggravation and Gretzky visited again and again, even though McNall was moved from Lompoc in California to Safford in Arizona and then to Milan in Michigan.

On one occasion, Gretzky's visit had just begun when the penitentiary went into a lockdown. McNall was taken away and three hours elapsed before he returned to the visiting area. Gretzky was still sitting there, waiting.

Many of those McNall had considered to be friends deserted him. Not many of the players went to visit him, but some did—including Rob Blake. I tried, but journalists were never allowed to visit, so we stayed in touch through the mail.

In 2002, when Gretzky had his number, 99, retired by the Kings, there were many who wondered why it had taken so long. The answer was simple: Bruce McNall.

"It's just remarkable that Wayne waited like this and held it up until I was available," McNall said. "That's Wayne. Friendship is something that's a rare commodity in the world, especially when things are not going well. Wayne was always right there, always the first there.

"I kept saying to him, 'Wayne, what about retiring your jersey?' And he said, 'No, I'm going to wait. It's not right yet.'

"And finally, when they announced that they were going to do it, he said, 'I wanted to wait until you were available.' It was very heartfelt. I was very taken by it all."

At the gala dinner that was part of the retirement ceremony, McNall was one of the speakers and thanked Gretzky for sticking by him. "It means a lot more to me than you can imagine," he said.

In typical fashion, Gretzky shrugged it off. "It's a lot better visiting you here than in Lompoc," he said with a laugh.

CHAPTER EIGHTEEN

In 1994, the New York Rangers won the Stanley Cup for the first time in more than fifty years and the National Hockey League was suddenly a red-hot commodity on the United States sports scene.

Like it or not, the New York media dictate the agenda for the whole continent, and with the Broadway Blueshirts on top of the hockey world, the sporting intelligentsia were all but unanimous that the NHL was finally poised to make the breakthrough it had sought for so long.

Rangers captain Mark Messier was the hottest name on the New York sporting scene and the media could hardly wait for the 1994–95 season to begin.

So Gary Bettman locked out the players.

The owners needed a better deal, he said, and until one could be hammered out, there would be no season.

By the time baseball staged its World Series in October, the dream of hockey's ascension into the American sporting Valhalla was nothing more than a bitter, distant and faded memory. The New York media— not to mention the city's sports fans—had shunted hockey aside once again. And since New York called the tune, hockey interest was fading rapidly all over the United States.

To Wayne Gretzky, this development was nothing short of torture. He was thirty-three, still in the prime of his hockey life, and he couldn't bring himself to sit idly by while the future of the season—if there were to be one—was debated by lawyers.

He considered organizing a goodwill tour of Europe with a hand-picked team of friends. He didn't want an NHL all-star team because it was his intention to tour Scandinavia playing against established club teams and he didn't want to steamroll the European teams or make them look inept in front of their fans. He just wanted to stage some exhibition games—his team against theirs—and promote the NHL in Europe.

He started to think of the concept as a reality, but a ray of optimism on the labour front changed his mind. He let it slide. Then, as negotiations dragged on, he considered it again. Once more, the prospect of a settlement seemed better. He dropped it again.

But when an agreement continued to be elusive, he finally decided to stage the tour.

For some now-forgotten reason, he and I and Mike Barnett, who was his agent at the time, were flying to Los Angeles and sitting together at the back of an almost-deserted business-class cabin. "You can't write about this yet, Strach," Gretzky said, "but we're going to make a European tour and I want to ask a bunch of guys to come along. They won't get paid, but we want to make sure everybody has a good time."

We started to put together a list of names, a fairly easy task. There were plenty of candidates who either were, or had been, Gretzky's teammates. Then we added veteran players who would be good draws in Europe. Sergei Fedorov was on that list. So was Al MacInnis. Russ Courtnall was another. And Steve Yzerman.

Doug Gilmour was on the original list too, but as it turned out, he went to Europe on his own and joined the Swiss team Rapperswil.

We were well into the proceedings and had washed back a couple of beers to help accumulate a pretty comprehensive list. The beers necessitated a washroom dash, and while I was there, I ran through a few more names in my head. Suddenly, for some reason (definitely not related to the surroundings), I thought of Mario Lemieux.

He was out of hockey at that point and no one knew if he would ever return. As a result, no one had thought of considering him.

When I went back into the cabin, I said, "What about Mario?"

"Wow, I hadn't thought of him," said Gretzky. "Do you think there's any way he can play?"

Lemieux had been plagued by injuries and illness. In early 1993, he had been diagnosed with Hodgkin's lymphoma, a form of cancer. That year, he missed two months of action. Then, in the summer of 1993, he underwent his second back surgery and, during the course of the subsequent season, missed fifty-eight games as the back problems continued. As a result, in the spring of 1994, when the Rangers were making their march to the Cup, Lemieux announced that due to the cumulative effect of his ailments—the back problems and the fatigue associated with the chemotherapy treatments he had undergone to deal with the lymphoma— he was taking an indefinite leave of absence.

That was why neither Gretzky nor Barnett had thought of him. But as soon as I mentioned him, they were enthused. After all, he wouldn't be facing the rigours of the NHL. In a Scandinavian goodwill tour, he was unlikely to be checked. He could come along and have a good time, playing only when he felt like it but adding so much to the tour's impact by his mere presence.

Lemieux's name almost completed the first draft list of potential players, so while Gretzky and I chatted, Barnett got on the phone and started working his way down the list.

Actually, it's incorrect to say he worked his way *down* the list. The first call he made was to Lemieux, whose name was near the bottom.

Lemieux considered the idea, but felt that he needed rest and recuperation. Therefore, it would be best if he stayed home. Also, there were some logistical issues that could not easily be resolved.

Those were the days of twelve-dollar-a-minute air-to-ground telephone calls, and for most of the flight, Barnett was on the phone.

"He's using my credit card for this," said Gretzky. "I hope they settle the lockout soon so I can pay this bill."

Then he laughed. "My dad would be proud of Mike. My dad used to work for Bell but now that he's retired, he's involved in so many things that he's on the phone all the time. He says his Bell bill now is bigger than any paycheque he ever got from them."

Over the next few days, the concept came together. Doug Messier, a hockey lifer who also happened to be Mark's father, was to be one of the coaches. Mark himself was to be an alternate captain. The head coach—although that categorization elevates the status of the post somewhat—was Doug Wilson who was a year into retirement after an outstanding NHL career that included a Norris Trophy.

Eventually, when all the calls had been made and all the willing participants had agreed to go, the group gathered in Pontiac, Michigan, for an exhibition game against the Detroit Vipers, an International Hockey League team. Right after the game, Gretzky's group boarded a bus for Detroit Metro Airport and the charter flight to Europe.

When we arrived at the airport, we greeted three Detroit Red Wings who had been waiting on the plane for forty-five minutes and had sat out the game to avoid creating any unnecessary animosity with the NHL—Fedorov, Yzerman and Paul Coffey. The rest of the Gretzky and Friends team boarded the plane as a lively, spirited group.

Half a day later, tired, bedraggled and disoriented, they disembarked 4,500 miles away in Helsinki, Finland. But they were no longer a formless group. Now, they were a team with a sense of purpose.

Mark Messier had already let it be known that he was something less than happy about the 4–3 loss to the Vipers. Even though he fully understood that he was embarking on an exhibition tour aimed at spreading goodwill, Messier had no intention of being embarrassed in the process.

"Well, that was our last loss," he announced to his teammates with a somewhat ominous note of finality.

Nevertheless, Gretzky and Friends knew that on the ice, they wouldn't have an easy time of it in Scandinavia. Simply getting to Europe had proved taxing. The flight on their Boeing 727, chartered for their two-week tour, was gruelling, even by Los Angeles Kings standards.

The first leg got them into Goose Bay, Labrador, at 3:15 a.m. Eastern time and at 6:40, they touched down in Keflavik, Iceland. Finally, at 11 a.m. Detroit time, they dragged themselves off the plane in Finland. It was 6 p.m. in Helsinki.

From the airport, they went straight to the rink for a quick skate, then headed back to the hotel for a 9 p.m. charity dinner before finally heading off for some long-overdue sleep. There wasn't time for a lot of rest—the opening faceoff of the first game of the tour was scheduled for 3 p.m. in Finland (8 a.m. in Detroit).

But the players all accepted it with equanimity. On a long flight of that nature, a kinship builds. Players who have known each other only on the ice strike up friendships. Players who have been close friends rekindle relationships that have ebbed during the course of the summer and the two-month lockout.

As they flew through the night, stories were exchanged, card games sprang up, camaraderie grew and the realization developed that this was to be an experience of a lifetime. Going on a barnstorming tour with Wayne Gretzky would be a chance that would probably never come again. It would be to a hockey player what touring with Babe Ruth would have been to a baseball player.

Gretzky himself saw the chance to fulfill a long-held dream and grabbed it. Looking out the window during the first refuelling stop, he said, "If you'd told me in June that I'd be in Goose Bay in December, I'd have said you were crazy."

The players were all aware that once the rigours of the NHL resumed, they would get back into their regular uniforms and those friendships would be put aside. But for the time being, they were hockey's ambassadors, taking the game back to a region that provided many of its elite players.

For the opening game against Jokerit, tickets were sold out within an hour. "We could have sold fifty thousand tickets," said a team official.

The arrival of the Gretzky team stirred up a sizeable local dispute.

Many fans wanted to see a reunification of Gretzky and his longtime linemate, Jari Kurri, the most revered player in Finland. Many others wanted Kurri to remain in the Jokerit lineup and play against Gretzky.

After heated debate, fans were given a vote—not an option Bettman and the NHL governors were considering back in North America as the lockout dragged on. Helsinki's hockey fans opted to see Gretzky and Kurri together. To add to the nostalgia, Messier became the third member of the line.

With Kurri playing for the Ninety-Nines, as the team was calling itself now, Gretzky and his friends breezed to a 7–1 victory over Jokerit. Even so, they needed a spectacular performance from goaltender Grant Fuhr. "It could have been 7–5 without Grant," said Teemu Selanne, the other elite player on the Jokerit roster. "Some of our guys were nervous about playing against stars. They wanted to get autographs before the game."

In Europe, all was well. But back in North America, bitterness was starting to surface.

A minor squabble was started by Gretzky's former teammate Luc Robitaille whom the Los Angeles Kings shopped all over, with an extra push in the direction of the Canadiens and Quebec Nordiques, before finally unloading him on Pittsburgh.

Robitaille was critical of the tour, telling a French-language newspaper in Montreal that Gretzky was anti-Québécois because the team had no French Canadians. In fact, the first person Gretzky and Barnett called on to join the team was Mario Lemieux, whose insurance agreement ruled him out. The first goalie Gretzky called was Patrick Roy, who turned him down because he had a chance to play golf with Fred Couples.

Gretzky then asked Kirk Muller about the availability of Vincent Damphousse, but Muller said Damphousse was committed to a team in Germany.

Therefore, the team had no French Canadians.

As for Robitaille himself, Gretzky said, "Montreal and Quebec didn't want him, so why would I?"

A much more relevant attack came from New York, and it had implications for years to come. Up to that point, Gretzky and NHL commissioner Gary Bettman had coexisted peacefully. But Bettman's response to the Scandinavian tour marked the beginning of the ill feelings between the two that grew and grew over the years.

It was no accident that, more than a decade later, after Gretzky stepped down as coach of the Phoenix Coyotes, he stayed out of hockey and was not offered an NHL job, not even as a roaming ambassador.

The Ninety-Nine All Stars Tour was a huge boost to the NHL's presence in Europe, but the head-office bigwigs, who like to be in the forefront of everything hockey-related and usually screw it up, decided that rather than lend support, they would go on the attack.

"They have done everything in their ability to stop us," said defenceman Marty McSorley, who, later in his career, was handed the longest suspension in NHL history by Bettman. "I think the NHL was desperately hoping that this tour wouldn't happen."

Gretzky and his close associates had been trying to avoid the subject, preferring to keep the tour on a totally positive note, but once McSorley made his views public, they didn't have much choice in the matter. One by one, they told me that they found the NHL's actions "shameful," "a disgrace" and "despicable after all Wayne has done for the game."

It became evident that players had nothing but scorn for the people who were running the league. Their derision even extended to the ones who weren't New York lawyers, such as then NHL vice-president Brian Burke, a Boston lawyer.

Chuckled one long-term NHL veteran, "I talked to Brian Burke for an hour and found out I didn't know anything about hockey."

"It's not a question of who's right and who's wrong," said Gretzky diplomatically. "It's a question of the people, the public, the fans. They just want to see the best they can see. I'm disappointed about the story that someone is leaking out now that the players are trying to delay negotiations to get this tour in. That's definitely not true. I've told them all along that if they get a deal, we're coming back home."

The story to which Gretzky referred had surfaced in a newsletter distributed by Stan Fischler, the New Yorker the NHL had intended to hire as a PR man a couple of years earlier until a storm of protest from team public-relations executives forced a sudden reversal.

Fischler was a strong backer of Bettman and his regime, to put it mildly, even to the point of writing that the United States' contributions to hockey over the years have been just as significant as Canada's.

The NHL also sought to minimize the impact of the Gretzky tour by forcing TSN to keep the Scandinavian tour's games off the network in Canada. At that time, TSN was trying to get a foothold in NHL telecasts and acquiesced to the league's demands. League executives also told *Hockey Night in Canada* that they didn't want any Gretzky games to be shown, but *HNiC,* being much more established than TSN, ignored their demands. NHL brass then approached the prime sponsor, Molson Breweries—with the same result.

NHL teams were told by the league in writing that absolutely nothing was to be done to accommodate the Gretzky goodwill tour. As a result, the players had to supply everything from equipment to trainers.

In order to make sure the players had the best of attention, Gretzky offered to pay the salaries of trainers and administrative personnel while they were on tour, thereby relieving the clubs of the obligation.

It wasn't a terribly intelligent move on the league's part to withhold NHL trainers, even though the ones who were brought in from other professional sports were extremely competent. Still, the league's vitriol was at such a level that common sense was ignored.

McSorley, who was a vice-president of the NHL Players' Association and was therefore privy to information that might not be widely disseminated, said that two high-ranking NHL executives, one of whom was vice-president Steve Solomon, even travelled to Europe to try to scuttle the tour by threatening the teams who were to provide the opposition.

NHL executives also tried to force Rene Fasel, head of the International Ice Hockey Federation, to withhold his sanction, but Fasel reluctantly refused to do so, more for political reasons than out of any sense of fair play. He wanted NHL players to participate in the 1998 Winter Olympics, and at that point, the matter was very much up in the air.

It is widely conceded that, were it not for Gretzky, there would be no NHL teams in Anaheim, San Jose, Dallas, Miami or Tampa Bay. In fact, there are even those who say that without Gretzky's arrival in southern California in 1988, the Los Angeles Kings would have packed up soon and gone elsewhere.

Gretzky was always a first-rate ambassador for the game. He was easily the most accessible team-sport superstar in the world and he gave his time freely for the game he loves.

There had been times when Gretzky had flown coast to coast to have his picture taken for a magazine cover at the league's urging. He had made a promotional video for the NHL cause. He had appeared on countless sports-interview shows in the United States on his own time.

But the vindictive bottom-liners who ran the NHL—and in some cases still do—chose to reward him for his years of devotion by sabotaging a pet project that he had tried to initiate on two other occasions.

Little wonder that Bettman's approach to the tour gave birth to an animosity that has never been overcome.

Throughout the Scandinavian tour, Gretzky always remembered its overriding purpose—to take the game to those who love it but might otherwise never be exposed to it. He and the other players spent time with local hockey officials, attended functions, played their games with a sense of ambassadorial sportsmanship and, most important, spent as much time as possible with the kids.

Wherever the team went, hockey was a popular local sport and the sporting-goods stores were full of NHL paraphernalia. In Stockholm, for instance, it was much easier to buy a Mighty Ducks sweater or a Blackhawks hat than a Djurgarden sweater.

Gretzky himself was mobbed. Whenever the tour arrived in a city, he was greeted by two new bodyguards (always dubbed Hans and Franz) who flanked him until he boarded the plane for the next city.

Gretzky would have preferred to handle the crowds himself, and he repeatedly frustrated the guards by stopping to sign autographs, but the crowds were such that, for his own safety, he needed support. By the end of the first week in Europe, it had become abundantly clear to the players why the NHL worked so hard to sabotage their road show.

The players were quickly finding out what the NHL had known all along: that Europe was wealthy, hockey hungry and on the verge of a communications explosion. Those three factors add up to a potential bonanza, and the NHL owners wanted to make sure they were the ones who hit pay dirt. The longer they were able to keep the players in the dark, the better. Negotiations on a new collective bargaining agreement were under way, and in the years to come, labour-management battles were going to be an ongoing feature of the NHL landscape. On the table would be revenues from European TV rights and international events— the Olympics and visits from NHL teams, for instance. As far as the NHL was concerned, the less the players knew about the lucrative aspects of these areas, the more likely they would be to make European concessions at the bargaining table.

That's why they did everything they could to prevent Gretzky's tour from taking place, and that's why their disinformation machine sprang into action with stupid stories about the tour forcing an extension of the lockout and Gretzky being the prime beneficiary of the spectacle.

Prior to the trip, NHL players had only suspected they could be popular abroad. Now, they saw it first-hand, and the magnitude of their popularity astonished them.

They saw the mob scenes that developed whenever they appeared in public. They saw a press conference that drew 100 media people in a city of 170,000 on a Sunday morning. They saw the packed arenas, even though they were staging only a small goodwill tour of exhibition games against a few club teams.

They learned that the communications industry in Europe was about ten years behind North America and poised for an explosion in cable TV and satellite TV, both of which had already taken place in North America. They became aware that network executives would soon be crying out for high-level entertainment and paying accordingly.

When all those factors were put together, the inescapable conclusion was that, not far in the future, high-quality professional hockey in the form of a rival to the NHL would evolve in Europe. As it happened, they were right. Roughly a decade after the Gretzky trip, a number of Russian oligarchs established the Kontinental Hockey League, paying big money to top-flight elite-level players, mostly of European origin.

Whether the NHL can maintain its position as the world's best league in the face of that challenge remains to be seen. But at the time of the Gretzky tour, the players were more concerned with having their eyes opened than extending the vision for years into the future. They began to realize that every league has owners and players. But to have the best hockey league in the world, you must have NHL-calibre players. You don't have to have NHL owners.

That's why the owners fought so hard against the Gretzky tour. They had locked out the players to force them into agreeing to the labour landscape they had established. The last thing they wanted was a bunch of high-profile players finding out just how much they were worth.

Throughout the tour, the league's misinformation machine relentlessly implied that Gretzky was hindering a settlement, even though out-clauses were part of every arrangement. Gretzky even paid five times the cost of commercial air travel to guarantee the use of a plane that could get every player to training camp within forty-eight hours of a lockout settlement.

Another story surfaced suggesting that Gretzky had staged the tour in order to line his pockets. In fact, he risked $500,000 of his own money in non-refundable costs to get the event rolling. Had the tour been cancelled after one game, Gretzky would have lost a lot of money. Once it reached the halfway point, he was off the hook.

As it happened, the tour played to its conclusion and raised about $300,000. One-third went to the retired players' pension fund and an equal amount to the NHL Players' Association. The remaining $100,000 was given to charity.

In addition, money was raised for European charities. In Helsinki, for instance, the children's hospital was the recipient of the proceeds from the dinner. It also got a visit from Gretzky after the game.

To suggest that Gretzky staged the tour for his own financial benefit was nothing short of ridiculous. During the tour, Gretzky received four offers to appear in European club games. He could have cleared about $1 million by staying for another week or so, but wouldn't because, "We came as a team, we're playing as a team, and we'll go back as a team."

In contrast, Philadelphia Flyers owner Ed Snider was among the NHL governors most vehemently opposed to the tour. The Flyers even prohibited their minor-league European players from taking part in any games. Nevertheless, when Gretzky and Friends played in Oslo, they did so in the Spektrum, a facility managed by Spectacor, one of Snider's companies. As a result, Snider made a tidy profit off Gretzky's appearance.

Not long after Gretzky and his friends returned from Europe, the players and owners hammered out an agreement. Perhaps a threat made by Mark Messier that the players were considering starting their own league was a factor. Perhaps the owners wanted to stem the rising tide of player independence before it became too entrenched. Either way, it was ironic that, even though the NHL did everything it could to sabotage Gretzky's goodwill tour, it was the tour's biggest beneficiary.

"It's very obvious that the NHL could come over here and be tremendously successful," said Gretzky as the tour wound down. "We opened a lot of doors, so to speak. We always knew that hockey was big here, but now it's clear that the NHL is very big in Europe.

"I think it surprised all of us that hockey is so popular over here. When Team Canada came over in '72, the people didn't know what to expect. But guys like Borje Salming and Jari Kurri and the other European players who were successful in the NHL really opened the doors by getting people to watch our game. Now there's such a following that the people knew most of the players, probably all of the players."

Gretzky gave himself an incredible workload. The trip was gruelling for everyone, but, by choice, he assumed added responsibilities—kids' hockey clinics in every city, hospital visits, television interviews and so on.

For the most part, Gretzky was happy with the tour.

"It was a lot of fun," he said. "There was a lot of good hockey and a couple of really good games. I think we surprised some people with how hard we played, and the response of the players was fantastic. Every time we asked somebody to do something, we got full cooperation."

His one disappointment?

"The fact that we didn't get to play the Russian all-star team. They had wanted to play us and we wanted to play them, but these games are all approved by the Players' Association and we couldn't get that one arranged."

When the tour ended, so did Gretzky's career as a tour organizer. "This is my last tour," he said. "I had fun and I enjoyed it, but I told Mess he can arrange the next tour and I'll jump on board."

CHAPTER NINETEEN

A s 1995 wound down, so did Gretzky's contract with the Los Angeles Kings.

At the end of the 1995–96 season, he was to become an unrestricted free agent, able to sell his services to any interested party.

He had lived in greater Los Angeles since 1988, and his three children had been born there. But at the same time, the desire to win another Stanley Cup still burned. The Kings had been plagued by a series of financial problems while he was on their roster, not the least of which was McNall's imprisonment on fraud charges. The subsequent ownership had declared bankruptcy.

New ownership was now in place, but it was unclear whether the financial commitment necessary to win a Stanley Cup was also present. When those new owners were in the process of acquiring the team the previous summer, promises had been made that as soon as the sale was finalized, free agents would be pursued with a vengeance. But by the time the lawyers had finished their usual clause-by-clause analysis (which, coincidentally enough, raised their fees) and the ownership was formally transferred, most of the worthwhile free agents had signed elsewhere.

Accordingly, it was agreed that on January 20, 1996, Gretzky's agent, Mike Barnett, would meet with the Kings' new owners to listen to offers.

If the two sides weren't in the same ballpark, it seemed safe to assume that Gretzky would be traded within a month or so. After all, if the Kings were liable to lose him in the summer for no compensation, common sense would dictate that they should trade him and get something in return. Like most teams unwilling to spend big money on free agents, the Kings had been musing about "rebuilding" and initiating the ever-popular "youth movement." But Gretzky was a few days away from his thirty-fifth birthday. He had no interest in being part of a youth movement.

The status of the game's premier player was widely known, and a number of teams approached either Barnett or the Kings about the possibility of acquiring him.

The Vancouver Canucks showed serious interest. Also making a pitch were the Toronto Maple Leafs, Detroit Red Wings and New York Rangers. There were even discussions involving Philadelphia Flyers owner Ed Snider despite the fact that, at the time, the Flyers were not big spenders and Gretzky was earning nine million dollars (two million plus a seven-million-dollar signing bonus) a year. But in what came as a surprise to most hockey fans, the most active pursuers of Gretzky's services were the St. Louis Blues.

And as an indication that he still had considerable value on the open market, in the week the story about the impending meeting broke, Gretzky was named the National Hockey League player of the week.

To the average fan, the decision was a simple one: the Kings would either deal Gretzky or they wouldn't. And if they did, they had to try to get the best possible deal.

But as is often the case in matters of this nature, political considerations were being brought to bear. For one thing, even though the NHL owners were terrified of showing the kind of collusion that could bring on an antitrust suit, a good deal of pressure was being exerted on some of the more generous owners to keep salaries down. Only a few months earlier, NHL commissioner Gary Bettman had imposed the first of his three lockouts and killed three months of the season in an attempt to reduce payrolls. If Gretzky, as the league's highest-paid player, were to be the focus of a bidding war and be given another whopping contract, the reverberations would be felt throughout the league.

On the other hand, as far as his personal finances were concerned, Gretzky would be willing to play for less than nine million dollars. But he, too, felt an obligation to his colleagues—in this case, the members of the NHL Players' Association. If a big Gretzky contract would drive up salaries throughout the league, a small Gretzky contract would drive them down. Even though Gretzky loved the game and wanted to continue playing, he wouldn't do it if the offers were too low.

There was also some animosity within the Kings organization. Before Gretzky arrived in Los Angeles, the Kings tended to be a happy, cozy, country-club team. Salaries were high, the climate and lifestyle were enjoyable, anonymity was easily acquired, and the fans were not at all demanding. For people like Dave Taylor, Rogatien Vachon and some of their friends, this was a great life.

But when Gretzky arrived, he not only stole what spotlight there was, but, by his very presence, changed the whole atmosphere. Some players didn't like it, and some of the broadcasters, whose opinion could influence fans, didn't like it either.

So while it would be difficult to move Gretzky out of a hard-core hockey market, that was not the case in Los Angeles, even though the Kings wouldn't be able to get anything close to equal talent in return.

After all, there wasn't much time left on Gretzky's contract, even though the Kings were on the hook for deferred payments until February 15, 2015. For another thing, the salary-first concept that dominates today's hockey had already established a significant foothold in 1996. To illustrate that point, Patrick Roy and Joe Nieuwendyk had recently been traded for a small return, as far as hockey talent was concerned. NHL teams were starting to be run by the accountants. The hockey people—all of whom would love to have Gretzky—usually were well down the chain of command.

In St. Louis, however, the guy who was the driving force behind the decisions was most definitely not an accountant. He was Mike Keenan, the coach and general manager of the Blues. He not only wanted Gretzky, he wanted him in a hurry. With the meeting to determine Gretzky's future originally planned for January 20 and then moved up to January 16, Keenan intended to make a deal the day after the meeting.

A week before that meeting, I was in Philadelphia, where the Blues were playing the Flyers. After the game, Keenan and I went out for a couple of beers. With the understanding that his comments on this particular matter were for attribution, he made his intentions as clear as was humanly possible without earning a million-dollar tampering fine from the NHL. "If Wayne Gretzky is made available by the Los Angeles Kings," he said, "then the Blues would be very interested in having him. Very interested . . . that's all I can say."

In fact, the Blues had already held a high-level management/ownership meeting and had unanimously agreed to do everything within their power to make Gretzky a member of the Blues as soon as possible. They had even agreed to offer him something in the range of nine million dollars annually—on a two-year deal. The signing bonus, if any, was to be arranged. They felt that they could recoup much of that money and possibly even earn a bit extra through increased ticket sales.

Although the Blues' announced home attendance in that era was usually in the seventeen-thousand range, a more honest figure would be closer to fourteen thousand. Their arena, then known as the Kiel Center, seats about twenty thousand, and with Gretzky in the lineup, all the seats were likely to be sold.

Furthermore, Gretzky's presence would vastly improve the Blues' chances in what could be a lucrative playoff run. Player salaries end with the regular season, so with each home game realizing about a million dollars from ticket revenue alone, the Blues envisioned a sizable windfall.

The Blues' biggest fear at that point was that they might be outbid. The New York Rangers were also interested in Gretzky and reportedly were offering Mattias Norstrom and a first-round draft pick.

It was the Blues' intention to offer the Kings a selection of young players and draft choices—as many as five if Gretzky were to bring along a friend or two. The Blues had in mind Marty McSorley and Rick Tocchet, operating on the assumption that if the Kings unloaded Gretzky, they had made a decision to rebuild and would therefore put other senior players on the block as well.

I called Gretzky and asked him if he knew about the Blues' interest. He said no one had told him directly, but he did know.

The week before, the Blues had sent scout Jim Pappin to Los Angeles, and his appearance at the Kings' practices caused a good deal of consternation among the players. Finally, Gretzky went over to him, laughed, and said, "Jimmy, you don't have to hang around here all week. Go back to St. Louis and tell Mike I still work hard in practice."

Usually, trade negotiations are secret. But I had published the details of this one in the *Toronto Sun* and now, there were almost daily updates. On the hockey front, most of the teams in the league had given some thought to their chances of acquiring Gretzky.

The Kings' management, meanwhile, was under assault for answers, even though the proposed meeting between Barnett and the team was still a week away.

In a city like Los Angeles, image is always a factor. The team didn't want to be seen as throwing away its short-term Cup hopes and insisted that Gretzky admit that the trade was his idea—which he did. Then the team had to say that it was trying to keep Gretzky, whether that was the case or not.

"We are prepared to offer a contract extension as early as tomorrow to Gretzky's agent, Mike Barnett, to show our intent to keep him," Kings general manager Sam McMaster told an L.A.–area radio station on January 14. "Ownership has told me we can increase our budget right now to acquire a veteran player."

That was true. But what he didn't say was that this was not a policy change. The money had been there all season. McMaster simply didn't spend it.

On the same day, Gretzky spelled out his concerns during an ESPN interview. "My priority is to see if this new ownership group would be willing to go out and add a couple of guys," he said. The "couple of guys" he had in mind, he explained, were a fifty-goal scorer and a defenceman of Paul Coffey's calibre.

"If we aren't going to better our team, then, yeah, I would just like to win a championship," Gretzky added. "I'm not twenty-two years old anymore. I'm not at an age where I can play for another ten years. It doesn't make a whole lot of sense to keep Wayne Gretzky around as a presence if we're not going to go out and win a championship. It doesn't make a lot of sense for the Kings to pay me what they're paying me if we're not going to try to win."

Up to this point, all the factors pointed not only to a Gretzky trade but to an imminent Gretzky trade. When the long-awaited meeting between the two sides finally took place, however, it did not go well. Gretzky did not attend, but was represented by his lawyer and Barnett. The Kings' representatives were McMaster, alternate governor Rogatien Vachon, and hockey operations head Bob Sanderman.

The fact that this trio represented the Kings was in itself ominous. The top two people in the Kings' organization were not present, although perhaps the absence of majority owner Philip Anschutz should not have come as a surprise. In his four months of ownership, he had never attended a game, so it wasn't a shock that he didn't attend a meeting concerning a team he had never seen in action.

Afterwards, the Kings issued the following statement: "We had a productive meeting today with Wayne Gretzky's representatives. We discussed many things including a contract extension for Wayne but there is no timetable as to when such an extension may be completed.

"We understand Wayne's desire for the Kings to be a winning team.

It is our desire as well. Our goal is to build a winner and keep Wayne Gretzky a part of the Kings' organization. We are working hard to accomplish those goals.

"Meetings between both parties will be ongoing."

In the news business, that kind of statement usually translates as "We're miles apart." It contained no indication that any progress was made. Furthermore, the Kings were clearly unable to suggest that Gretzky had any intention of signing the contract extension to which they referred.

All of a sudden it became clear that the Kings and Gretzky were not on the same page. They weren't even reading from the same book.

In his ESPN interview, Gretzky had said, "We will have a good idea where everybody stands by the end of the week. I'm sure something will happen by then."

But two days later, McMaster announced that he expected no further meetings until after the all-star break, which was coming up that weekend.

Thus began more than a month of half-truths and innuendoes, of one step forward and two steps back, of dawdling and indecisiveness.

The all-star weekend, which, naturally enough, usually centred around the all-star game, instead focused on the state of the Gretzky-trade negotiations.

By this point, the Blues weren't saying much. They were still in the forefront of the talks, and they were still pulling out all the stops to get Gretzky. But Keenan, certainly not one of commissioner Gary Bettman's favourite people, had been told to shut up about it. It was Keenan—and only Keenan—who spoke for the Blues.

Keenan knew what he wanted. Gretzky knew what he wanted. But the Kings, lacking any experience in such matters, had no idea which way they should turn and were caught in an internal battle between their hockey people and their financial people.

McMaster, in only his second year in the NHL, was under the kind of intense media pressure that he had never encountered in junior hockey.

Coach Larry Robinson, like the new owners, had been in place for only four months. As a result, the hockey people couldn't make up their minds what they wanted, and the financial people couldn't understand that deals can't be done in a vacuum. If you get involved with big-time contracts during the season, it usually has a negative effect on the team.

So by this time, Gretzky was worn down physically and emotionally, McMaster was constantly flustered, the management couldn't decide which move would be best in the long term, and the Kings were in the tank. Each game, there were thousands of empty seats in the Great Western Forum, and the Kings were giving every indication that they would miss the playoffs for the third consecutive year.

The only course of action that made sense was to put Gretzky up for auction and get the best possible package—and to do it quickly, because his contract was running out. Unfortunately for the Kings and their fans, there was no one in the team's upper echelon with enough hockey acumen to get the ball rolling. Instead, they were seriously considering offering Gretzky a contract.

Why they would even think of doing that remains a mystery. Well, actually, it's not a mystery. They simply didn't understand the situation. The team needed a major overhaul, and the most valuable asset to deal was indisputably Gretzky. If they thought they could sign him and trade him at their leisure, they were wrong. But they didn't know that. Every time Barnett was asked what Gretzky wanted, he told them to make an offer. In fact, Gretzky wanted a no-trade clause, thereby negating any sign-and-trade options for the Kings.

But the clock was ticking, and the longer the Kings waited, the less the Blues and the other suitors would offer.

Nevertheless, there followed a month that, from a psychological point of view, was probably the darkest of Gretzky's career. No trade was made, and there were almost daily reports of yet another deal being put up for consideration.

In 2013, we spoke about that segment of his career, not one of the most pleasant. "My heart was in L.A. when I went there," he said. "A lot of people say I went there to change hockey. Well, I didn't go there to change hockey. That was never ever in my mind. We went there to win a Stanley Cup and we were so close and we had such a great bunch of guys and Barry was such a great coach. Then it just sort of all unravelled, and then Bruce started to get into his trouble.

"I felt sick and bad for him with what he was going through, and I had so much respect for Larry Robinson, who took over from Barry as coach. Larry and I had played together and he was always so good to me. When he became coach, he was always honest with me.

"He said we had had a good year, and I understood that. When I met with the ownership of the Kings, they said, 'What do you want to do? Do you want to re-sign? We're thinking of going young.'

"I said, 'Hey listen, you guys have to go young. You can't patch this together to make a championship team.'

"I was devastated from the point of view that I felt I'd failed by not bringing them a championship. It bothered me in the sense that I knew I had to go and I knew that it was the right decision for the organization. But I was such a good friend of Larry. Larry and I had been teammates; it was a tough scenario for him, too, not just for me."

Gretzky remains close to Robinson, who, at the time we were speaking, was in his first year as an assistant coach with the San Jose Sharks. "Larry loves hockey," said Gretzky. "He'll do a great job in San Jose. All he does is win Stanley Cups. They couldn't have a better teacher than Larry. He helped me as a player and he helped me as a coach."

The state of affairs in Los Angeles during the 1996 negotiations was murky, to say the least. The general manager was telling his colleagues that he was accepting bids for Gretzky. The team president said he was testing the market. But the man designated by the owners to run the team said Gretzky was going nowhere and the Kings wanted his name on a new contract.

Gretzky, because of his nature and his basic decency, said little, a fact that started the media vultures circling. He was accused of starting the rumours of his trade. In fact, the rumblings started when the Kings announced that they intended to have a top-level management meeting in early January to discuss his future.

He was accused of putting himself above the team. In fact, he approached the ownership in August and told them that, for the good of both parties, they should trade him if there were no immediate plans to build a winner. That stance made sense throughout the ordeal, but the team dragged its feet at his expense.

He was accused of manipulating the team. In fact, he was the one who was being manipulated. Team officials lied when they said they would build a Stanley Cup contender that season.

He deserved far better treatment than to be offered around the league like a fringe player with a hygiene problem. He deserved to be consulted as to his preference for a destination, should the bumblers who ran the Kings eventually find a way to finalize a deal. He deserved to have a swift conclusion to the deal, something that, as the matter dragged on and on, he finally requested publicly—but to no avail.

The situation became so unpleasant that his friend and teammate Marty McSorley spoke to me about it on the record—even though he was playing for the Kings at the time.

"I've heard a lot of people calling him selfish and self-centred and a lot of things like that," McSorley said. "I think people fail to realize the whole scenario. He's a total free agent this summer. If he were really self-centred and greedy, he wouldn't be going to the team and saying, 'Let's get some players; I'd love to stay.' Instead, he would wait until the summer when he'll be a total free agent. Then, nobody's going to say anything, because it's done in all sports. When you're a free agent, you have an opportunity to sign wherever you want for as much as you want."

So why did Gretzky ask for a trade? "Because he feels he has a vested interest here in Los Angeles," McSorley said. "He wants to see the team win. He meant no hostility.

"What people fail to realize is that Wayne is a winner. He hasn't broken all the records and kept driving on just because he just puts his skates on. He's a driven man and people still pay a lot of money to watch Wayne Gretzky play. The reason is that he wants to win a Stanley Cup. If he were less than that, if he were a guy who is just going to put his equipment on and not worry about winning, he wouldn't have been such a great hockey player."

As far as McSorley was concerned, Gretzky was trying to help the Kings, not hurt them. "It was a pretty simple statement he made," McSorley said. "In a sense, Wayne gave the Los Angeles Kings a gift by saying, 'If you're not going to be in a position in the summer where it's going to be attractive because we're not going to be in a position to win, then get something for me.'

"What he was meaning to do was assist the L.A. Kings, not put a gun to anybody's head."

From the time Gretzky joined the Kings in 1988, he was perceived as a de facto general manager. McSorley said that was another unwarranted criticism. "People talk about Wayne running the show," he said. "But the Kings traded Paul Coffey. They traded Tomas Sandstrom. They traded me [and then reacquired him]. Wayne never would have approved any of those trades.

"Wayne weathered the storm when Bruce McNall, his friend, had financial troubles. He weathered the team going bankrupt under Joe Cohen and Jeffrey Sudikoff" (who, like so many NHL owners, later went to prison. In his case it was a one-year term for insider trading).

"Finally, the team got into a position financially where they were talking about a new building. Everybody knows the Kings have stable ownership now. Wayne gave this team an opportunity to get back on its feet. And now he's getting all this criticism. It's not right."

Finally, six weeks after the story broke, more than five weeks after the meeting to determine the Kings' course of action, and more than four weeks after the all-star weekend in which the matter was originally to be settled, the deal got done. More or less.

It was a Saturday night, and I was on a business trip to Kingston, Ontario. I'm not sure about the time—although it must have been before 2 a.m. because I subsequently called the story in to the *Toronto Sun* and beat the last deadline. I was already asleep when the phone rang and a familiar voice said, "It's done."

As it turned out, there was a bit more fiddling to do, but essentially, the trade was in place. Gretzky would go to St. Louis for three young players—Roman Vopat, Patrice Tardif and Craig Johnson—as well as a first-round draft pick in 1997.

The reason the trade didn't get officially announced until four days later was that some internal financial details had to be worked out. One of them revolved around the fact that when Gretzky went to Los Angeles in 1988, Prime Ticket (which by that time had evolved into Prime Sports West) boosted its rights payments considerably, but threw in a clause saying that if Gretzky weren't in the lineup, the TV revenue for that game would be halved. The longer Gretzky stayed in Los Angeles, the more the Kings received in TV revenue. On the other hand, if he were to stay past the trading deadline, the Kings would get no players in return. The corporate people wanted to drag the matter out a bit longer.

There was also the matter of settling Gretzky's signing bonus and salary, much of which was deferred. He was still owed roughly two million dollars to complete the 1996 obligation, and there was also the matter of $20 million in deferred payments.

On the hockey front, Gretzky's feeling was that if he was going to go to St. Louis, he wanted to get there as soon as possible. Conversely, the Kings wanted to get their new players into the lineup just as quickly. The Kings were in the midst of a rough season, but so were a number of their Western Conference competitors, and a playoff spot was still within reach.

With three effervescent youngsters added to the lineup, the spark could perhaps be enough to get the Kings back into playoff contention. But it was abundantly clear from the team's play during the Gretzky affair that until the matter was resolved, the Kings were going nowhere.

But even then, the matter wasn't settled. The Kings had one more wrench to throw into the machinery. They refused to give Barnett permission to talk to the Blues.

The Blues, of course, wanted to sign Gretzky to a long-term deal. They certainly didn't want to part with four bodies for a player who would be free to go back on the open market four months down the road.

Therefore, the trade could not be completed until the Blues and Barnett agreed to terms, something they could not do until they met. And they couldn't meet until the Kings gave permission.

The Kings' motivation was that they had decided to make one last-ditch offer to Gretzky: a ten-year deal.

By the Tuesday following the Saturday-night phone call, the deal had still not been finalized and the Kings were playing the Jets in Winnipeg. The next day, Gretzky was going to fly back to Los Angeles to meet with Sanderman to discuss the Kings' proposal.

After the Jets game, the crowd had filed out of the Winnipeg Arena, and Gretzky and I stood in the penalty box talking—the only place where he could be sure that we were the only two taking part in the conversation.

"I'm not supposed to tell you everything that's going on," he said. "It's pretty nearly done, but I promised them I wouldn't say what's happening."

"Well, my only concern is that I'm not sure where to go next," I told him. "I want to be there when you play your first game with your next team, but I don't want to be flying all over the continent while it drags on."

He winked. "Be in Vancouver on Friday," he said. "I'll see you there."

The Blues were playing in Vancouver on Friday.

CHAPTER TWENTY

O n Thursday, the deal was finally announced, and that afternoon, I was sitting in my hotel room in Vancouver when Gretzky called from his home in Encino.

"I'm ecstatic," he said. "I'm thrilled to be going there. It's going to be exciting."

The long-awaited deal was the one that had been announced earlier, with a slight change. When McMaster saw that the details had been revealed in the Sunday *Sun*, he insisted that Keenan throw in a later-round draft pick just so that the *Sun* couldn't brag that it had nailed the deal. He wanted a fourth-rounder, but Keenan insisted on nothing higher than a fifth-rounder, and McMaster settled for that.

With the deal done, Gretzky was finally free to give his side of the affair, something he had been unable to do while under contract with the Kings. He said the split was more of a philosophical disagreement than a financial one. Under his original Kings contract, much of his salary was deferred, and in the previous August, when the sale of the team to the Anschutz Entertainment Group came about, a clause in the contract gave him the right to be paid immediately, instead of down the road.

But Anschutz wanted to keep the deferral clause in place. "They told me they wanted to go out and get players, and I said that was fine by me. I wanted to make it work. We started out pretty well, but I didn't see any new players coming in."

By late November, the Kings were fading noticeably and the media were asking Gretzky about his future, questions he repeatedly dodged.

Throughout December, McMaster and Keenan talked frequently, and Gretzky, who rarely missed any worthwhile NHL gossip, was fully aware of it. Meanwhile, his relationship with the Kings was deteriorating. "I said, 'Well, you promised me since August—and that's why I deferred so much money—that you'd buy some players or dip into the free-agent market.'

"But they didn't. They just said, 'Trust us.'

"I couldn't do that anymore. I thought that this time, I needed some proof before I signed. They had been saying since August that something was going to happen."

With a stalemate appearing to be looming, Gretzky finally made a proposal: "I told them, 'Let me play until July 1 [when he would become a free agent without compensation] and I'll give you first priority [on the new deal]. This is where I want to play. This is my home. I don't want to pack up and move.'

"That's when they made it clear to me that wasn't an option," Gretzky said. "I was a little hurt that people were saying that it was just over money and that I was being greedy," he continued. "I deferred close to 70 per cent of my salary. Here's a guy [Anschutz] who just got a cheque for $1 billion [in a Los Angeles land deal], who paid $115 million for the franchise, and who's talking about a new stadium for $250 million, and he asks me to defer my money.

"I said, 'No problem,' and I did it. For people to say it was just over money, it was ridiculous. That part hurt me the most."

Gretzky didn't know who his Blues linemates would be, but when I told him that Keenan had already suggested it would be Brett Hull and Shayne Corson, he replied, "I sure hope so.

"I'm ecstatic about being able to play for Mike," he said, "and I'm looking forward to playing with Brett. He and I are friends, and I've talked to him many times over the past few weeks. I had dinner with him after the game Saturday. There's nothing wrong with that, but I wouldn't talk to Mike or anybody else in the Blues organization."

Hull was just as delighted about the deal as Gretzky was. "He adds a dimension that I don't think anybody understands in St. Louis," he said at a press conference in St. Louis.

Keenan was relieved to have pulled off the deal. "I worked on that thing every day for two months," he said in a 2012 interview. "They were nervous. Sam McMaster had experience in junior hockey, but he didn't have much experience at the NHL level. I had to give him a verbal water-boarding to keep him on track every day until he finally gave in."

As a measure of the respect that Gretzky's new St. Louis teammates accorded him, Corson announced he had relinquished his captaincy of the Blues and had handed it over to Gretzky.

In the midst of all the optimism in the St. Louis organization, it went almost unnoticed that the Blues were so frustrated in their dealings with the Kings and so impatient to end the wait that they never did have any contract talks with Barnett. They would later regret that decision.

There was another nagging question: If Gretzky was so eager to win another Stanley Cup, why would he go to the Blues, who were a .500 hockey team? "Well, the first thing I would say," Keenan remarked as we chatted on the bus to the rink for Gretzky's first practice with his new team, "is that there has been an excessive number of injuries and they were a new team to begin with, so they really haven't had a chance to jell."

With Gretzky in the lineup, Keenan saw nothing but a bright future. He said it was not unreasonable to assume that Gretzky's presence could boost the Blues' output by a goal a game on average.

"If we had, at this point after sixty games, sixty more goals on the ledger, we might have twenty-five more points," he speculated.

"Brett Hull's value just went up immensely," Keenan said, "because now he has someone who sees the same hockey game that he sees. That's a big plus."

And let's face it, Gretzky had an impact on all the players, not just the stars. "There are all the subtleties," Keenan said. "All the subtle little things that already are having an impact. One guy came up to me, and I won't identify who it is—oh, maybe I'll tell you. It was Tony Twist. Normally, the guys wear jeans to practice, but he said, 'Maybe we should get dressed up today because this is special.' That's a subtlety that surfaced right away. It shows Wayne's presence and the respect that the players have for him.

"Players are going to put in more when they see how hard he works," Keenan said. "A guy like Chris Pronger is not going to dare to have a bad practice now, and that's what players like Wayne Gretzky bring to your team."

Keenan said he could see the Blues coming together just the way Team Canada '87 did. "These guys just don't know it yet."

Neither did most other people. The Blues certainly did not immediately start to dominate the league, even though, in most ways, Gretzky looked like Gretzky.

He still wore the same style of Jofa helmet, one much loathed by NHL officials because it was basically useless. It was often said that if someone threw an egg at it, the helmet was more likely to crack than the egg.

But Gretzky—who, like most hockey players didn't like to modify equipment—loved it, and the league's grandfather clause allowed him to use it for the rest of his career.

That style of helmet had been out of production for a decade or so. In fact, every year the company's representatives made a point of sending a letter to the few NHL players who still wore them. It was full of legalese that translated to "Please don't wear this helmet any more."

"We didn't have many because they didn't want to make them anymore," laughed Gretzky in 2013. "Every time they sent me one, they'd say, 'This is the last one.' When I was playing in New York, the Rangers went to their third uniform and it was that dark blue, and I didn't have a helmet that was that colour of blue, so I had to paint one.

"All the helmets had to match. But if you look at the old tapes of the Oilers, there were six or seven different colours of blue depending on whether the helmet was Jofa or CCM or Cooper or whatever. You can't do that now."

So it came as something of a surprise when Gretzky wore a blue Jofa helmet at his first Blues practice. Had the team's trainers painted his white one? If so, how had they got the paint to dry so quickly? He'd been in town only an hour or so before he hit the ice.

It was simple foresight. As soon as the trade was announced, the Blues' trainers dug deep into the storeroom in St. Louis and found a few old helmets in mint condition. They then packed some for the trip to Vancouver. The pleas of the Jofa representatives continued to go unheeded.

And Gretzky continued to use an aluminum Easton stick, although he told me the silver one he had used in Los Angeles was to be retired in favour of a blue aluminum version.

"I didn't know Easton made blue sticks," I said.

"They didn't make silver ones, either, until I went to L.A.," said Gretzky.

The specifications for the sticks of both hues were the same, and he continued to go through them at the usual rate.

But while the good news for the St. Louis fans was that Gretzky continued to look and play the same as he always had, the bad news was that the Blues as a team did too. They didn't change, and they certainly didn't appear to improve with his inclusion in the lineup.

In fact, when Gretzky arrived, the Blues were two games over .500. When the regular season ended, they were two games *under* .500.

He scored in the first period of his first game, and Keenan had him on the ice for almost half the game. "He wasn't in as good a shape as he should have been," recalled Keenan. "I don't know if they weren't pushing him that hard in L.A. or what."

The fact that Gretzky had lost twenty pounds during the course of the two-month negotiation, largely as a result of stress, was probably a factor.

"It might have been," conceded Keenan. "He went out for dinner after the game and the waiter said, 'What can I get you, Mr. Gretzky?' and he said, 'A bottle of oxygen.'"

Over the course of the eighteen games he played for the Blues in the regular season, Gretzky contributed twenty-one points. But the fact remained that the style he preferred to play wasn't the one Keenan liked. Dale Hawerchuk, another St. Louis forward, explained it this way. "Mike's style is very tight. You don't make too many chance passes. If you make a pass through the middle and it gets picked off, even if you're the first guy back, he doesn't care. He doesn't like that play. When I first came here, he sat me quite a bit to drill it into me, but that's the style he plays."

When I put the matter to Keenan, he said the prohibition might be eased a bit for Gretzky. "It's suitable for some and not for others," he said. "Most often, Wayne is not putting it on somebody else's stick."

There were other areas of adjustment, though. Shayne Corson said, "Wayne likes his wingers to come late, and I'm the type of player who likes to be up, to be ahead of the play a little bit more, to drive to the net a little bit more. With Wayne, you come late and he finds you. He's got eyes in the back of his head."

But Corson conceded that, from a defensive point of view, Gretzky's approach had its advantages. "With Wayne, you want to be high to get a good chance to shoot the puck," Corson said. "If you're already high and the puck gets turned over, then you're already there to make it a lot easier on yourself."

There was also the on-ice relationship between Gretzky and Brett Hull to consider. Although Gretzky was a great sniper in his own right, he felt that in this case, he would contribute more as the set-up man with Hull doing the sniping, the same sort of arrangement he'd worked out to great advantage with Mario Lemieux in the 1987 Canada Cup.

"Brett has to learn to play off me in the sense that I'll give him the puck," Gretzky explained. "He doesn't have to spend time trying to chase down loose pucks and getting the puck. Now he's got to spend more time getting open. I think it's going to make his game easier."

There was another area that required modification. Keenan was in the forefront of today's style of hockey—short, hard shifts of forty seconds. Gretzky certainly wasn't stuck in the earlier era of three-minute shifts, such as those played by Phil Esposito, but he felt comfortable staying on the ice for ninety seconds.

"He's still going to get his ice time," Keenan said. "He'll get twenty-seven minutes or more each game. But I want them in shifts of forty seconds or so."

Keenan always had a habit of being totally unpredictable because he felt it kept players off balance. It was a concept he had learned from Scott Bowman, the idea being that if a player never knows what to expect next from the coach, he's more alert and more determined to do the right thing.

Keenan's explanation of his system included the assertion that the only unbreakable rule is the one that says no rules are unbreakable. "You don't implement a system and say, 'This is my system,' or, 'This is our system.' What you do is adjust to the personnel you have. Variables are great because it's hard to defend against them.

"You make the adaptation as a coach to the personnel you have—at least, that's my philosophy. We've got to have a semblance of order and discipline and structure, but at the same time you've got to create an environment that allows the creative abilities of athletes to surface."

Nevertheless, as the Blues struggled towards the end of the eighty-two-game season, there was no indication that they would cause any ripples in the playoffs. Keenan purported to be unconcerned.

"The only game I want to be ready for is Game Eighty-three," he would say.

CHAPTER TWENTY-ONE

Towards the end of that eventful 1995–96 season, the Detroit Red Wings whacked the Blues 8–1. Those expecting a Keenan meltdown were disappointed. He disappeared seconds after the game and went to Vail, Colorado, where he owned a hideaway on the ski slopes.

Those who knew Keenan well just chuckled. "I wouldn't say he's intentionally lying in the weeds," said one, "but I wouldn't underestimate him for a minute."

Sure enough, the Blues opened the playoffs with a series win over the Toronto Maple Leafs. At first glance, that might not seem like a great achievement, but by virtue of having more wins in the regular season, the Leafs had been given the home-ice advantage.

Furthermore, every pre-series assessment included a statement along the lines of "The Blues must have Grant Fuhr playing the way he tends to play in the post-season if they're going to be a factor." But in the second game—with Fuhr sporting a 0.89 goals-against average, Nick Kypreos fell on Fuhr in a goalmouth scramble. Fuhr's knee was injured so severely that he was out indefinitely.

"When Grant Fuhr got hurt, that kind of changed everything for us and the team," recalled Gretzky in 2013. "I had thought we had a really good chance."

Nevertheless, the Blues won the series in six games and advanced to the next round. This one figured to be much more onerous. Detroit was by far the best team in the league that year, having finished with 131 points. The second-place team, the Philadelphia Flyers, had 103 points. The Blues had 80.

If the Blues were to knock off the Wings, it would not only be an upset, it would be the biggest upset in the history of the National Hockey League.

To do it at all would be astonishing. To do it with Jon Casey in goal would border on miraculous. Casey had been outstanding in a playoff run five years earlier, but his talent appeared to have fallen off considerably, and, on average, he allowed a goal a game more than the injured Fuhr.

Did Kypreos do it intentionally? "Absolutely," said Keenan in a 2012 interview. "Absolutely. I've always said that if Kippy didn't destroy Grant's knee, we might have won the Cup. Gretz says that too. I still see Kippy and I tell him he did it on purpose. He just laughs. He says, 'I accidentally fell on him on purpose.'

"God bless Jon Casey. The guy played as well as he could play, but he was not Grant Fuhr. When we lost Grant, the team got a little edgy defensively. They were nervous. You could sense that they stayed back instead of going for it like Gretz and those guys could do.

"If we had Grant, I don't know if we would have won the Cup, but we would probably have beaten Detroit. And for that matter, I don't know if Scotty Bowman would have lasted as their coach."

It was in that setting that one of the greatest series ever played kicked off. Had this been a Stanley Cup final, it would have been the stuff of legend. But because it was only the second round, it gets written off as remarkable but not great. That is an underassessment of the first degree.

It started off as many suspected, with the Wings winning the first game at home, but the pot-stirring by the two coaches was well under way.

The matter of injuries was under discussion. Gretzky was reportedly hurt, but pretending not to be. Wings star Sergei Fedorov was pretending to be hurt when he wasn't. "He's a disgrace," snorted Keenan.

Bowman, who doesn't miss much that takes place on a hockey rink, left no doubt as to his view. "Gretzky's hurt," he said flatly as we sat in his office with the door closed. "He's wincing. He was in real pain. Every time he came by the bench, I was watching him. He's really hurt. He only played nineteen minutes, and that's unusual for him."

In Game Two, the good news for the Blues was that their first-period power play was operating at a 50-per-cent clip. The bad news was that Jon Casey's save percentage was only slightly better. And since Casey faced eleven shots from the Detroit Red Wings, that put the Blues down 5–1 after only twenty minutes. The final score, when the afternoon's proceedings dragged to their merciful conclusion, was 8–3.

Now it was the turn of the Blues' players to feel the sharpness of Keenan's tongue. "Casey played very poorly. He was awful," he said.

But the fault was certainly not all Casey's. The Blues' two big stars, Hull and Gretzky, also played poorly.

"Wayne let his man go twice, and they got two goals off it," said Keenan. "That was pretty much the end of the hockey game. It was over in five minutes."

"He's right," Gretzky said. "I stink. The second goal was definitely my fault, and the other night was my fault as well. I missed a breakaway when it was 2–2." Needless to say, Gretzky wouldn't admit to being injured. That was something he never did, always saying that if you were healthy enough to go on the ice, there were no excuses.

Keenan moved on to other targets—Chris Pronger being one. "That was a very undisciplined penalty he took early on," Keenan said. "A selfish penalty." Was it a humiliation? "That would be a pretty good summary, fairly accurate," Keenan conceded. "We haven't got a chance to win a play-off series if our best players, including Brett Hull, play like that."

As far as most fans were concerned, they didn't have a chance anyway. The Blues saw it differently. Looking like a completely different team, they shut down the Wings 1–0 in the next game, with Gretzky getting the goal. It came on a breakaway, and he didn't bother with any fakes, choosing instead to simply blast the puck between the legs of Detroit goalie Chris Osgood.

"That was my Joe Sakic snap shot," he said with a laugh. "Actually, I've had four or five breakaways in the playoffs, and when I had one against Osgood, he moved to the side. I felt as soon as I got the puck tonight that I was going to go for the five-hole."

It was his first playoff goal since June 5, 1993. Was it a relief?

"It was probably more of a relief for you guys than for me," he smiled. "For the first five games in the Toronto series, I feel I played as well as I can play. The first game in this series, I was mediocre, and in the second game, I played poorly. But all of a sudden, it's starting to roll again."

It rolled for Gretzky and the Blues in the next game. And the next. Suddenly, the hockey world was noticing. The Blues were one game away from knocking off a team that had finished fifty-one points ahead of them!

It wasn't overly pretty. The defensive plan, as explained by Blues forward Craig MacTavish, was simple: "Everybody go to the front of the net and start chopping."

But really, the Blues were doing everything that needed to be done, paying total attention to detail and, as a bonus, getting great goaltending from Casey. They still needed one more win, however, and they knew it wouldn't be easy.

Hull's statement on the matter was typical. "Confident?" he snorted in answer to a question. "We're playing the best team in hockey."

The Blues produced a great effort, and with less than five minutes to play, trailed 3–2, but lost 4–2. That sent the series back to Detroit for Game Seven, and now, to darken the outlook even further, Casey's participation was questionable.

At least Keenan said it was, but that didn't really mean an awful lot.

"It's uncertain at this point," he said on the off-day.

As expected, Casey did play. And he was outstanding. At the other end, so was Osgood. The Wings had the better chances, though—and a lot more of them—and Casey was repeatedly called upon to stop shots that looked like sure goals.

After one period, the score was 0–0.

After two periods, the score was 0–0.

After three periods, the score was 0–0.

After the first overtime, the score was 0–0.

In the second overtime, the Wings went to the attack right away, and Fedorov had a glorious chance from the edge of the crease. But Casey, as he had done all night, shut the door. Moments later, the Wings were coming out of their zone down the left side when Gretzky, reaching back one-handed, almost intercepted a pass that probably would have sent him in alone. But the bouncing puck skipped over his stick and went to Steve Yzerman, who raced across centre ice with Gretzky in hot pursuit, moving towards the right point. Once there, he unleashed a shot that rocketed over Casey's shoulder into the upper corner.

In some accounts of that game, Gretzky is blamed for a turnover, but that was hardly the case. Keenan saw defenceman Murray Baron as a much greater contributor to the Blues defeat than Gretzky.

"Murray Baron!" he said with some vehemence. "I can still see it. The guy lifted his leg. If he just keeps his foot on the ice, the puck bounces off his shin pad."

"It was going to be a goal like that that won it," Hull said, "or a goal where someone went wide and then put it out front to a guy coming in. There's nothing anybody can do about a shot like that. Jon was screened and it took him a while to pick it up."

In 2013, I asked Gretzky if he had indeed been hurt. "My pride was hurt," he said ruefully. "No, I wasn't hurt. I can't lie. I played well in that series after the first two games when we were down 2–0. I played really well the next three games that we won, and I thought I was okay in Game

Six. I thought I was okay in Game Seven, too, but we lost 1–0 in double overtime."

It was a heartbreaking defeat for the Blues, who had started to believe they could pull off the biggest playoff upset in NHL history.

"You sit on the bench and there's nothing but positive things going through your mind," said Hull. "You picture the team winning, and you see yourself scoring the winning goal. Then, all of a sudden, it's over and you're numb."

That was Gretzky's last game with the Blues.

No one had ever expected it to end that way. When the Blues acquired Gretzky, they had intended to keep him around for at least three years, and he himself had intended to finish his career there. His wife, Janet, was from St. Louis, and he considered it to be a great place to raise a family. He had even started looking for a house.

"The day I got traded, we met with the ownership and the general manager," said Gretzky in 2013. "I wanted to get a deal done that day. They kept saying, 'We're going to do it.'

"A week later, they were still saying, 'We'll get a deal done,' and before we knew it we were into the playoffs and I said, 'You know what? Forget about it. Let's see what happens in the off-season.'

"It had nothing to do with Mike Keenan. He was sort of on the outside. He was coaching and sort of acting GM but the ownership, they just wouldn't sit down with us and ink a deal.

"I wanted to sign the day I got traded. I wanted them to fly to Vancouver and get the deal done, but it never got done."

Rumours exist that Gretzky and Keenan had a major blowup, but Keenan denies it. "No," he said flatly when asked if that was the case.

In 2013, I asked Gretzky about it as well. "Did I have any problems with Mike? No. To this day, Mike and I are still really good friends. He did a lot of good things for me as a hockey player. I didn't agree with everything he said or did, but he was the coach and I understand that. There's no animosity between Mike and me, no."

The two had their confrontations, but Keenan locked horns with all his players. That sort of challenge wouldn't stop Gretzky from playing for Keenan or anyone else. He had some extremely nasty confrontations with Glen Sather in Edmonton as well. He saw that as a coach's job.

"I always considered myself lucky to play for Glen in Edmonton," Gretzky said in 2012. "He really pushed players. He would often tell guys, even at the age of twenty-two or twenty-three, 'Listen, I'm really pushing you because one day, you're going to be a Hall of Famer.' Players don't think about that at that age, but Glen did."

"Obviously, you communicate with a player of that ability a lot, which I did," Keenan said in 2012. "The only star player I ever had a tough time dealing with was Brett Hull. Other than that, I got along with all of them. They love the way I play them. They get all the ice time.

"And also, Wayne was the type of guy who would walk around the world twice to avoid a confrontation. He liked to win, so he didn't care if you pushed him hard."

The problem between Gretzky and the Blues was financial. Blues vice-president Jack Quinn, armed with the lucrative contract that he would have presented to Gretzky before the trade if the Kings had given him permission, was not expecting any problems. The Blues were willing to give Gretzky a three-year contract for $22.5 million in salary, a $1 million signing bonus, a 1-per-cent ownership of the team, 1-per-cent ownership of the Kiel Center, a corporate box and a few other perqs. But the deal was never consummated.

"What happened as far as I know, and as Jack explained it to me," said Keenan in 2012, "was that Wayne's financial advisor [Ron Fujikawa] asked for half the money in a signing bonus. Today, that's nothing, but back then, it was unusual.

"Jack said, 'What am I going to do if Wayne breaks his leg in the first game and I've already given him half the money? Then I've got no explanation for the owners.' That became the stumbling block. They could never resolve it."

The mention of the contract produced a chuckle from Keenan. "I was mad at myself because when I got fired there, they came in with security guards and escorted me out of the building," he said. "The day before, I'd been going through my desk, and I came across the proposal for Gretzky's contract. If I'd taken it home, I would have had it, and it would have made a nice memento. All these years later, I'm still mad at myself."

After his contractual battles with the Kings and seeing the team go bankrupt, Gretzky wanted financial security. The Blues, on the other hand, were not a rich team and felt that a signing bonus of eleven million dollars was too much of a gamble to take.

CHAPTER TWENTY-TWO

A few weeks after contract talks with the St. Louis Blues collapsed—on July 1, 1996, to be precise—Wayne Gretzky became a free agent. He was up for auction, and a number of teams privately expressed interest while telling the public they were not in the market.

One such team was the Mighty Ducks of Anaheim. President Tony Tavares tried to sign Gretzky, but insisted that his general manager, Jack Ferreira, be kept in the dark about the negotiations. In public, however, Tavares said that Gretzky had called the Ducks, but the team had no interest.

Gretzky himself wanted to go to Toronto. He had grown up as a Leafs fan, considered Maple Leaf Gardens to be a hockey shrine, and dearly wanted to come back to what was more or less home, only commuting distance from Brantford. He also got along well with Toronto general manager Cliff Fletcher.

"Toronto was my first choice," he told me in 2009. "It was really where I wanted to go.

"We called Cliff and asked if he was interested. He said he was, but if I was looking for big money, it was not going to happen. The owner was trying to save money and put it towards a new arena.

"So I said, 'Just put together a reasonable offer, and we'll see what we can do. He came back with a deal for three million dollars a year with some money deferred. We said 'Okay, we like that.'"

"But Cliff came back and said he had taken it to the owner [Steve Stavro] and the owner nixed it."

Fletcher had been elated about the prospect of getting Gretzky for what was one of the rare decent Toronto teams of that era, and he thought that Stavro would jump at the opportunity.

But Stavro, a cash-strapped grocer who had taken ownership of the team through a succession of moves that met with widespread disapproval in many circles and were considered by some to be outright illegal, concerned himself only with the bottom line.

"How many seats will that sell?" he asked Fletcher.

The answer, of course, was zero. The Leafs always sold out no matter how bad they were, and Stavro wasn't about to add Gretzky to the payroll, even though Gretzky was offering a hometown bargain price.

But Gretzky was still in demand elsewhere. "Bob Gainey called from the Dallas Stars," recalled Gretzky, "but I felt I'd already played in the southern United States, and I didn't want to do that again. At that time, Dallas wasn't as established as it became later. Bob gave me a firm offer and it was a good deal, but I'd been through the thing of building a team in the south and I just wanted to go to a team that was more established."

The next offer was from Vancouver, a team that was reconfirming the interest it had shown a few months earlier. When Gretzky was still with the Kings, the Canucks, like everyone else, knew that he was on the market. With the Kings having recently declared bankruptcy, Canucks owner John McCaw Jr., a Seattle billionaire who was listed on the *Forbes* magazine list of the 400 wealthiest Americans, tried to acquire Gretzky in the old-fashioned way. He tried to buy him.

NHL commissioner Gary Bettman vetoed the deal, saying that if Gretzky were to move, it had to be a trade, not a purchase.

But once Gretzky became a free agent, a trade was no longer necessary. Now McCaw was free to buy him.

Accordingly, Gretzky met with Canucks general manager Pat Quinn in Seattle and discussed the nature of his potential involvement with the team. Quinn was in a foul temper because he had been on vacation in Singapore when McCaw called him and demanded that he return to North America to sign Gretzky before he went somewhere else.

Both Quinn and Gretzky favoured a style of play that used speed as a weapon, and both were totally opposed to the neutral-zone trap used by many teams.

In its basic form, the trap is an easy defence to utilize. You set up your three forwards like a diagonal picket fence so a team trying to move the puck out of its own zone is channelled towards the boards between the blue lines. Once the puck carrier gets there, he's trapped. Hence the name. The puck carrier's best option is to dump the puck into the offensive zone before the trap snaps shut. Then the other team tries to move the puck up ice against the trap, and the whole process is repeated. It's not exciting hockey. In fact, both Gretzky and Quinn felt that the trap would kill the sport if it weren't eliminated, either by legislation or by smart coaches finding ways to make it ineffective.

With so much accord between the two sides, it seemed inevitable that Gretzky would join the Canucks. All day long, Gretzky's advisors, Barnett and Fujikawa, met with Quinn and assistant general manager George McPhee.

Gretzky and McCaw, meanwhile, sat in an outer office and chatted amiably about all kinds of topics. Every so often, their functionaries would emerge to bring them up to date, then head back into the office; and McCaw and Gretzky would resume their discussion.

"He's a great guy," said Gretzky of McCaw. "I really liked him. We got along great."

As midnight approached, the talks were continuing, and Gretzky headed back to his hotel. The negotiations were progressing well and were in the hands of those he paid to perform such functions. There was no need for him to stick around.

Shortly afterwards, the Canucks added a year to their proposal, making it a three-year deal, and bumped up the money to about five million (U.S.) dollars a year. Gretzky's advisors then went back to the hotel bearing the offer, and the three agreed they would accept the terms and sign the contract in the morning.

But all of a sudden, the phone rang. The Canucks wanted an immediate answer, and if it was in the affirmative, they required an immediate signature. Quinn wanted to get back to his vacation, and McPhee disliked and distrusted Barnett.

Gretzky told them he would accept the offer, but he was going to bed. He gave them his word that he would do the deal, but the formalities would have to wait for the next morning.

That was not good enough for Quinn. He told Gretzky he had to take it or leave it. Immediately.

Apparently, the Canucks felt that Gretzky intended to use their offer as a lever to force a better deal from the New York Rangers. Once again, it was an instance of people attributing their own ethical standards to Gretzky, not realizing that his word is his bond. Once he had said he would sign, he would sign.

He had no plans to use the Canucks' offer as leverage, but once he was delivered an ultimatum that clearly implied a lack of trust, he balked. He decided that he had no intention of playing for a team that opted for confrontation over conciliation. And the Canucks under Quinn were notorious for being such a team.

Gretzky very much liked and admired McCaw; he liked Vancouver and wanted to play there. But when the team put a gun to his head for no good reason, he decided that life would be a lot easier elsewhere.

In New York, the Rangers, captained by his old buddy Mark Messier, were still an option, and it was a city where star power is paramount. It was a logical place for him to play, even though the salary was lower than the St. Louis offer.

"My instincts were that maybe money wasn't all that important," he said when he got to New York. "What tipped the scales was to play with Mark and with a team focused on winning a championship. I wanted to come here and I'm thrilled they wanted me."

He added with a laugh, "I'm probably the only free agent to come to New York for less money."

CHAPTER TWENTY-THREE

The 1996 World Cup was to be more than just another international tournament. It was to be a changing of the guard, a passing of the torch.

After having been so instrumental in creating the Canadian legacy, Gretzky was now going to be instrumental in making sure that it was perpetuated.

The old Edmonton Oilers–based order, so capably led by Gretzky and staffed by stalwarts like Mark Messier, Paul Coffey, Bill Ranford, Grant Fuhr and the other heroes over the years, was going to stand down. It was time for rising stars like Eric Lindros, Ed Jovanovski, Keith Primeau, Scott Niedermayer and Martin Brodeur to become not only the core of the 1996 team but also the core of Team Canadas over the next decade.

The World Cup also marked a transitional phase in international hockey, because it was the first time this name was used for what was essentially the latest instalment of the Canada Cup.

The Canada Cup, which involved all the world's top hockey-playing nations, had been held every three to five years since 1976, but there was widespread feeling that a name change to the World Cup would elevate its status, especially among Europeans who held soccer's World Cup in such high esteem.

The last Canada Cup had been played in 1991, but because of the 1994 lockout that killed half the season and created a high level of animosity among the various factions involved, the first World Cup was delayed.

The Canada Cup had always held a certain mystique in the eyes of North American hockey fans because it was the only time they would get to see players from the Iron Curtain countries. But by 1996, the Iron Curtain had gone. Now, Russians, Czechs, Slovaks, Latvians, Ukrainians and other formerly inaccessible players were displaying their skills in the NHL.

As a result, there was some concern in the media that such a tournament was irrelevant in that it no longer opened any doors. But that feeling was nothing more than a reflection of the unfamiliarity of hockey fans with the concept. It was no more irrelevant than Wimbledon would be to tennis fans or the British Open to golf fans.

"It's more of a show now than a learning process," conceded Gretzky. "I think that the trade-off that we used to get from '76, '81 and '84—where we would learn from the Soviets and Europeans and they would learn from our game—was to the benefit of all countries.

"Now, let's face it, this is really an NHL tournament. Most of the guys on most of the teams are from the NHL, and now what we're doing is selling the sport.

"That's why they changed the name from the Canada Cup to the World Cup. It's hard for Canadians to accept, because we know the Canada Cup tradition and the history of it. That's special in Canada, all the way back to the '72 Summit Series, if you want to count that.

"The name change was a stepping stone to selling the game. It benefits the owners and benefits the players."

By 1996, Canada's first fully professional foray into the Olympics was only two years away, and hockey was becoming increasingly important on the world stage. It was time to create a legacy and establish a heritage.

As was always the case, Canada was at or near the top of the international rankings, but no matter how good a country might be, it can't win every time. There will be bad bounces. There will be off-years.

Still, even if you're not unbeatable, you can create a legacy of being the single dominant hockey country in the world. That was the goal pursued by Team Canada '96.

It was also the goal pursued by coach–general manager Glen "Slats" Sather, who, like the veteran players, was part of the transition. Just as this was to be the last Team Canada to be built around the Edmonton Oilers dynasty, it was also the last to be managed by Sather, the man who built that dynasty.

For that reason, even though Brodeur was only twenty-four, he was named to the team to back up Curtis Joseph because his NHL performances had indicated that he was to be Canada's goalie of the future. By playing for Team Canada at that age, he would learn the international game from the best. He would get involved with guys who had been through it all before and knew what was required.

Had Sather made the easy choice of Patrick Roy, who was almost the same age as Joseph, Canada would have been faced with the problem of breaking in two internationally inexperienced goalies in the not-too-distant future. Had Paul Kariya not been injured, he too would have been one of the younger stars in the lineup.

Said Sather, "All these guys who are here now are going to learn from the older guys. That's why they're here. They're going to learn truckloads from these guys. By hanging around them. By osmosis. It's wonderful."

The veterans knew what was expected of them and acted accordingly. When Messier, Coffey and Gretzky went golfing in the afternoons, they took Lindros along to make up the foursome.

When the team got together for dinner, one of the regular topics of discussion was Canada's hockey heritage and how it was the responsibility of the younger guys to perpetuate it. Sather used the veterans as teachers. Sometimes the lessons were major; sometimes they weren't. "There was a small thing the first day," said Sather a few days after camp opened. "I said, 'Who wants to lead the exercises?' When Mark started, he would have said, 'I will, but show me some exercises.' This time, he said, 'Okay,' and he had half a dozen stretching exercises that he already knew all about.

"He's an experienced, veteran guy who jumps in and takes over the leadership. Only the veteran guys can do that stuff."

Sather also set up the accommodation list so that veterans roomed with youngsters. He set up a stall arrangement in the dressing room that sandwiched first-timers between veterans. During practices, seniority had no relevance in the determination of linemates.

"From the point of view of planning of the team's future, there has been a lot of that," Sather said. "We're trying to get the young guys incorporated into the same philosophy that some of the older guys have had—the feeling of the importance of the team, of having the same mental attitude that Mark has, the feeling that's going to be carried from the tradition of all these guys who have been so great for the last ten or twelve years throughout their careers, and passing it on."

Gretzky was totally in favour of the concept. "You've got to be excited about playing for your country," he said. "That's the first thing to pass along. I honestly feel as much excitement now as I did back in 1981.

"The next thing you have to do, you have to show players that when you come here, it's hard work, and that you have to be dedicated for the time that you're here.

"Through that, too, you get to know the other people. But I think the biggest thing of all is dedication and what it takes to win because it's imperative as Canadians that we win."

There was no gradual ramping up in that tournament. The players arrived in game-shape condition at the training camp in Whistler, British Columbia, on Wednesday, August 14. That evening, ice was made available for a light skate, but the concept of a light skate was quickly forgotten. Even though many of the invitees were still en route, the earlier arrivals engaged in a full-tilt, high-speed scrimmage.

This was a new approach for Team Canada. In previous tournaments of this nature, forty-five or fifty players would show up at the beginning of August. Then, over the following two weeks, a training camp would be held to serve the dual purpose of eliminating half the players while allowing the others to get in shape.

This time, there was no surplus, and every player on the squad was told to be ready to go when he got to camp, partly because the players had said, through their NHL Players' Association leaders, that they wanted to play for their country but didn't want to give up two weeks of their summer only to get cut in camp.

Hockey had evolved into its modern phase by then. In the six-team league, and even for years afterwards, players spent the summer relaxing, and then came to training camp to lose weight and get in shape. Often, they didn't accomplish that goal by the time the regular season started. Many a coach would blame an early season loss on the fact that "our guys aren't really in shape yet."

By 1996, those days were mostly gone. Many of the players—and Gretzky was one of them—had personal trainers who kept them in top condition during the summer. "I worked out every day," Gretzky said after one of the practices. "You just have to. When you come here, there's no time to get into shape. This is not a training camp. We're right into practices now."

Even so, Gretzky suffered a slight groin pull, which gave Sather an opportunity to tee off on his favourite target—the NHLPA.

This was another area in which the NHL was evolving. Now that Bob Goodenow was running the Players' Association, it was the end of the cozy relationship between the PA and the league that had existed under Alan Eagleson, who had been jailed for defrauding players. In his six years on the job, Goodenow had already forced the league to boost the average salary from $190,000 to $1 million, and he had instituted a number of rules regarding the manner in which players had to be accommodated.

"I don't think it's particularly right that you've got some lawyers in Toronto telling you how to organize your training camp and in what period of time the players are going to be in good enough shape," Sather said. "I think it will be a real travesty if somebody gets hurt here because of a lack of conditioning."

When asked why he didn't bring the team to camp sooner, Sather said, "We didn't have anything to do with that. It was done by [Goodenow's assistant] Ian Pulver. They're making rules that you can practise for only four or five days. For the most part, these guys train hard. But they don't train under the kind of tempo and conditioning that you're going to see here.

"They need at least five days of this. They need a couple of days to get into it and a couple of days to wind down."

When asked why he didn't ignore the rules, as coaches from Russia and the Czech Republic did, Sather said, "The PA basically runs the NHL. All we are is the caretakers. We have to do what they say because they control the players. If you're going to have anything done, you have to have the co-operation of the players.

"If they say you're going to be here on the Wednesday, you'll be here on the Wednesday."

Despite all the bombast, Sather and the players—and the PA, for that matter—were all on the same page. Style-wise, there would not be much difference between the Edmonton Oilers of the 1980s and Team Canada '96.

The four basic rules of that Edmonton dynasty would be followed to the letter:

Go to the net once you've passed the puck.
Move up the ice when you pass to the forwards.
If you lose the puck, stop. Don't go for a skate.
Move into the open area on the ice.

It was not likely that Team Canada '96 would be engaged in any titanic defensive struggles. "We're trying to develop a team-flow style that is aggressive and offensively designed," Sather said. "We're not going to lay back and wait for the opposition. We're going to create the opportunities."

For Gretzky, the early phase of the tournament—the camp and the exhibition game that Canada won 3–1 over the United States—wasn't overly demanding. Janet was there with his three children, and they had something of a family vacation.

But then the team travelled to San Jose for the opening of the tournament, and Gretzky had time for a chat about his role. He was no longer hockey's shining star, but he was certainly its elder statesman. He was the Team Canada veteran with four Canada Cup appearances to his credit, one more than Messier and Coffey, and he was fully aware that his role had changed.

"It's a lot different this time," he said. "I mean, let's be honest. When you look in this locker room, you don't just look at me or maybe Mess, like you would have in 1987 or 1991. I don't mean to put pressure on guys, but you look in this room, you see Eric Lindros. He needs to play his best hockey for us to win. We need Joe Sakic. It's not just a question of looking in this room and seeing myself. We need Steve Yzerman. We need all our weapons.

"No longer am I the guy you can walk in and say, 'Well, he had two hundred points last year.' My role has changed in a lot of ways, but the bottom line is I still come to work and contribute as best I can."

In all his years, Gretzky had never turned down a request to play for his country.

"Years from now, when I look back at it, I'll be thrilled that I played," he said. "I'd be disappointed if I didn't. The thing about this tournament is that there are so many guys who want to be here who don't get invited. To get invited, I think, is an honour, so I'd rather be here.

"It's up to the individual. It's your choice, but I think it's their loss, the players that don't come. I think it's something they'd always remember and would be a great thrill for them."

In the 1981 Canada Cup tournament, just out of his teens and learning from the likes of Bobby Clarke, Bob Gainey and Guy Lafleur, Gretzky was in awe. By 1996, he was the player who inspired the awe in others, but the learning process still continued.

"And Slats is still yelling at me," Gretzky laughed. "I learn a lot. The game changes all the time—the way teams forecheck, how they handle the power play. As for the game itself, the fundamentals of the game are never going to change, but the things you're going to do, that changes, and you need to stay abreast of it all the time.

"Our team is a solid hockey club," he said. "We have some great young superstars. The problem is the other teams have some great young superstars. The Americans are a great example. You take guys on their team like Keith Tkachuk, Mike Modano, Gary Suter and Brian Leetch. They're all-stars.

"For us to be successful in this tournament, it has to be a mistake-free tournament. We can't take unnecessary penalties. We can't give up the puck in certain situations. We have to play a quality tournament. We're not a dream team like people want to think it is, because other teams are on a level that is very comparable to ours."

As usual, Gretzky had assessed the situation accurately. It was no insignificant matter, therefore, when Team Canada started to lose defencemen to injury. At some levels, they could win easily with a depleted squad. But this was hockey at its highest level.

Al MacInnis had been ruled out before the training camp opened; then, in quick succession, Coffey, Adam Foote, Eric Desjardins and Rob Blake all went down with injuries of varying degrees.

The team desperately needed Raymond Bourque, but Bourque did not share Gretzky's approach to international play. He had played in the Canada Cups of 1981, 1984 and 1987, but then decided he had done enough. Even though Gretzky and Messier had both pleaded with him to join Team Canada in 1991, he had refused to do so. In 1996, he refused again, even after Canada had become desperately short on the blue line.

"He should be here," said one of the 1996 players. "I don't know why he didn't come in the first place."

His answer was that he wanted to spend time with his family.

Mario Lemieux wouldn't play, either. He opted for golf over Team Canada, but at the time, his absence didn't seem to be as critical as Bourque's.

Even with a depleted defence, Canada had little trouble winning the opener 7–4 against the Czech Republic in a game played in Edmonton.

In international tournaments, only one star is selected after the game, not three, and in this case, it was Gretzky. "He looked good, didn't he?" asked Sather. "He was really dancing. The funny thing about being around Wayne is that you can see the gleam in his eye when he's going to have a good game."

Gretzky gave credit to the locale. "How can you not feel good when you've been here and won championships? I've missed it."

But Canada lost the next game 5–3 to the United States and, as a result, found itself facing the horrific prospect of being eliminated from the tournament in the opening round. This kind of ignominy was supposed to be reserved for the likes of Germany and Norway, not Canada.

It was also supposed to be reserved for the likes of Slovakia, who, after two periods, were leading Canada 2–1.

From coast to coast in Canada, fingernails were being bitten and fans were shouting at television sets. But according to the Team Canada players, there was no serious concern either in the dressing room or on the bench.

Finally, Team Canada banged in a pair of third-period goals to escape the disaster of a first-round exit, but not a single player would say that there had been the slightest doubt about the outcome.

"Never," announced Vincent Damphousse, when asked if he had considered the repercussions of a loss. "Everybody was calm. Everybody was confident. Nobody panicked."

"It's a lot harder on the people watching than it is on us," Gretzky admitted. "We're so into what's going on on the bench and who's up next that the possible consequences don't occur to us."

And the dressing room between the second and third period?

"It was quiet and calm, nothing out of the ordinary," said Steve Yzerman, who salvaged Canadian pride by scoring the winner. "There was really not a whole lot said."

Getting the crucial win was no easy task for the Canadians, who were dog-tired. As Brendan Shanahan said after Air Canada had failed to deliver the chartered plane on time, "I'm not one to make excuses, but all these ridiculous screw-ups and sitting on a runway until 3 a.m. take their toll."

"Fatigue does play a part," Yzerman said. "When you play back-to-back games on the road in the regular season, it always takes some time to find your way into the game. And we needed some time tonight."

"You just try to go out and battle," said Theoren Fleury, who put his finger on the reason that Canada had persevered. "It was a real heart check, gut check there in the third period that got us through."

Nevertheless, it was clear that the original philosophy was going to have to change. An offensive approach requires offensive defencemen, but because of all the injuries and Bourque's refusal to play, Canada was desperately short in that regard.

As a result, Team Canada could no longer count on long, crisp, trap-beating passes from its defencemen and would have to use another method to defeat the trap. They would have to get the puck low and use their physical presence to keep it there.

Said Sather, "We have to play a simple game. We have to fire it in. We have to chase the puck, and we have to crash the net."

By this time, Team Canada had been together for two weeks. That meant that Sather and Gretzky had been together for two weeks. Their relationship, which had once been so tight but had shattered, was now becoming tight again.

In the 1980s, the skinny kid with his dazzling moves and the smirking mastermind behind the bench had changed the face of the hockey world. A decade later, their faces were creased, and neither carried himself with the carefree grace that was once so evident. But the rift between them had been healed. Gretzky and Sather were back together, fighting side by side for the nation's hockey glory.

The media had focused on the reunification of Gretzky and Messier and, to a lesser degree, Coffey. But those three had been together a number of times since Gretzky had left the Oilers—in all-star games, in the 1991 Canada Cup and in the barnstorming European tour during the 1994 lockout.

But Gretzky and Sather together was a different story. Gretzky felt betrayed when he was sold to the Los Angeles Kings in 1988, and it took years before he became convinced that Sather had played only a minimal role in the affair.

On a number of occasions when I challenged him, Sather swore that if the decision had been his alone, Gretzky would have played his entire career in Edmonton. It was a message I repeatedly passed on to Gretzky, but he was not easily convinced.

Sather insisted that he became involved only to make the pot as sweet as possible after Oilers owner Peter Pocklington had struck the basic deal. Although there were some ill feelings between Gretzky and Sather, there had never been a loss of mutual respect. Even when he was angry at Sather, Gretzky always conceded that Sather prodded him into his best performances. In turn, Sather always said he felt that Gretzky was the greatest player the game had ever seen.

"My entire career was built around him," Sather said three years later when Gretzky retired. "All the success I've had has come directly from Wayne. If someone wasn't playing well, it wasn't, 'Get a psychologist and straighten him out.' It was, 'Let him play with Wayne.' Suddenly, a kid would get four or five goals in a week and he would be straightened out."

As far as coaches are concerned, Sather knew Gretzky better than anybody.

"I set a standard," he said. "I expected them to play up to it all the time. I wouldn't take any excuses, so they accepted that standard. Even in practices, I wouldn't let them slack off."

Sather knew how to use Gretzky to maximum advantage and how to spur him on. And he was doing it again in the World Cup.

"That's a pretty fair assessment," Gretzky said. "First impressions are lasting impressions. It's like with my dad. You get this sense of not wanting to let somebody down, not wanting to fail.

"I don't think there's any question that in my career, because of my stature, because of the way I'm built, a lot of coaches might not have given me the same opportunity that he gave me. He pushed me. He enjoyed the good times with us, and a lot of times were fun. At the same time, a lot of times were tough."

That elicited a rare burst of modesty from Sather.

"I would not give me any credit," he said. "Wayne does it on his own. The only thing I feel about Wayne is that there's a sort of chemical link between us. I know when he's feeling good. I know when he's not feeling good. I have that sense with Mark, too, but with Wayne, probably more so because I think he feels the same thing I'm thinking a lot of times."

Both Gretzky and Sather enjoyed the reunification, Sather out of his sense of Canada's hockey heritage, Gretzky out of his sense of respect for those who helped him along his way.

Sather was not the first choice to coach Team Canada '96, but he took over when Scott Bowman backed out. Others were available, but one consideration pushed Sather into the job.

"I did it," he said, "because I knew it was going to be the last opportunity to be around Wayne and Paul and Mark—the last chance to be back with them."

All three players had very close relationships with their fathers, so it would be unfair to say Sather was like a father to them. But he did exhibit many fatherly qualities. He knew when to spur them with criticism and when to reassure them, because even though the Oilers, and especially Gretzky, had accomplished so much, there were still times when they needed help to overcome their nervousness.

Most people wouldn't expect Gretzky to still feel nerves, but Sather knew better.

"Oh yeah," said Gretzky forcefully. "You still get nervous. Adam Foote and I were talking about it on the ice. He said, 'Oh, I'm so nervous out here.' I said, 'Hey, it's my fifth one and I still feel the way I did in 1981.'

"When I got here, I didn't know what was going to happen. You always have to show people you can play all the time, every time you step out there. I don't know if lack of confidence is the proper word, but yeah, I was a little bit unsure."

After all he had accomplished, he was still unsure?

Gretzky paused for a moment, and in a tone that reflected an unexpected vulnerability, said, "I just don't want to fail, you know?"

Sather knew. He had always known. In the discussion about his relationship with Gretzky, he had referred to Gretzky's initial "lack of confidence." He always had been able to handle Gretzky like no other coach.

In the late 1970s, Sather acquired a bunch of kids, and by the end of the 1980s had transformed them into the men who were the elite of the hockey world.

"I had to pat them on the back and give them the odd boot in the pants once in a while," he said. "Players always think they're giving a hundred per cent, but you have to push them to get them to give a little bit more."

To Gretzky, there was little change between the Glen Sather who ran the Oilers and the Glen Sather who ran Team Canada. He spoke of Sather's reaction when Canada was trailing 2–1 to Slovakia after two periods. "He was strong, but he didn't panic," he said. "That was always kind of his forte. When you thought he may panic, he didn't."

After the near-disaster against Slovakia, the Canadians were anything but overconfident in their first elimination-round game against Germany. After all, if the Germans were capable of getting to the second stage of the tournament, they had to be taken seriously, especially since they had a Canadian coach, George Kingston, who was quite familiar with Sather's methods.

The Canadians responded with a strong game—a 4–1 victory—and moved on to their next hurdle, a single game against Sweden that would determine which team qualified for the three-game final series.

As was becoming the norm in this tournament, the Canadians did little to makes their lives easy. They took a 2–0 lead into the third period, only to see it evaporate as the Swedes sent the game to overtime.

A number of factors were in play, the most obvious being that the Swedes were a good team. Also, the dearth of healthy defencemen had forced Canada to play a chip-and-chase game that was nowhere near as explosive as their much-preferred freewheeling, quick-passing game.

But Canadians, whether players or fans, feel that the more difficult the circumstance, the more likely it is that the Canadians will come out on top. They feel that their skills might fall a little short some days, but never will another team show more heart or courage.

In this case, the teams battled through an overtime period with no scoring. The second overtime was also showing signs of settling nothing, but in the late stages, the Swedes bottled up the Canadians in their own end, and as the defenders became more and more tired, a Swedish goal became more and more likely.

Sweden's Johan Garpenlov ripped a shot that beat Canadian goaltender Curtis Joseph, but the puck hit the crossbar dead centre and bounced out. In those days, a team was able to ice the puck and get a line change, but when Coffey took possession, he was not ready to capitulate.

Instead, he skated the puck out and passed it to Theoren Fleury, who fired it into the net with 12.5 seconds left. Canada was off to the finals.

Even after blowing a third-period lead, the Canadians never lost their poise or composure and kept coming at the Swedes.

"I wish people could actually see what it's like in here after regulation time, or after an overtime period," said Gretzky, hunched over by himself in a back hallway and watching the pool of sweat build up on the floor, drop by drop. "It's very calm, very relaxed, and yet very efficient. Nobody really said anything, but when it was time to go out, everybody said, 'Well, we'd better go out and win.'"

Was it as draining as the 1987 Canada Cup, with its high-tempo overtime games against the Russians?

"About the same," gasped Gretzky. "But there's a difference of about nine years."

The manner in which Team Canada had progressed had not been well received in some segments of the media. Even Gretzky, despite his brilliant start, had come in for some criticism, a fact that infuriated Sather. After delivering a couple of expletives, he said, "Do you expect a guy to paint a Mona Lisa every day? Most people do one. He has done thousands."

Gretzky shrugged it off. "We've been taking a lot of heat—some deserved, some not," he said. "But we're the first team in the finals."

Canada's opposition in the final was the United States—a dream matchup for the organizers. It was also a dream matchup for the two teams involved. It is not a subject that gets a lot of media attention, but in the NHL there is constant conflict between the Canadian and American players.

Canadians see themselves as having a God-given right to hockey supremacy, whereas Americans don't narrow down the field quite as much. They see themselves as having a God-given right to supremacy.

Americans sincerely resent the fact that Canadians see themselves as having a proprietary right to hockey, a sport in which they will occasionally allow others to participate as long as the interlopers don't get delusions of grandeur. If the rest of the world wants to have high-level stars like Pavel

Bure, Teemu Selanne and Jaromir Jagr, that's fine. But as far as Canadians are concerned, only they can provide the true elite—Gordie Howe, Maurice Richard, Mario Lemieux, Wayne Gretzky, Bobby Orr and Guy Lafleur.

It's not a subject that players often discuss publicly. After all, Americans and Canadians play on the same NHL teams. Creating rifts over nationalism is counterproductive.

But when the Americans found out that they were going to have an opportunity to knock the Canadians off their perch in a three-game, best-against-best, head-to-head tournament, they were delighted. "They hate us, and we hate them," Team USA forward Keith Tkachuk said. "It's going to be hard-hitting."

That was fine with Sather. "We've got to play good, emotional, tough, old-time hockey," he said. "Just get the gloves off and get it on."

Sather also employed one of his favourite psychological tricks: the portrayal of his team as an underdog.

"They're definitely the team to beat," he insisted. "They're the favourites. They're strong in every aspect. They've got great forwards and an exceptional defence. I don't see any holes in that team. They've got everything going for them. The first game is in Philadelphia. They're younger. They're hungry."

The Canadians got off to a good start, winning the first game 4–3 in overtime, but the Americans won the second game 5–2 in Montreal. It wasn't a lack of effort on Canada's part; it was a matter of too much effort. "The biggest thing," said Gretzky, "was that in the second period, we seemed to get ourselves into trouble by being too aggressive.

"All our chances in the past have come from getting the puck in deep and grinding it out and getting our opportunities. For about twelve minutes in the second period, we broke down a little bit and they took advantage of that. In the third period, we went back out, went back to dumping it in and chasing, and we were much better."

To this point, the team that was built in the model of the 1980s Oilers was true to form. The Oilers never followed the easy path. Instead of delivering knockout blows, they invariably let the opponent off the canvas for a while and then administered the KO.

"I just hope the end result is the same as the Oilers of the eighties," Gretzky said.

As expected, play in the deciding game was intense, and the outcome was in doubt for most of the proceedings. But then came the controversial play, one that Americans accept without question but which Canadians still say tainted the result.

Brett Hull, who is a Canadian by any reasonable standard but always played international hockey for the United States, broke the tie when he deflected a shot into the net with a high stick.

To most Canadians watching the proceedings, there was no doubt that the apparent goal would be disallowed. It was covered by Rule 58(b): "A goal scored by an attacking player who strikes the puck with his stick which is carried above the height of the crossbar of the goal frame shall not be allowed."

As the CBC replay showed again and again, when Hull deflected the puck, his stick was even with his shoulder—or, at worst, his armpit. The crossbar is four feet high. Therefore, unless Hull was four foot nine with his skates on, the goal had to be disallowed.

Replay judge Alex Thompson and officiating director Bryan Lewis were looking at replays when American GM Lou Lamoriello arrived on the scene and started insisting that the goal had to be allowed. Seconds later, Brian Burke, an American who was an NHL vice-president at the time, sprinted from his seat, barged into the room and started shouting that Hull's stick was in a legal position.

Burke was the boss of both Lewis and Thompson. The goal was allowed to stand.

"There's a natural letdown when you're in a situation like that," said Sather. "We had been hammering them all night long, and to get a goal scored like that against you on what was basically a nothing play is tough."

The Canadians were deflated, and seconds later, another goal went in, this time off a skate. Again, the play was approved on the video replay.

Sather said, "Then they get another one that a guy punts in and you just have to assume it was a matter of fate."

Gretzky refused to make any excuses. "They came back," he said, "and when you come back, it's gutsy."

Gretzky, as Canada's leading scorer, was not accustomed to losing in a major international tournament. But he had lost. He would never win another.

CHAPTER TWENTY-FOUR

J ust as the style of hockey changed during the course of Wayne Gretzky's career, so did the technology affecting the game's equipment.

For the most part, Gretzky was a traditionalist. For his entire NHL career, much to the consternation of league officials—especially commissioner Gary Bettman, who sees the game only through a lawyer's eyes—he insisted on wearing a tiny Jofa helmet that was all but useless as head protection. He liked to wear the same pair of hockey pants he had worn for years. His dinky shoulder pads were ragged from wear.

But he was fussy about his sticks and constantly made modifications, even when he wasn't switching models. When he played in the world junior championships in 1978, he used a CCM stick. He had no choice; CCM was a sponsor and provided the sticks.

But by the time he got to the NHL, he used a Titan TPM 2020, which was as different from today's sticks as a war club is from a chopstick.

It was basically wood, but nothing like the ash sticks that were a staple in the NHL until the late 1960s. Those were simply two pieces of ash glued together. The Titan was slightly lighter and definitely stronger.

The shaft had a fibreglass core covered with wood; the blade was composed of laminated wood over a plastic-sole insert that went right up into the heel of the stick to prevent cracking or splitting at the bottom. Once the two parts were joined, they went into a press that bonded the units together. They were then coated with a fibreglass and wood finish.

The stick was durable, but it had what some players perceived as a drawback in that the plastic in the blade prevented any modifications. This was not a concern for Gretzky, who used a stick that was almost straight. A curve would make backhand shots more difficult and, thanks to the treasured advice he got from Gordie Howe as a youngster, a backhand shot was a major part of Gretzky's arsenal.

The only change he made to the blade was to cover it with black tape and then add a light coating of talcum powder.

"There are two reasons I do that," he told me in 1984. "One is superstition; I like to have powder on my stick." When he was a youngster, he had seen another player do it and, for no good reason, he followed suit. He played well that night and a superstition was born.

"The second reason is that the powder will stop loose ice sticking to the stick so you don't have to knock the snow off the stick or worry about it affecting the puck."

The powder wouldn't last for an entire game, but since Gretzky changed sticks frequently, using two each period, that didn't matter.

Even though he left the blade alone, the shaft of the stick was another story. He modified that constantly.

"I use the sticks exactly as they come from the factory, except that I cut them down a bit," he explained. "The longer the season goes, the more I cut off.

"Earlier in the season, I use a longer stick because you're still a bit out of shape and you're sometimes behind the play a bit. With a longer stick, you can reach a bit further. I gradually cut off a bit more as the season goes on, and by the playoffs, I'm cutting off about four and a half inches."

We were once out for a social evening, not long after Sammy Sosa of the Chicago Cubs had been caught using a corked bat, and our discussion turned to baseball. Sosa's defence had been that he didn't know the bat was corked. I suggested that he might be telling the truth. Gretzky gave me a look of stunned disbelief. "He knew," he said flatly.

To a guy playing pickup hockey, a slight change in a stick goes unnoticed. But to an astute professional like Gretzky, playing at the elite level, the stick is almost an extension of the body. He clearly felt that Sosa would be as familiar with his bat as he himself was with his stick.

John Pagotto, who was the product manager for Titan when Gretzky was their most famous customer, told me a story that clearly illustrates this point.

"One time we sent him some sticks," he said, "and the guy in the factory had sanded about an eighth of an inch too much off his blade. Wayne noticed it right away and called me the same day he got them.

"He said, 'There's something wrong with my sticks. Can you check on it?'

"I went back to the factory, because we always keep one stick after we send them a few dozen. He was right; there was something wrong. An eighth of an inch! He's incredible."

Gretzky used the Titan stick until the end of the 1989–90 season. That summer, he attended the Greg Norman Challenge, a golf tournament, and afterwards joined in a bit of light entertainment with Norman, Ivan Lendl and Larry Bird in which he used an Easton aluminum stick.

With an athlete other than Gretzky, that fact would be perceived as inconsequential. But when Gretzky endorsed a product, he would never be seen in public using a different brand, let alone on network television.

Sure enough, his contract with the Finnish company Karhu-Titan had lapsed, and Gretzky had switched to Easton, an American company. Furthermore, he had switched from wood to aluminum. I reported the development in the *Globe and Mail* at the time, but it was ignored by the rest of the Canadian media until October, when Gretzky made an official announcement. As was so often the case, the media then jumped to base-less conclusions and criticized him.

On CBC Radio, it was decreed that Gretzky had made the change for financial reasons. Anyone who knew Gretzky would know that there was not the slightest chance that he would risk his hockey reputation, not to mention his personal reputation or his thirty-million-dollar NHL contract, for a relatively small endorsement fee from a stick manufacturer.

The critics also said that it was an indication of Gretzky's deteriorat-ing skills that he needed an aluminum stick to provide a harder shot. In fact, aluminum sticks don't provide a harder shot. Until an eye injury forced him out of the game, Al MacInnis routinely won the hardest-shot competition using a wooden stick.

"Obviously, it's a big change for me," explained Gretzky, "but the two things I like in a hockey stick are consistency and stiffness. I was able to get that with the Titan, but I've found that the aluminum stick has that at half the weight. That's what I'm really excited about—that I can get the things I want in an aluminum stick, but it's not as heavy."

The Easton stick he used in Los Angeles was silver, and there were a few half-hearted complaints from general managers and coaches around the league that the glare negatively affected their players. Nobody took them very seriously.

Gretzky had hoped to use a chrome-blue Easton stick in St. Louis, but he didn't stay there long enough for the sticks to be delivered. However, when he moved to the New York Rangers for the following season, the blue stick matched the team's colour scheme perfectly.

In between, he played in the 1996 World Cup, and used a black, white and red Easton stick.

While he was in New York, Gretzky bought a share of a stick-manufacturing company in southern Ontario that had brought back the Hespeler brand, once the choice of many players in the six-team NHL. By that point, when he had become more of a playmaker and less of a scorer, he found that a return to a wooden stick served his purposes better than an aluminum stick or the composite sticks that were becoming the mainstay in the league. As well, the new wooden sticks were mostly a Styrofoam-wood laminate and a fraction of the weight of the old Titans.

Gretzky would never use a composite stick. While it would allow him to shoot harder, it would make puck-handling and pass receiving more difficult. Shooting harder was not his priority.

The Hespeler 5500 that Gretzky used in New York had blue trim. His 1998 Olympic stick was the same model, with red trim. He would have preferred to have the Olympic rings in the design on the shaft, but was aware that the five-ring logo is jealously—and legally—protected. In fact, the Olympic logo was at the heart of one of the major battles between the NHL and the International Olympic Committee when participation in the 2014 Olympics was being discussed. The NHL wanted the right to use the logo, but, as usual, the IOC was withholding permission.

To avoid any such battle, Gretzky had a design burned into the stick's butt end that had three interlocking rings and a rounded WG instead of the other two rings. To prevent counterfeits, each stick was numbered.

Unfortunately, no one will ever know how that particular stick would work in a shootout.

CHAPTER TWENTY-FIVE

F or years after he won his first Stanley Cup in 1984, Wayne Gretzky repeatedly said he had only one remaining hockey dream: He wanted to play in the Olympics and, if the dream were to be fully realized, win a gold medal.

For most of his career, there was no hope of that dream becoming reality. Canada sent only amateur teams with an occasional sprinkling of borderline professionals to the Olympics, and Gretzky didn't qualify on either count.

But in 1998, it appeared that he would finally get his chance. Even then, it was no sure thing.

Every aspect of Olympic participation is always heavily politicized, and in the case of Canada's 1998 hockey involvement, the political manoeuvring resulted in what can only be called a disaster.

Right from the start, the signs pointed to an impending fiasco.

More than a year before the Olympics were to begin, there was nothing but confusion about the manner in which the plan to put together Team Canada would be implemented. This was the first time that an elite-level professional team would represent the country, and naturally enough, the professionals wanted to run the team. But the bureaucrats who ran the amateur hockey establishment weren't ready to go gently into that good night.

In December, 1996, Murray Costello, the president of Canadian Hockey, asked Glen Sather to be in charge of the team. He told Sather he would be the executive director.

But within days, the vista changed. "Costello offered me the job, but now the job is being part of a committee," explained Sather.

Because Olympic involvement was within the purview of Hockey Canada, it was decided that its vice-president, Bob Nicholson, and a squad of general managers would pick the team and coach. Then the GMs were to disappear and leave the operation of the team to Nicholson.

"I don't want to be involved if that's the situation," said Sather who had fired the rest of the managerial committee formed to run Team Canada in the 1984 Canada Cup.

"I have no problem being involved in the committee," he said in what was at best a stretching of the truth and at worst an outright lie, "but whoever is in charge of this committee has to be an NHL general manager. Bob Nicholson may turn out to be the best general manager in the world, but it doesn't matter. It has to be an NHL general manager."

That was the end of Sather's short-lived involvement.

Eventually, it was decided that there would be a managerial committee, but it would have a lot more authority than had been proposed originally. In keeping with that decision, three NHL GMs—Bob Clarke, Pierre Gauthier and Bob Gainey—were named.

It's worth noting that Sather had put together more championship teams than that entire group combined. In fact, a single championship would have been enough to top that trio's output. At that time, neither Clarke, Gainey, Gauthier nor Nicholson had created a Stanley Cup winner, a Canada Cup winner or any other kind of winner at the professional level.

As is almost always the case in groups of this nature, one personality would emerge as the strongest. This time, Clarke was that man.

The author, with Number 99 (and some of his dogs) at his California home,
five months after he retired.

Mike Keenan, head coach of the Philadelphia Flyers, was selected to coach Team Canada in 1987.

The celebration after Number 99 set up Mario Lemieux for the game-winning goal in the 1987 Canada Cup final game against the Soviets. The other Canadian player is Larry Murphy, who provided a decoy on the play. Gretzky joked that his father, who was in the stands, had a better chance than Murphy of getting the pass.

Gretzky married Janet Jones in Edmonton on July 16, 1988. A crowd of thousands cheered on the couple outside of St. Joseph's Basilica.

Wayne Gretzky and Bruce McNall during the press conference on August 9, 1988, when Gretzky was traded to the Los Angeles Kings.

*Victorious: celebrating a
hat trick in a 1993 playoff
game against the Toronto
Maple Leafs.*

*Gretzky's idol had always
been Gordie Howe, the man
known as "Mr. Hockey." A
year after arriving in L.A.,
Gretzky broke Howe's
all-time scoring record. Seen
here together after filming a
commercial in Culver City.
"I played with him and it
was a treat," said Howe
afterwards. "Those passes
come over nice and flat, no
wobble, just the right speed."*

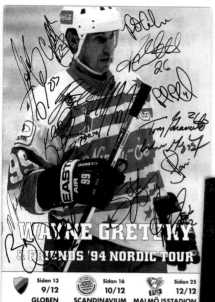

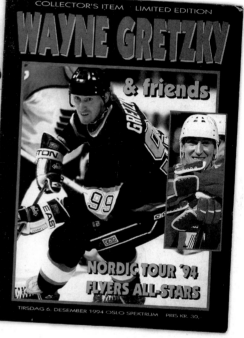

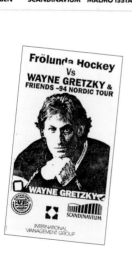

"You can't write about this yet, Strach," Gretzky said, "but we're going to make a European tour and I want to ask a bunch of guys to come along." Gretzky's goodwill tour throughout Scandinavia during the 1994 NHL lockout was a huge success. Elite players such as Mark Messier, Steve Yzerman, and Jari Kurri played for the Ninety-nines, and proved that there was enormous interest abroad in hockey. The tour was an overwhelming success and fulfilled its main purpose: to take the game to those who love it.

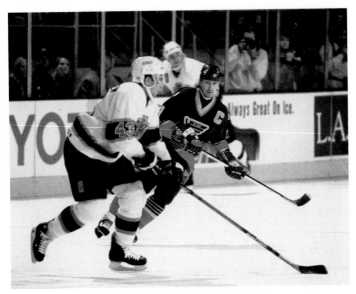

Gretzky, playing for St. Louis, in his first game against the L.A. Kings.

Gretzky was thrilled to play for his country in the Nagano Olympics. Aware that he wouldn't be allowed to make use of the Olympics logo on his stick, he had a design burned into the stick's butt end that had three interlocking rings and a rounded WG instead of the other two rings. To prevent counterfeits, each stick was numbered.

Gretzky with his father, Walter, his main inspiration, in a pre-retirement ceremony in 1999.

Retiring from the New York Rangers – and hockey – before a crowd of grateful fans.

Canadian royalty and British royalty: Queen Elizabeth II prepares to receive the ceremonial puck prior to the Canucks–Sharks game in Vancouver during her royal visit in 2002.

Always a proud ambassador of Canada, Gretzky carried the Olympic torch during the opening ceremony of the 2010 Vancouver Olympic Winter Games.

Gretzky and assistant coach Ulf Samuelsson forcefully make their case to the officials during a Phoenix Coyotes game in 2008.

Consequently, when it came time to build the team, it was built around the player Clarke most revered at the time: Eric Lindros.

This was before the many battles between Clarke and Lindros erupted, before all the insults, charges and counter-charges flew, before Bonnie and Carl Lindros became the two highest-profile parents in Canada. At this time, Lindros was seen as the cornerstone of the Philadelphia Flyers and was expected to maintain that status for years to come; and Clarke, as the GM of the Flyers, wanted to do everything he could to elevate the status of that team—not to mention its profits—by turning its biggest star into the league's biggest drawing card.

The Olympic team didn't have to be finalized until December 1997, and during the months leading up to the announcement, there was no shortage of speculation about the status of a pair of high-profile Team Canada veterans, Mark Messier and Gretzky.

Messier left no doubt as to his feelings on the matter. "I would love to play for the Olympic team," he said. But the GM triumvirate was not moved. Long after it had been made clear that the top three centres would be Lindros, Joe Sakic and Steve Yzerman, it was finally decided that Gretzky would be on the team as well.

Messier, however, didn't make the cut.

In many ways, it was not an unreasonable decision. For much of the NHL season, Messier's play had not warranted his inclusion. But Messier's leadership value, which never waned, could have been invaluable. In a tournament of this nature, playing in unusual surroundings under unusual rules and unusual governance, it was important to have the stability of someone who had encountered almost every conceivable hockey circumstance and who never accepted anything less than total commitment. The role was tailor-made for Messier.

When the press conference was held to announce the team, many questioners brought up the issue of Messier's absence.

"I think the players understand the difficulty in selecting this team," said Clarke. "It certainly doesn't take away from their accomplishments in the National Hockey League or what they've done for Team Canadas and international hockey and everything else.

"We had to make some decisions, and they were really difficult decisions. But they had to be made, and we made them."

The decision didn't stun only Canadians. "I can't believe he is not on the team after all he has done for Canada," said Team USA defenceman Chris Chelios. "He'd be on my team in a heartbeat. I'm going to call [Team USA GM] Lou Lamoriello and ask him if we can get him a green card."

The Canadian executive board—mainly Clarke—also made the decision to name Lindros captain.

"It's Lindros because he seems to be the young horse that Canada wants to ride now," said Clarke in explaining the decision. "Steve Yzerman and Joe Sakic will be the alternates because they're the captains of the past two Stanley Cup winners."

No one on the team had as much high-level international experience as Gretzky. He had been captain of the 1996 World Cup team and the three previous Canada Cup teams. But he couldn't even wear an *A* this time. Gretzky, the greatest scorer in the history of the game, was to be just another player. It was an indication of the anti-Gretzky sentiment that prevailed among the management group, and in the end, it would cost them—and Canada—dearly.

Nevertheless, Gretzky was thrilled to be on the team. He said he fully accepted his new role, and as the Olympics approached, he made no effort to hide his enthusiasm. "I'm excited about it," he said. "I think the whole hockey world is excited about it. It's the first time professionals from every country get to participate in it, and it's the first opportunity I've had to participate in it."

When the National Basketball Association started to participate in the Olympics, the players insisted that they be accorded suites in a luxury hotel. Team Canada was to stay in the Olympic Village.

"I'm looking forward to that," Gretzky said. "That's the fun of the Olympics. We're paid well enough that you can travel the world and stay in nice hotels anywhere you go. But how many times in your life are you going to get to stay in the Olympic Village?

"All of our guys want to do it. Nobody has said, 'Why are we staying in the village? We've got to be in a hotel.' Not one guy has said that, and I think it's exciting. That's part of what makes the Canadian team unique. Everyone is looking forward to being together in a room—three guys in some rooms.

"I wanted to be somewhere close by the action. That will be the fun of it."

The American hockey players, unlike their NBA counterparts, accepted the situation but would have preferred a bit more seclusion. Not Gretzky. "My wife always tells me I'll sit down and gab with anyone," he laughed. "It doesn't bother me. I don't know why it doesn't. There are times when there'll be a crowd of people and I'm with a couple of friends and I'd like to sit down and be alone a little bit, but all in all, I wouldn't trade my life for anything."

Still, Gretzky knew that the Olympic experience was going to be a lot more than merely a carefree vacation. There were NHL games on February 7. The players were to leave for Japan on February 8, arrive on February 9, and play their first game on February 13.

"Our travel is bad," agreed Gretzky. "It's going to be tough on everybody, but it's going to be such a big thing that I think everybody's going to enjoy it. It's going to be such a big high for everybody."

It would also be a major challenge to Canada's hockey supremacy.

"There's obviously going to be pressure on Canada," Gretzky said. "There's always pressure on Canada. Look at all the debate we had when they named the team. There were four or five players that people said should have been on the team and other players that people said shouldn't have been on the team. That's a good example of why there is always going to be pressure on Canada. We look at it so closely.

"What makes it exciting is that so many good players from all over the world are going to be taking part and that everybody is on even ground. There are going to be at least four good hockey teams—Sweden, Canada, Russia and the United States.

"I think it's going to be a huge boost for hockey, a big stepping stone to the next Olympics in Salt Lake City. Undoubtedly, the next Games in 2002 is going to push it to a whole other level.

"Kids who grew up in Canada always said, 'I want to win the Stanley Cup and play in the NHL.' By having guys like Eric Lindros and myself in the Olympics, kids are now going to grow up with two dreams. One of the dreams will be to win the Stanley Cup and the other will be to play for Canada in the Olympic Games. That's good for the country."

And, as was always the case whenever Gretzky played for his country, he did so eagerly and with pride.

"One thing you know about Canadian people is they're proud to be Canadian," he said. "My kids were born in the United States. They should be proud of their country, and they are, but I'm a Canadian. I was born in Canada and I'm proud of my country. That never leaves you.

"I've always looked at it as a privilege. We're all thrilled by it. We're all big kids at heart. We all love to play the game. I don't think that ever changes for anybody."

Canadians were not only happy to see Gretzky in the Olympics, they wanted him to be the flag bearer. When Sun Media's internet site, SLAM! Sports, asked for opinions as to who should be the flag-bearer for Canada, Gretzky finished with twice as many votes as second-place Elvis Stojko.

A couple of weeks previously, *The Hockey News* staff selected Gretzky as the top player in history by only the tiniest of margins, but in a subsequent poll of fans, he was a runaway winner.

It would have been a memorable moment in Canada's sporting history: the best-known athlete this country had ever produced leading the nation's Olympic entourage into the stadium, proudly bearing the Canadian flag. Granted, there was a conflict with the schedule of his NHL team, the New York Rangers, but had an overture been made to the NHL to modify the Rangers' schedule accordingly, it would probably have happened. After all, the Olympic schedule had been in place for four years. There was no need for a last-minute alteration.

Instead, the usual political correctness of the COA (officially the Canadian Olympic Association, but widely known in sporting circles as Can't Organize Anything) came to the fore and a French-Canadian free-style skier got the honour. It didn't even go to Stojko, the figure skater favoured to win a gold medal.

Any anguish that Gretzky might have felt at being shunned by the COA (very little) was more than compensated for by the response of the Japanese people when he arrived in Nagano. The crush was so great that there were serious fears for his safety.

"I've been in a lot of places, but I've never seen anything like this," said Gretzky after escaping a crowd that even surpassed anything he had encountered in his heyday with the Edmonton Oilers, when he invariably needed a police escort to leave NHL arenas.

As soon as the Canadian team started emerging from the train that had brought them from Tokyo, there was a crush of Japanese fans. But when Gretzky emerged, it was a stampede. Older observers compared it to the scenes out of *A Hard Day's Night* when the Beatles had to dodge mobs of screaming, hysterical fans. Younger observers compared it to scenes they had witnessed of some of the worst sale-day crushes at big department stores.

The crowd surged in on Gretzky, who was surrounded by a phalanx of television cameramen, and it was a miracle that no one was knocked down and trampled. Finally, the police moved in and cleared a path for Gretzky, who made it to the team bus while waving to the crowd and smiling at the screaming girls.

Not long afterwards, the Canadian organizers staged a news conference, and once again, their anti-Gretzky attitude came to the fore.

The event was held in an amphitheatre that was packed with media representatives from all over the world. This was their chance to hear directly from the famous hockey icon, and they weren't going to miss it.

First, the brass sat at a table and answered questions for fifteen minutes. Then three players came out and followed the same format. Gretzky wasn't one of them.

The world's media sat patiently through the management's segment, then listened fairly patiently to Yzerman, Sakic and Lindros.

There were shouts of "Where's Gretzky?"

That was not a surprise. If Clarke and friends hadn't realized before they left Canada what an international attraction Gretzky was, they should have managed to figure it out when they saw the mob scene at the train station. But they wouldn't put him on the stage that night and give him a microphone, because to do so would suggest that he was at least Lindros's equal, a view that would run counter to their declaration that Lindros had taken over Canadian hockey's leadership reins from Gretzky.

Finally, the rest of the team was brought out onto the stage and stood well back from the apron. That was supposed to be the end of the affair, and many disgruntled journalists left. A number of us, knowing that Gretzky would accommodate us if he could, approached the stage, which had been declared strictly off-limits.

Gretzky saw me there, and without a word but with an inquisitive look and a pointed finger, asked if I wanted to come up. I nodded affirmatively, at which point he went over to whisper in Bob Nicholson's ear.

Nicholson looked over, walked to the front of the stage and said, "Wayne says if you want to come up, he'll talk to you." I went up, a number of people followed, and Gretzky, in a move that no doubt annoyed Clarke—and infuriated the IOC officials—but delighted the media who had stuck around, answered everyone's questions. As far as I know, it was the only time in Olympic history that the media were allowed up on the stage to do an interview after a formal press conference.

Once the tournament began, Gretzky made his usual contributions. He killed penalties; he worked hard; he sparked the offence. Team Canada breezed through the qualification phase, winning all three games by a cumulative score of 12–3.

The quarter-final game against Kazakhstan posed no problems, either—a comfortable 4–1 victory.

But now there was to be serious competition. In the semifinal game, the Canadians were to face the Czech Republic.

A few days earlier, in a casual chat with the great Russian star Igor Larionov (inducted into the Hockey Hall of Fame in 2008), I had suggested that there were four top teams at Nagano—Canada, Russia, the United States and Sweden.

"Don't forget the Czech Republic, Al," Larionov said.

The Czech Republic didn't seem to have an awful lot going for it.

"They've got Dominik Hasek," said Larionov. "Any time you've got Hasek, you've got a chance."

It was a prophetic remark, and a warning that was not challenged by the Canadians. In their preparation for the game, they made it clear that, even though they had to be aware of the scoring prowess of Jaromir Jagr, Hasek was their primary concern.

"He's a great player," Gretzky said. "He's one of the great players in the game. He's right up there with Eric Lindros, Teemu Selanne, Peter Forsberg and Jaromir Jagr. He's good.

"One guy doesn't make a team, though. We believe in our team and we have to keep going at him. Obviously, he's a big part of their team, but so is Jagr. We have to be solid defensively and, when we get the puck, go to the net.

"We have to crash the net, do what we can. He's a good goalie, but we have to beat him."

Even though the Canadians had rolled to this point, their offensive plan left much to be desired. The team had been built with a defensive priority and an expectation, based on the 1996 World Cup result, that the United States would be the team they'd have to beat. When the tournament didn't unfold as expected, the Canadians struggled.

The Czechs weren't much better. For almost fifty minutes, the teams cautiously engaged in a tight-checking affair, and neither was able to get a goal until Jiri Slegr put the Czechs ahead with a screened shot from the point. With ten minutes remaining, Canada appeared to be in trouble, but with only 1:03 left in regulation time, Trevor Linden tied the score to send the game into overtime.

In the NHL, overtime continues in twenty-minute periods until someone scores, but under Olympic rules, there were to be thirty minutes of overtime. If neither team could get the winner—and in this game, that was the case—the result was to be determined by a shootout.

It was the situation Canada dreaded: a shootout against Dominik Hasek with a spot in the gold-medal game on the line.

It was the middle of the night in Canada. The game had started at 1 a.m. Eastern time, but even so, much of the country was wide awake. The Canadian supporters in Nagano and those glued to their TV sets back in Canada listened to the announcement of the roll call of Canadian shooters.

Theoren Fleury. No problem. He's a shifty player with good moves.

Ray Bourque. Concern began to creep in. If a defenceman was to shoot, why not Al MacInnis, with his blazing—and goalie-intimidating—shot?

Joe Nieuwendyk. That made sense. A great player with lots of experience.

Eric Lindros. Well, of course. He had been deemed the saviour of Canadian hockey. Everyone knew he'd be there, and then Gretzky would finish.

Brendan Shanahan. What? Where was Gretzky? The greatest scorer in the history of the game, and he's not shooting?

Only the beginning of the shootout itself stilled the buzz over the decision. Fleury tried a high snap shot, but Hasek deflected it.

Robert Reichel deked Patrick Roy, and the puck hit one post, slid across the crease, hit the other post, and settled over the line. The Czechs led 1–0.

Bourque's shot was almost identical to Fleury's and was also deflected by Hasek.

Nieuwendyk deked to the right, but missed the net with his shot. Lindros tried the left side, but hit the post.

Along the way, Vladimir Ruzicka, Pavel Patera and Jagr had been stopped by Roy. That left it all up to Shanahan. He, too, missed the net.

All five Canadian shooters had picked up the puck at centre ice and moved directly towards Hasek, even though European shooters usually skated far to the left or right on penalty shots and then came in for the shot. This forced the goalie to come out at an angle, then skate backwards and hope that he had the right alignment.

Joe Sakic, one of only two players to beat Hasek on a penalty shot during the league's all-star skill competitions, missed the game with a sprained knee and wanted to get a message to the shooters, but he was in the upper reaches of the arena and no one had a phone. He tried to get down to ice level, but couldn't get through the crowd.

His strategy was to start towards Hasek at speed. Hasek would come well out, but then go back quickly to counter the speed. At that point, the shooter should slow down. Hasek would be well back in his crease, giving the shooter large open areas of net and time to pick a spot.

But without this guidance, and with a questionable lineup that saw both Gretzky and Steve Yzerman left on the bench, the exercise was a futile one for Canada.

The Czechs advanced to the gold-medal game, and Canada's Olympic dreams were shattered.

In the postgame press conference, the scrutiny centred on two things: the loss and Gretzky's exclusion from the shootout.

Team Canada coach Marc Crawford made the usual coach-like noises about the former and refused to explain the latter.

"When it comes down to penalty shots, you go with your gut instincts," he said. "We prepared a list before the game."

That made the decision even worse. Not only had they made the wrong decision, they'd had plenty of time to mull over the situation. Yet they'd still got it wrong.

And if they *had* prepared such a list, perhaps it might have been wise to let the participants in on it. In a subsequent quiet moment, players confirmed that the bench was in full-scale panic mode after overtime ended. None of the players knew who was going to do the shooting, much less the tactics or the order in which they would shoot.

After the game, Crawford said, "When the ice is heavy like it is after thirty minutes of play on the same sheet, you've got to have some guys who not only have the ability to pick the corners and then make the clean shot, but also have the strength to get through the shot."

Gretzky wouldn't?

"We won't second-guess that decision," growled Crawford. "If you people want to, that's obviously your prerogative."

Except it wasn't second-guessing. At the moment the lineup was announced, there was no shortage of negative reaction in the press box—and, for that matter, probably throughout the hockey world. But after a little thought, the situation started to become clear. The management group had done everything it could to minimize Gretzky's impact. Why would they stop when it came time for a shootout?

They were determined that the reins of leadership be handed over to Lindros, even though he had never won a single Stanley Cup—or, for that matter, a scoring title. Even before the team was picked, the management floated stories that Gretzky might not be chosen. But his NHL play was so good they had to select him, even though they didn't want to.

They wouldn't give him the *C* or even an *A*. They tried to keep him out of the opening press conference. So when the time came to pick the shootout participants, they certainly weren't going to risk the humiliation of having Gretzky be the hero after all the things they had done to indicate that he was just another player. They left him off the list.

They really showed him. They won the battle. But they lost the war.

The loss was so demoralizing that Canada didn't even beat Finland in the bronze-medal game. That's usually the Canadian way. They go into these competitions expecting gold. Once that possibility ends, the intensity level drops.

A shoddy goal Roy allowed seventeen seconds into the third period stood up as the winner in the 3–2 game.

"We're tremendously upset that we didn't win," Gretzky said. "We'd like to have everything start all over again. I like our team. We really played hard. The bottom line was we didn't win.

"I don't care what level you're playing at, whether you're at youth hockey or the National Hockey League or here, especially the elite players, all they have to think about is first place. Nobody ever thinks about second, third, or fourth. We came here to get a gold medal and we didn't get the job done."

For Canadian fans, the poor Olympic result was made worse by the fact that everyone knew it would be the last time they would see Wayne Gretzky in a Team Canada uniform.

For years, he had worn the jersey proudly. He had provided some of the country's greatest international hockey moments and he had been on hand for some of its worst.

The fourth-place finish in the Olympics wasn't good, but it wasn't one of those terrible moments. The 8–1 loss in the final game of the 1981 Canada Cup certainly was, and the loss to the U.S. in the deciding game of the World Cup final was no treat, either.

But Gretzky always was there when asked, in the Canada Cups, the World Cup, and even in the world championships—which most National Hockey League players put on a par with the bubonic plague.

"I just think that whatever sport you're in, whatever you do, if you can play for your country, it's a privilege," Gretzky said after the Olympics. "At sixteen, I played for Team Canada in the world junior tournament, and I felt the same way playing on this team as I did on that team. It was a great thrill, and I was very proud to be a part of it.

"Every time you put on a Canadian uniform and play for Team Canada, anything but gold is not acceptable. That's a pressure and a fact that our team lives with, that maybe no other country has. When you win, the roses are tremendous. When you lose, you have to stand up and take your lumps. And we're taking our lumps."

More of the lumps were being taken by the management team, and especially Crawford, after the shootout debacle. But Gretzky, in typical fashion, refused to cast aspersions.

"That's unfair to the guys," he said. "I think we probably could have had twenty guys out there, and nobody would have scored. I think the only thing that hurt us was Joey Sakic's injury. Joey would definitely have been one of the shooters. There were a lot of guys that it could have been. If one of the guys would have scored, what a great decision. I really don't believe I would have made any difference."

But he sat on the bench long after the loss, staring into the distance, stunned by the defeat.

"I don't think there's any question that was one of the worst losses of my whole career, just because I felt that the team played hard and did a lot of great things and lost in a shootout," he said. "To say the least, we're devastated.

"We haven't gone through that feeling before. We've never experienced that as players before. You play a Game Seven, you go into overtime. You keep going. This was a whole different feeling. We were in shock when we lost. We didn't know what happened. It was a tough loss for us to swallow. You keep it forever."

It took a year to get to the bottom of what really happened during the events that led up to the infamous shootout decision. Crawford said it was a group decision. Clarke said it was a coaching decision, not his. "I felt against the Czechs that if we were going to win it, it was going to be because of Gretzky," Clarke said. "He was the one guy who kept giving us chances with the puck."

The matter would not go away. In the hockey community, it was a burning question: Why had Gretzky not been in the shootout?

Again and again, once anonymity was promised, the name of assistant coach Andy Murray surfaced. Three direct Olympic team sources and other indirect sources said that Murray told the others on the coaching staff that Gretzky had asked to be excluded from the shootout.

Gretzky categorically denied making any such request. "I don't have any bad feelings about not being picked," he told me in a private conversation. "When I was sitting on the bench, I was pulling for all the other guys. But I never, ever turned down a chance to shoot. That's one hundred per cent not true. To say that I turned down a chance is definitely wrong."

What is not wrong is that there was total confusion within the workings of the team. The whole process was a mix-up—probably more innocent than malevolent, and not unusual in everyday affairs, but something that shouldn't happen in such circumstances.

With so many fingers pointing at Murray, he appeared to be the only one who could shed some light on the matter. He said that, about three days before the game against the Czechs, he and Gretzky were having a lighthearted chat in the dressing room. He jokingly said to Gretzky, "Are you ready for the shootout?"

Gretzky's response was typically modest: "There are better guys than me."

When the coaching staff was putting together the list of shooters, Gretzky was not on Crawford's original list—presumably for the reasons already mentioned—but at that point, the list was still subject to revision. When the possibility of inserting Gretzky was raised, Murray related their conversation of three days earlier.

Gretzky's remark apparently was interpreted as a request to be left off the list, and, as a result, he was not included.

Murray vehemently denied the widespread belief within the hockey community that he insisted Gretzky be excluded.

"I have far too much respect for Wayne to do that," he said. "The ultimate decision was Crawford's, and he simply never bothered to ask Gretzky."

Prior to the Olympics, Clarke and Gretzky had interacted in only the most minimal way. They were involved in the same league and each knew of the other, but their careers had never directly overlapped. They had never been involved with the same team.

But after the Canadians staggered home without so much as a medal, Clarke, never a man known for sugar-coating a situation, was aware of two things: one, he should not be involved in the next Team Canada, the entry in the Salt Lake City 2002 Olympics; two, Gretzky should.

"When you lose like we did, I don't think that I should get another crack at it," he said. "I really don't. I think when you lose like that, someone else should come in as a manager."

He was being a bit too hard on himself. Others were involved, and Sather, the architect of the previous national team, saw that as the problem. "You can't do a job like that by committee," he said.

Clarke not only headed a managerial troika, but to make matters worse, there was considerable involvement—some would say meddling—from Canadian Hockey. Bob Nicholson played a large role in the proceedings, and the team followed a game plan provided by Andy Murray, who had been appointed by Canadian Hockey. To put it simply, that plan was a disaster. The Canadian players did their best without complaint, but they didn't like that game plan, and ultimately, it became clear that it didn't work.

"You can look back and say if we'd had a healthy Paul Kariya and Joe Sakic, we might have won," Clarke said. "But we didn't lose a game, we lost a shootout."

Theoren Fleury put it another way. "Perhaps next time, they can set up a Scrabble board at centre ice and we'll play Scrabble to see who wins."

"The mentality of the Canadian players probably put us at a little bit of a disadvantage against the Finns," Clarke conceded, "because a bronze medal doesn't mean too much to Canadians in hockey. I think that it should, and that next turn around, maybe the team going in will realize that just getting a medal at the Olympics is something special."

That would be one lesson. But there were others, and Clarke rhymed them off.

"You have to keep better control of the team when you're at the event," he said. "There were families and friends and agents and NHL sponsors and everybody. I think when the game's over, you should take the players and wives and go somewhere and give them a couple of hours together.

"I think also, knowing that a shootout is part of it, we should have practised it. You should identify the guys who could end up in that position and have a plan.

"Each guy who went in on Dominik Hasek did exactly the same thing. He went right down the middle of the ice. We should have said, 'Maybe we should send one guy down the right side, one down the left. Let's see if we can't make him think a little bit.'

"Again, it's hindsight, but I think for next time, there should be a lot more time spent on that kind of planning."

With Clarke never having had any firsthand contact with Gretzky, he had been less aware than some of his potential contributions. But he was won over.

When I asked him about favouring Lindros at Gretzky's expense, he said, "I think you're reading that wrong. It probably turned out looking like that, but it was not intended that way. It was our intent to not put the responsibility of the whole team on Wayne Gretzky again.

"Gretzky is a guy you can count on regardless of whether he's the captain or not. You know what he's going to give you. You know what he's going to do for you. You know how he's going to conduct himself.

"We felt he had carried so much for so long that some of the other guys—by being put in the position of captain or assistant captain or spokesman or whatever—would rise. They're going to be the guys who have to carry us the next time."

It wasn't just Gretzky's on-ice performance that impressed Clarke; it was his total involvement. On most days, for instance, Gretzky would walk from the Olympic Village to the rink, stopping to chat with admirers and well-wishers on the way. By the end of the Olympics, he had regulars who waited for him to come by. I suggested that it was the first time in years that he had been able to wander freely along urban streets.

"I wouldn't say that," he said with a laugh. "But I don't mind it. I'm used to it. It's part of my life, but it's not just me. Everybody gets asked for a picture or an autograph."

Living in the athletes' village had also been a pleasant experience. "I think our whole team really enjoyed it," he said. "All our guys rallied around the whole Olympic team—the speed skaters, the skiers, everybody. They seemed surprised that our guys are so friendly and outgoing, but I don't think that should be a big surprise to anyone who knows hockey players."

There was no doubt that Clarke had become a convert. "I think we should go out of our way to make sure that a player like Gretzky—and his wife—should be part of our next management or coaching group," he said. "With their knowledge and their class, they're such a strong representation of Canadian hockey. What they have to offer is so much. I think they have to be either a part of the management or part of the coaching team—in a serious role. I'm not talking token. Maybe Gretzky should be the manager or the head coach—depending on what he's doing at the time, because we're talking three years down the road."

Clarke was so moved by Gretzky's contributions that he couldn't let the matter rest.

"I wrote him and his wife a personal letter," he said, "because I think it is important for young players in hockey to see how a guy like that, who is the best player that hockey ever has had, and his wife, conduct themselves with decency and humility.

"To me, that's what's so important to Canadian hockey: that you can be as great as that and conduct your personal life with your wife and kids properly and be so humble about what you've done. To me, that was so impressive.

"I hadn't really spent a lot of time with him. I had never met his wife before. It was really wonderful."

CHAPTER TWENTY-SIX

Wayne Gretzky was always acutely aware of the location of all the other players on the ice. This not only made him a more effective player, it also made him a healthier player because he rarely took any serious hits.

For his first eight seasons in the NHL, he missed an average of one game a year, even though he was out for a six-game stretch right after he set the consecutive-game scoring mark of fifty-one.

Whether it was through good fortune or skill, Gretzky was able to avoid the debilitating knee injuries that negatively impacted the careers of many great athletes. Bobby Orr is hockey's best example, but Pavel Bure is also on the list.

Oddly, it was a knee injury that first set Gretzky down for a prolonged stretch—sixteen games in 1988.

During a game against the Philadelphia Flyers on December 30, 1987, Gretzky was on the attack near the crease when he got crunched.

"It happened as I shot the puck," he recalled. "Kjell Samuelsson kind of slid under me and Mark Howe blocked me. I wrenched the knee, I snapped it. But I didn't hit the post like some people said, and nobody landed on me."

The original club announcement, which made direct reference to the knee injury—unlike today's ludicrous "upper-body" or "lower-body injury" announcements—speculated that Gretzky might miss a game or two. He knew differently.

"As soon as I came back to the bench, Mess asked me how I felt," he said. "I had heard it pop. I said, 'It's bad, Mess.'"

He knew that everyone who plays in the NHL learns to accept injuries as a fact of life. "There's no question that I've been terrifically lucky," he said.

In fact, the injury had its benefits. "The first week, it was really a nice rest," he said three weeks into the recuperation. "Now it's getting to be kind of boring. I can't burn off energy. I can't play squash. I can't do anything."

But he could watch hockey, and by that time, he had a satellite dish, so he watched game after game while his knee healed, and, in the process, picked up all sorts of useful information about the tendencies of players around the league.

Also, he got some rest. He had played in the Canada Cup in the fall, and a midwinter break wasn't likely to do him any harm.

As it happened, he was rested and dominant when the playoffs started. He not only led the Oilers to another Stanley Cup, he won the Conn Smythe Trophy as the MVP of the post-season.

Gretzky's luck continued to hold for three more seasons, but then he suffered a back injury that was not only the most serious injury of his career, it even threatened to end his career.

It came in a Canada Cup game against Team USA in September 1991. Gretzky had outraced Chris Chelios to a loose puck in the corner and was squirming away from Chelios with his back to the play.

At that point, Chelios's defence partner, Gary Suter, rammed Gretzky into the glass. Just that summer, the NHL had decreed that checks of that nature would be punishable by a five-minute major. In today's hockey, a suspension invariably accompanies the major. But in international hockey in 1991, Suter got away with it.

"It was a legal hit," protested Suter afterwards. "If it had been anyone else in the world, we wouldn't be talking now. I guess that's just the stature he has."

Team Canada coach Mike Keenan disagreed. "It was an illegal hit, no question about it," he said.

Suter seemed surprised by the controversy. "It's unbelievable," he said. "It's a game of hits. Any other player but him. I don't think it was a cheap shot."

Few would agree, especially those who grew up with today's rules. And if it weren't for the fact that international rules preclude enforcers and impose onerous punishments on fighters, there's no doubt that Suter would have been forced to answer immediately for his indiscretion.

But whether the check was legal or not, the resultant back problem continued to bother Gretzky. He played through it for the entire 1991–92 NHL season, but by the following September, it was determined that he not only needed a back operation, but his career might be over, and he was even in danger of being paralyzed.

Hockey players' backs tend to take a lot of punishment. The legal bodychecks are bad enough, but the cross-checks are worse, and in Gretzky's era, they were all but ignored, especially if they were delivered near the net, where Gretzky spent a lot of his time.

The NHL's best scorer prior to Gretzky was Mike Bossy. A back injury forced his retirement. The NHL's best scorer after Gretzky was Mario Lemieux. A back injury forced his retirement.

Lesser stars of the era, such as Wendel Clark, Rod Gilbert, Paul Reinhart, Craig Simpson and many others all suffered debilitating back injuries.

Gretzky battled severe pain for the entire 1991–92 season and expected that, once the hockey stopped, the pain would as well. It didn't. It got worse.

In early September, it got so bad that he was admitted to hospital and given intravenous painkillers.

When I spoke to him in mid-September, he was despondent. Hockey had always been his great love, and he had been told there was a very real danger that he might never play again.

But that was a secondary concern. "The first thing I've got to worry about is me," he said. "At last I know what I have. All year, I thought it was a torn cartilage in my ribs. Now that we know what it is, we can start to clear it up. It's not like it was last week. It's not unbearable any more. The doctors say they're not going to do anything until the pain goes, and they're saying that should be in a week or ten days. But the last time I had this, the pain didn't go away in a week. It was three months."

Once again, he had a bit of luck. He had entered hospital at just the right time and got his back examined a day before a major conference of back doctors opened in Seattle. Gretzky's doctor attended and took along the pertinent data. As a result, many of the top specialists in North America were apprised of Gretzky's problem, and they offered advice.

It was determined that he had a form of herniated thoracic disc and was told that it was a one-in-a-million injury. Herniated discs are usually much lower in the spine. It was also decided that he would need an operation, but for various medical reasons, it could not be performed right away.

In the interim, Gretzky undertook a rehabilitation program to help reduce the inflammation. At times, it seemed to be working; at times it didn't. When he did a *Hockey Night in Canada* interview that aired on November 7, he strongly implied that he was facing an imminent operation followed by a lengthy period of recuperation, possibly as long as a year. When I talked to him two weeks later, he was much more optimistic.

"The rehab program seems to be progressing," he said, "which is great news. They can never sit across from me and tell me there is no risk, but we're so much further ahead than we were a month ago. A month ago, they were telling me, 'You've got to have an operation.' That sort of thing."

The operation never happened, and Gretzky explained his pessimism during the *HNiC* interview by saying that his rehabilitation had been going well, but the day before the taping, he "kind of hit the wall."

At that point, he said, "I didn't know what was going to happen, but I was extremely concerned, naturally."

When he spoke to his doctors, they told him that the temporary setback was a normal occurrence. "Things look really positive now," he added.

"I still get pain when I move, but it's kind of diminished. I've got more mobility now. I get the pain in the front. There's no pain in the back at all. It's the inflammation in the back that blocks the nerve that comes out. You know how when people hurt their back, their legs go numb? Well, my injury is the nerve that goes around the front. That's why I kept thinking it was my ribs that were hurt, and that I had torn a cartilage there."

Even though the future appeared brighter, there were no guarantees. Gretzky had been riding an emotional roller coaster ever since he entered hospital. Sometimes, the outlook was positive. Sometimes, it was negative.

"When it happened, I said, 'I don't know where I'm going to be or what I'm going to do. I might not even skate this year, let alone play. I really don't know.'

"Two months ago, they said, 'You're done for this year.' Four weeks from now, when I get into a healthier condition, I could get the pain back. Then there's no choice. They'll have to operate."

Again, he was lucky. The pain didn't come back. With the use of MRIs—which were still an innovation—exercise, steroid injections and some world-class medical advice, he was able to return to the NHL on January 7, 1993. He had missed thirty-six games—almost half the season.

When you're gone from the NHL for that long, there's invariably a negative reaction, even if you're Wayne Gretzky. Not long after the layoff, he lost his confidence. Perhaps the two weren't related. Perhaps what happened next was nothing more than coincidence. Either way, it was another difficult stage of Gretzky's most difficult season.

"I lost my confidence a couple of times in my career," he admitted four years later, "but the worst was when I came back from my back injury. I was all gung-ho and I got going with a good eight- or nine-game run. Then, all of a sudden, sixteen games—nothing. I mean nothing. Not even a chance. I wasn't involved in the play most of the time."

Eventually, he broke out with a six-point night, but he never forgot that slump and its impact upon him. "The craziest thing about professional sports," he said, "is that whether you're the best player in that sport, border-line or the weakest, if you don't play with confidence, you can't play."

In 1999, just before he retired, he missed twelve games because of a back injury, but that one involved a different area of his back and was not related to the previous problem. The injury evolving from the Suter hit was the worst he ever experienced.

CHAPTER TWENTY-SEVEN

With the 1998 Olympics having been such a disappointment for Canadian hockey fans, the nation's hockey establishment was determined to pull out all the stops in 2002.

The Olympics were to be held in North America, the next best thing to home turf, in the year that would mark the fiftieth anniversary of Canada's last gold-medal win. What better time could there be for the nation to regain its hockey pride?

And who, the organizers asked themselves, would be a better man to run the team than Wayne Gretzky?

Gretzky had retired as a player in 1999, and with his far-reaching connections, his hockey knowledge, his corporate ties and his experience—not to mention his availability—he was the perfect choice.

It was an honour that Gretzky was eager to accept, and he took his responsibilities extremely seriously. As far as he was concerned, this was not to be a ceremonial position, nor was it to be approached in a lackadaisical fashion. The country's hockey reputation was on the line, and by extension, so was the hockey reputation of Wayne Gretzky himself. Over the course of his career, everything he did made it clear how important that was to him.

Accordingly, more than a year before the opening game of the 2002 Olympics—on February 2, 2001, to be precise—Gretzky and his staff met in Denver to put in place the first building blocks of what they hoped would become a gold-medal team and, at the same time, try to cast aside a few other obstacles that were in the way.

To the average viewer, the Olympics are a fascinating sporting spectacle. But to anyone involved in them, they are a mystifying, complex maze of politics, kickbacks, under-the-table deals, intrigue and deceit. There is never a straight line from A to B in the Olympics. The path is always winding and circuitous—and it usually leads to a back door.

Over the course of the next twelve months, Gretzky would become painfully aware of that fact. And he would also learn that not all of his Olympics difficulties would be created by Olympics people themselves. Sometimes, they would come from those who were supposed to be his allies.

Even a year before the Games, he discovered that what he expected to be the straightforward matter of arranging practice time for the team was not just a matter of arranging practice time. That would be far too simple. That would not be the Olympic way.

For starters, his longtime adversary Gary Bettman stood in his path. The NHL commissioner had not only shortened the Olympic break compared to 1998, he had insisted on a full slate of games on Wednesday, February 13, 2002. But Canada was scheduled to play its first Olympic game on Friday, February 15 against Sweden.

As the adage goes, the enemy of my enemy is my friend. So Gretzky approached Bettman's biggest enemy for help. He didn't get any. "Our agreement for all players in all countries," said NHL Players' Association head Bob Goodenow, "is that there will be no tryouts or practices prior to the Olympics."

Either way, Gretzky seemed stymied. He wanted the team's prospective players to get together at some sort of camp in August, but the way Goodenow had explained the situation, that was impossible.

If Gretzky hadn't named the team by August, then a training camp would be considered a tryout. If he had named the team, it would be considered a practice. Neither was acceptable.

Gretzky next turned to Mario Lemieux, who was in the unique position of owning a team and therefore being one of Bettman's bosses. Gretzky's compromise, which he and Lemieux intended to present jointly, was that the full Wednesday NHL slate would be shifted to the preceding Sunday, which had a fairly light load. The Sunday games could be squeezed in elsewhere, and the Olympians could at least have a couple of days in Salt Lake City before the first puck was dropped.

Bettman turned that down too.

On the Olympic-provision front, there was the requirement that players be named to the team in April—ten months before the Games—so that the International Olympic Committee could maximize its revenues by involving the players in marketing and promotion over the summer.

It wasn't hard for Gretzky and his advisors to come up with eight surefire names, but those men had to agree to the responsibilities that went along with being named. They had to help with the previously mentioned marketing and promotion. More important, although this consideration was never mentioned in public, once they had been named, they were subject to random, unscheduled Olympic drug tests.

NHL players, who battle through a rigorous eighty-two-game schedule, want to play the game and get on the charter flight or go home. They don't want to sit in a room and submit to a drug test at the whim of an Olympic official while their teammates are kept waiting.

They weren't worried that the testing would uncover any serious drug use. But these guys were flying all over the continent all winter long in airplanes that recirculated germ-laden air. They got colds, and they took over-the-counter remedies that are available to all of us. Some of those remedies are banned by the IOC and would lead not only to a suspension, but also to the embarrassment that comes with being labelled a druggie.

The Denver meeting also had to determine the Canadian Olympic team's overriding philosophy. Was it to be an all-star squad or was it to be a mixture of stars and specialists? Was it to be composed only of veterans, or would some youngsters be tossed into the mix? While it wouldn't be totally defensively oriented or totally offensively oriented, how was it to be weighted?

Once those and other similar factors were determined, the management group had to come up with a list of the best forty players who fit the bill, fully expecting that no one would turn them down. In that regard, they were right.

Gretzky made the calls himself, and there were, he said, "about three or four players" who, upon receiving his call, said something along the lines of "Yeah, right," thinking it was a friend pulling a practical joke. But once they realized that it was indeed Gretzky they were talking to, they were delighted.

Because coach Pat Quinn wanted Team Canada to have an offensive leaning, and because most of the candidates played for coaches who tended to stress the defensive side of the game, Gretzky desperately wanted his team to have a pre-season training camp and a couple of practices before the Olympics began.

But since he couldn't get either, he was prepared to bite the bullet as long as there was no cheating anywhere else. Widespread rumours suggested that the Scandinavian teams intended to hold tryouts under the guise of calling them summer camps, but with Gretzky's proposal in that regard having been turned down, that arrangement came under scrutiny, and it was agreed that they would not be allowed to do so.

"We are in the same position as all the other countries preparing for this tournament," Gretzky said. "We would like to have a summer camp of some sort, but we understand the position.

"Whether it's organized or unorganized, if other countries are having some sort of camp, we want to be on the same page. That's our concern."

In late March, when Gretzky had to announce the names of his first eight players with the Olympics still almost a year away, there were no major surprises.

Al MacInnis, who had been seen initially as an automatic choice, had to be left off the list because of lingering questions about the state of his injured eye. His replacement was Scott Niedermayer, a highly versatile, swift-skating defenceman who, like MacInnis, was at home in both ends of the rink. This was revealing because one of the failings of the 1998 Olympic team was that the defencemen were sufficiently sound when it came to keeping the opposition off the board, but when Team Canada needed some offence and wanted the defencemen to join the attack, they fell a bit short. Chris Pronger and Rob Blake, the other two defencemen named, were as capable of joining the rush or quarterbacking the power play as they were of clearing the front of the net or blocking a shot. Also, they were all powerful skaters, an important aspect to consider since the Olympics were to be played on a European-sized ice surface, even though the venue was Salt Lake City, Utah.

The inclusion of Steve Yzerman was also a revealing development. In his youth, he was almost purely offensively minded, but he had evolved into the best two-way forward in the game.

In the post-Olympic soul-searching that swept Canada and its hockey establishment in 1998, there was widespread agreement that the team had not been sufficiently versatile. It had been geared to think defence first and was built with the specific aim of being able to handle Team USA in a gold-medal game. But the Americans imploded long before the medal round, and the Canadians found themselves playing a defensively oriented game against a bunch of Czechs who weren't of NHL calibre but played solidly as a unit.

This time, the Canadians intended to be ready to produce whatever would be needed, whether it was offence or defence. They intended to be ready for any team in the tournament, not just one.

The four players who rounded out the early selection list—Lemieux, Joe Sakic, Paul Kariya and Owen Nolan—further illustrated the intentions of Gretzky and the management team.

No goalies were named because at that point, there were too many good candidates, the top five being Patrick Roy, Martin Brodeur, Roberto Luongo, Curtis Joseph and Sean Burke.

All summer long, Gretzky worked on getting a summer camp, and eventually he got his way—but it wasn't easy.

He started by calling players on the list and asking if they considered an August training camp to be acceptable. It's a simple fact in the hockey world that the respect for Gretzky is such that no player would turn him down. They all said, "Sure, Wayne, no problem. We'll do it."

However, some of them called the NHL Players' Association and said, "I've just told Wayne Gretzky I'll go to a summer camp. How can I say no to a guy like him? But there's no way I want to be there. You have to help." Accordingly, the NHLPA issued a public denunciation of an August camp.

But as the summer passed, there were quiet negotiations. Gretzky learned that it was the date of the camp that was unpalatable, not the concept. If he held it immediately before the NHL teams opened their camps, he discovered, there would be no problem.

As one of the players said, "At that stage of the summer, we'd be going full speed if we were back in our hometowns. We'd be skating with a group of guys and getting into the final stages of preparation for training camp. We're skating every day anyway, so why not do it with the best players in the world?"

So that's when it was held.

Along the way, the NHLPA quietly pulled out of the proceedings. Naturally, there was no news release on the matter. But those conversant with the hockey world knew that as soon as the players withdrew their objection, there was no further reason for the NHLPA to intercede.

And the ban on "tryouts or practices"? Gretzky had found a way around that too.

It transpired that Canadian officials had never got around to signing the agreement between the International Ice Hockey Federation, the NHLPA and the Canadian Hockey Association that covered participation in world championships and the 2004 World Cup.

The document that had been signed was a letter of understanding from the CHA to the NHLPA and the NHL. It had four clauses relating to training camps, one of which said that teams were allowed an "optional orientation meeting that will occur over a forty-eight-hour period, excluding travel time."

That was the clause Canada used to stage its training camp.

Did it matter? Well, consider this: the camp was held in Calgary, and when Simon Gagne reported, he was nursing a previously unreported injury; so a last-minute call was made to Jarome Iginla, who lived in Edmonton.

"I'd watched the first day of camp on TV," said Iginla, "and I'd seen the highlights on all the sports channels. I went out to dinner with my brothers and my dad. My wife—my fiancée at the time—called me, and she said, 'Wayne Gretzky just called and he'd like you to come down to camp.'

"I said to her, 'Are you sure it was Wayne Gretzky? I can just see some guys playing a prank on me.' I said, 'What are the chances?'

"I told her there were some guys who thought it would be a pretty good joke to have me go in there with my equipment bag and everything. When I get there and they ask what I'm doing there, I'm supposed to say, 'Oh, I want to try out.'"

Iginla was so sure he was the victim of a practical joke that he refused to call the number Gretzky had left. Instead, he called Kevin Lowe, who assured him that his presence was indeed required.

He got up at dawn the next morning, drove to Calgary, and was so impressive, despite his shortened exposure to the selectors, that he made the team. In the Olympic tournament, he was one of Canada's best players and scored two goals in the gold-medal game. Without that training camp, Iginla would not have been on the team.

The evolution of the team seemed to be progressing smoothly, but in November, Gretzky faced a major setback. Patrick Roy, by that time the odds-on favourite to be the first-string goaltender, called Gretzky at his Los Angeles home to tell him that he would not participate. He wanted to rest.

Roy had been Canada's starting goalie in the 1998 Olympics in Nagano and had played every minute of every game. He compiled a 4–2 record with a 1.46 goals-against average.

But this time around, Roy prioritized his commitment to his NHL team, the Colorado Avalanche. "My reasons are simple," he said. "I wanted to take the time to prepare myself to have a good playoff and finish the season strong." Roy was thirty-six at the time, and because of the Olympics, the 2002 playoffs could run until June 20. He felt that the grind would be too much and that the Avs, who were paying him $8.5 million to do the job in goal for them, would be cheated.

Gretzky tried to put the best possible face on the development. "I respect his decision," he said. "Obviously, he was one of the goalies that we were looking at, but the other goalies we had in camp are very capable as well. He showed a lot of class. He showed up in Calgary, and he participated and worked hard. He played in the Olympics once, and it's his decision that he doesn't want to do it this time. I can accept that."

The positive side of the announcement was that, by making up his mind in November, rather than after the twenty-three-man roster had been named, Roy allowed Gretzky ample time to fill the gap.

Nevertheless, the development gave Gretzky a hint of what was to come. The entire nation, it seemed, was suddenly in an uproar, partly because of the usual unsubstantiated observations that emanate from radio panel shows and partly because of a newspaper report in New York, of all places.

The urban myth that spread everywhere said that Roy had been mistreated—"dissed" in the jargon of the day—by Gretzky, and that's why he had pulled out. The newspaper report said that Brodeur might not be named to the team. The fact that there was not the slightest evidence to support either assertion seemed to trouble no one.

For the first allegation to be true, Roy would have had to lie publicly about his reasons for leaving the team. But Roy had never shown the slightest aversion to being forthright, as anyone who remembered his days with the Montreal Canadiens would have known.

In fact, Gretzky had approached the matter this way. First, he told Roy he would be named to the team. Then he told him that he would have the inside track to the first-string job—that it would be his to lose. And he told him that another goalie would play one of the qualifying games.

That was an eminently sensible approach. After all, if Gretzky unequivocally promised the full-time job to Roy, what would he do if Roy were in a slump in February? The Olympics are a single-game elimination tournament, after all.

As for Brodeur, it turned out that he had not been removed from the list of those being considered for the team.

But the level of hysteria that arose because of those two unfounded assumptions was ominous, to say the least.

As the deadline for naming the twenty-three-man roster drew close, Gretzky's decisions became even harder—not because of a shortage of players, but because of a surplus of quality players combined with a number of short-term injuries. Lemieux was the perfect example. He wanted to play, but he had a wrist injury. Clearly, he had to be on the team if he was healthy, but if it turned out that the injury didn't heal as expected, a roster spot would have been wasted. Other players—notably Derek Morris and Ryan Smyth—were in similar situations.

And what about players whose track record was good but whose recent play wasn't?

These were the kinds of decisions that Gretzky always knew he would face, but they were made more difficult by the Olympic bureaucracy, which created unrealistic deadlines and imposed needless rules.

Finally, the management group, led by Gretzky, assistant executive director Kevin Lowe, director of player personnel Steve Tambellini and head coach Pat Quinn, reached a decision.

"It kept coming back to the same thing," Gretzky said. "Just take the best players."

In the end, that's what they did. There wasn't always unanimity. Gretzky himself thought that Burke belonged on the list of the three goalies, along with Brodeur and Joseph, but around the room, the sentiment favoured Ed Belfour. So Belfour got the call.

"It got down to the fact," Gretzky explained, "that these are the three goalies the coaching staff was very, very confident with."

Any disagreements that did arise were minimal and within well-defined boundaries. Gretzky and his support staff had worked hard over the preceding year to whittle down the options—so much so that when they met in a Toronto hotel room to finalize the team, they needed only ninety minutes to do so.

After the goalies came the defencemen. There were the three named the previous spring plus MacInnis, Adam Foote, Eric Brewer and Ed Jovanovski. In addition to the five pre-selected forwards, Gretzky added Smyth, Iginla, Theoren Fleury, Eric Lindros, Mike Peca, Brendan Shanahan, Joe Nieuwendyk and Simon Gagne.

"We wanted speed," said Gretzky. "We wanted size. We wanted emotion. We really wanted emotion.

"Everyone loses. Everyone makes mistakes. But we wanted our mistakes to be made out of caring, out of wanting to do well. We wanted that to really be a part of our team."

Peca exemplified the concept. Despite missing the previous NHL season in a contract dispute, he had gone to Germany to play for Canada in the world championship, suffered a shattered orbital bone on his first shift, but continued to play and was named the game's most outstanding player.

"That kind of attitude, that kind of atmosphere, is what we really want," said Gretzky, "because it's a disease that spreads through the team and you want that. You want guys feeling that, 'I'm so happy to play for this country, and I'm proud to be on this team.' Those are the kinds of guys we wanted from day one, and I think we really established that."

Making the personnel decisions didn't end the meeting—far from it. For four more hours, the brain trust talked about every aspect that could possibly become relevant. They discussed possible line combinations. They worried about the ratio of right-handed shots to lefties. They debated the pairing of roommates. They considered the most recent (and probably not final) IOC edict regarding practice times. They pondered possible matchups against other teams. They worked out hypothetical defence pairings. They talked about the advantages and disadvantages of moving certain players to unaccustomed positions.

And on and on it went. "We really turned over every stone throughout this whole process," Gretzky explained.

But that was the Gretzky way. He tried to consider every possible scenario that might arise and how to handle it. It was the way he had played; it was the way he intended to run Team Canada.

In a task of that nature, the commitment has to start at the top, and if the gold medal did eventually find its way into Canadian hands, it would be because, along the way, every aspect of preparation had been done as thoroughly as possible.

Even then, with the team named and the tournament nearly two months away, it was not clear sailing. Once again, the rumour mill sprang to life. As stories spread like wildfire from coast to coast, an unmerited authenticity accrued to them as they were told and retold.

One such rumour had the Olympic organizers being on the verge of dumping Eric Lindros and Theoren Fleury and replacing them with Joe Thornton and Keith Primeau. Again, the stories appeared in print and were discussed on radio, even though they made no sense. "We would never do that to anyone," said Gretzky. "We have no intention of embarrassing any players. Those guys have been named to the team, and everyone named to the team will stay on the team unless they are genuinely injured. We won't be dropping anyone.

"These guys have pride and they have agreed to play for their country. We would never do something like that to anyone. It just wouldn't be right."

Those rumours had hardly been put to bed when another cropped up. This time, the organizers allegedly were determined to find a way to add Joe Thornton to the team. An emerging star at the time, Thornton had solid fan support, but once again, the rumour made no sense.

When the organizers made their original selections, they were fully aware of Thornton's ability. They had also spoken at length to Boston Bruins general manager Mike O'Connell. They knew exactly what Thornton would bring to the team. But they didn't select Thornton in December, and they weren't going to do it in January.

On paper, Canada had the strongest hockey team in the Olympics, but Gretzky knew that meant nothing. Canada was probably the strongest team in the 1998 Nagano Olympics as well, but they lost a shootout. If nothing else, that fact illustrated the potential importance of a single goal in the Olympic format. One more goal during regulation time against the Czech Republic in 1998, and Canada would have gone on to play for gold, a game it probably would have won.

In 2002, Canada intended to be ready for all eventualities. The preparation in 1998 was good; in 2002, the preparation was meticulous.

The simple fact that the Canadian professionals had one Olympic experience under their belts was seen as a big advantage. The Europeans were comfortable with the Nagano format, having been through it so many times. For Canada, it had been a novelty.

Another advantage would be the time and effort that the key people in Canadian management had devoted to preparation. Gretzky had, in effect, made the gold-medal quest his full-time job, whereas in 1998, most of the decision-makers thought about the Olympics only when they found some slack periods in their NHL workload.

Also, the assistant coach in charge of developing strategy in 2002— the "Xs and Os guy," in hockey terminology—was Ken Hitchcock, who was conveniently fired as head coach of the Dallas Stars fifty games into the season. That left his plate clear to concern himself with Team Canada's Olympic tactics.

But when the Olympics finally opened, there was no visible evidence that Canada had done any preparation whatsoever.

In the opening game, they got thumped 5–2 by Sweden, and if Gretzky and friends had thought there was an unreasonable uproar when Roy opted out, they came to realize that the country's reaction to a decision by one player was a drop in the ocean compared to the country's reaction to a decisive loss.

According to letters to the editor, talk shows, columnists (and not only sports columnists) and even unsolicited emails sent to media members covering the event, it was a disgrace. It was a national tragedy. It was an embarrassment. It was an outrage. Goaltender Curtis Joseph should be sent home immediately.

It was certainly an embarrassment. The players agreed with that. The rest of the criticism was well over the top, including the venom directed at Joseph. He hadn't been great, but he hadn't been bad, either.

Nevertheless, in the next game, Gretzky made the decision to go with Martin Brodeur. In theory, it was a group decision, but Gretzky led the way.

"Don't read into this that we're blaming Curtis for the loss," he said. "That's not the case at all. We didn't lose the game because of our goaltender. I don't care who was in net, we were not going to beat that team with the chances they had and some of the things they did.

"Their goaltender [Tommy Salo] made some key saves early in the game, and that seemed to be the difference. But I wouldn't blame our goaltender. I'm still not concerned about our goaltending being the weak link in this hockey team."

Judging by the reaction, he was the only Canadian who wasn't.

Two days later, Canada beat Germany 3–2. That did nothing to quell the uproar. The German team wasn't star-studded, to say the least, and a victory by such a small margin was not what Canadian fans wanted. Brodeur allowed two goals on twenty shots, but only seven were from NHL players.

Now, Gretzky had to make another difficult decision. Coming in, the plan had been to play Joseph—who, in the weeks before the Olympics, had been the better goalie—in the first and third games. Did Gretzky go back to Joseph? Or should he now reverse that decision and stick with Brodeur to see him against the Czechs, who represented much better competition than Germany?

He opted for the latter and was proved right. Brodeur was outstanding. Canada got a 3–3 tie and, in the process, qualified for the elimination round.

Had Gretzky let the matter end there, he would certainly have faced another storm of criticism. A loss, a tie and a one-goal win over a weak team didn't come close to satisfying the nation's demands for the three-game opening round, even though Quinn had been saying for months that, as far as he was concerned, those games were nothing more than a training camp for the subsequent elimination round.

But when that anticipated storm of criticism broke, it was dwarfed by the reaction to Gretzky's outburst after the Czech game.

In an uncharacteristic tirade during the postgame press conference, he blasted, among other things, stick use by the Czechs, inconsistent officials and American rumourmongers.

An incident late in the game was the flash point. Theoren Fleury, one of the smallest players in the Olympics, had absorbed a vicious cross-check from the lumbering Roman Hamrlik. The incident went unpenalized.

"I think the guy should be suspended for the rest of the tournament," fumed Gretzky. "If it was a Canadian player who did it, it would be a big story. A Czech player did it and it was okay."

He was rolling now. There was no slowing him down.

"I'm very proud of all the players in our locker room, and it makes me ill to hear some of the things that are being said about us."

He paused briefly, but there was more. "Am I hot? Yeah, I'm hot, because I'm tired of people taking shots at Canadian hockey and when we do it, we're hooligans. When Europeans do it, it's okay because they're not tough or they're not dirty. That's a crock of crap."

There had been some stories in the media concerning the fact that not all Canadian players were enamoured of Quinn's coaching. Gretzky had no interest in entertaining that view, either.

"American propaganda," he snorted. "If you want to talk about hockey, you want to talk about Canadians. We're the biggest story here. They're loving us not doing well. They loved the start we had. It's a big story for them.

"I don't think we dislike those countries as much as they hate us. And that's a fact. They don't like us. They want to see us fail. They love beating us. They may tell you guys something different, but believe me, when you're on the ice, that's what they say. They don't like us."

It was an outburst that made news around the world. In Gretzky's entire career as a player, he had never said anything nearly as contentious as this. Many in the American media were outraged, calling him a "crybaby" and worse. When I talked to him the next day, he had no intention of backing down or softening his comments.

"I have no regrets," he said. "I was trying to protect our hockey team. I said it with a great deal of passion for our game in Canada. I was upset at the cross-check. Had this been an American or Canadian player, a lot would have been made of it. I sat there for twenty minutes, and not one person asked me about that cross-check.

"If that had been a Canadian or American player, it would have been the first question asked."

He said that his complaint about the American media was not based on a specific instance but more of a cumulative effect.

"Every time I walked in, something new was thrown at me. There were all these stories, from coaches not talking to each other to Mario

Lemieux having gone home. I just had no idea where all this was coming from. I just had enough of it.

"For some reason, there were all these silly rumours flying around about our hockey team. It really started to wear on me, and it really bothered me, especially when our hockey team is here representing our country and doing what they can to win a gold medal and carrying themselves with a great deal of class."

This was a previously unseen facet of Wayne Gretzky. He was no stranger to the limelight, but when he played, even internationally, his remarks were more measured and his approach more diplomatic. Much more diplomatic.

"When I was a player, I was a player," he said. "Now I'm in a situation where I can defend our hockey team, and I feel obliged to do that. I'm no different than anyone else who has ever been involved here, whether it's Bobby Clarke or Glen Sather. That's what you do. You protect your team. That's what I was trying to do."

In Canada, the reaction was mixed. Some said he was trying to divert attention from his team's failure. Some said he was trying to divert attention from his own failure. Some said he was just a sore loser. Some said he had hurt the team by his remarks in that he had given them excuses.

Those were opinions. The unassailable fact was this: after that speech, Canada never lost another game.

Granted, they had some good fortune. But they could hardly be blamed for that, and no one can say that they would not have persevered without that good fortune.

One instance was the stunning upset of the Swedes by Belarus, who won in the dying minutes of regulation time when a shot from centre ice bounced off Salo's head and dropped into the net to break a 3–3 tie.

"We knew going into the Olympics that, first of all, the Americans were going to be tough," said Gretzky as he reminisced in 2012. "They had a good team, and the Olympics were in Salt Lake City, so we knew they'd be even better in front of a home crowd. They didn't have a really great tournament in Nagano, and we knew they wanted to make up for that.

"But the matchup that really scared us was Sweden. We just didn't seem to match up well against them, and they beat us 5–2 in the first game. It was a flattering 5–2 because they handled us easily.

"There's no question that we got a break when they got beat in the quarter final on a fluke goal. Playing the Swedes at that stage would have been a tough game for us."

The next piece of good fortune for Canada came in the first elimination game, when they were playing Finland.

Finnish goaltender Jani Hurme allowed an easy goal three minutes into the game to give Canada the luxury of playing with a lead for most of the evening. The Canadians eventually opened a 2–0 lead, but it lasted for only twenty seconds, so the pressure was on again. But Canada hung on and won 2–1.

As expected, Canada had little trouble beating Belarus in the next round to qualify for the gold-medal game. Goaltender Andrei Mezin, who had been brilliant against the Swedes, was somewhat less so against Canada, and the final score was 7–1.

Gretzky's team was now poised to win Canada's first hockey gold medal since the Edmonton Mercurys had done the job fifty years earlier. The competition was to be provided, as Gretzky had anticipated, by the United States—a strong, balanced team with Mike Richter in goal and dangerous snipers like Brett Hull and Jeremy Roenick up front.

Being in Salt Lake City at the time, I had not been aware of the feverish anticipation for the game back in Canada. We had heard so much of the negativity and the criticism, but now, phone calls to various locales in Canada revealed that, two hours before puck drop, every bar in the country was full. We had expected an approach similar to the fevered anticipation for a Game Seven of the Stanley Cup final. It seems this game was more than that. It was on a par with the 1972 Summit Series or the third and deciding game of the spectacular 1987 Canada Cup.

Even Gretzky got caught up in the anticipation. As he paced up and down before the game, he said, "This is the first time since I retired where I wish I could be out there getting ready for a game like this and just focusing on playing."

No game in history had more TV viewers. In the United States, NBC's coverage drew a 10.7 rating, which translates into about eleven million viewers. In Canada, another 10.6 million people watched at home, plus millions more in bars. As became evident later, Canadians all over the world were watching as well, no matter how inconvenient the time might be. People were watching it in English pubs, on Australian beaches and in South American villages.

The United States opened the scoring in that 2002 game, but even so, the Canadians seemed to be in control. To those of us watching at the rink, it appeared that the American goal had been nothing more than an aberration and that eventually the scoreboard would reflect the reality of the game.

Sure enough, it wasn't long afterwards that Lemieux made that now-famous play of letting a pass go between his legs to Kariya, who fired it past a surprised Richter. With eighty-seven seconds left in the first period, Iginla put Canada ahead 2–1. Both teams scored in the second period, but in the third, Iginla scored again to put the game out of reach, and in the dying seconds, Sakic made it 5–2.

In Canada, it was party time. Previously deserted streets were suddenly alive with revellers, and in bars from coast to coast, impromptu renditions of "O Canada" broke out. The nation celebrated. Pride had been restored. Canada was at the head of the hockey world again.

How much of it had to do with Gretzky's speech after the Czech game?

"Gretzky was the big force," said assistant coach Ken Hitchcock. "He took the heat off us. He took all the crap. He put himself in the position to be blamed. These guys wanted to play for him. They didn't want to let him down."

Gretzky himself wouldn't exactly admit that his rant had been "staged," as some in the American media had suggested, but he did concede that it hadn't exactly been a spur-of-the-moment outburst either.

"I learned that from Glen Sather," he admitted. "There are times when you have to stand up and take responsibility. At that time, I didn't think our team was very comfortable or relaxed. The hope was to take some heat off the guys.

"It did."

CHAPTER TWENTY-EIGHT

I t is the nature of Canadian hockey fans to be hypercritical. They expect their team to emerge victorious at every important international tournament, and if a different result should materialize, they lose all sense of proportion, all sense of reason and all sense of propriety.

Canadian fans are not unique in this regard. The concept is universal; it's just the sports that differ. In New Zealand, the nation expects the All Blacks to win every rugby tournament. Brazilians expect their soccer team to win every World Cup. The Americans expect their basketball team to win gold at every Olympics.

And if you're the prime mover behind one of those teams, there are no excuses, no extenuating circumstances. Lose and you're vilified.

Wayne Gretzky knew all that. When he ran Team Canada in the 2002 Olympics and the team got off to a slow start, the outpouring of vitriol was nothing short of appalling. Even though the meaningful games were yet to be played, the majority of the country's hockey fans not only seemed to feel that further involvement was hopeless but that Gretzky, the other management staff, the coaches and all the players were total incompetents.

Only when the team won the gold medal were the critics silenced, at least temporarily, and the victory quelled any disagreement about who would be the executive director of the 2006 Olympic team. It would be Gretzky.

The circumstances surrounding the launch of the 2006 team were unusual, to say the least. Gretzky held a training camp for thirty-seven players in August 2005, but the NHL had been shut down for the 2004–05 season, so some of the candidates hadn't played a meaningful game for sixteen months.

"We had a list of forty guys," said Gretzky at the time. "We've got thirty-seven guys here, and each and every guy here has a chance to make it. And there could be guys on the team who aren't even here."

In a way, the abundance of talent made management's job easier. But at the same time, it also made it more difficult. It would be easy to put together a strong team that would be seen as a gold-medal favourite. But if the players who were cut were allowed to form Team Canada II, that group would probably be seen as a gold-medal favourite as well. The potential for second-guessing was enormous.

Gretzky had a simple solution. "You take the best players," he said. "Talent is always tough to beat."

Still, at that level of competition, there are always subtleties. As Gretzky said on another occasion, "It's not just 'Pick every guy who can score fifty goals, and we'll win a gold medal.' You have to take the best possible players, but they've still got to fit within the team concept."

Even though Canada was the defending Olympic champion, the pros and cons of both the 1998 and 2002 teams were studied closely prior to 2006.

Gretzky tried to delay the naming of the team. "I don't want to get into a situation like we had in '02," he said, "where we had to pick the team so early, and then there's this huge controversy about so-and-so should have been on the team. We want to stay away from that as much as we can."

He was also aware of the potential impact on some players of having missed a year of hockey. The longer he was given to evaluate their current form, the better.

Head coach Pat Quinn looked closely at the evaluations from 1998 and 2002 and decided that the team was evolving in the right direction. There would be no positional specialists in 2006, just good players.

"Our theory for 2002 changed from 1998," he said. "We were going to take the guys we thought were our most talented guys. To me, philosophically, that was a big change for us. It proved to be right.

"Philosophically, we were a different bunch going in there because we were taking our best, and we were going to try to play a possession game and not be a fall-back trap team. We were going to see if we could do it that way, and we did. It took a while to get there, but we did."

As the date for the announcement of the team neared, Gretzky said, "I think the biggest change on our team today compared to 2002 and over the years is that before, we could take centremen and move them to the wing. You can't move them to the wing now. We have so many good wingers now, there's no room to move them.

"We have centres now and we have wingers, and that's the way it's going to be."

Gretzky was fully aware of the ramifications of such a firm decision.

"No matter what we do, there's going to be a controversy," he said. "The only way we're going to be right is by winning the gold medal. Other than that, you're not going to be right."

Wherever Gretzky went that winter, he ran into coaches and general managers who were lobbying for the inclusion of their players. Those he didn't meet in person, he heard from by telephone.

"Everybody wants to add guys to the team," he said. "And that's great, but who gets taken off? We can only have seven defencemen. We can only really have four centremen, and unfortunately, when you add guys, you have to take guys off, and that's where it becomes really difficult."

Canada has traditionally been extremely sparing when awarding spots to promising youngsters. It has been the nation's policy—one that proved fruitful in world championships, Canada Cups, the World Cup and the Olympics—to limit the turnover and lean heavily on players who had a proven record at the world-class level. In 2006, there were four youngsters who deserved serious consideration: Eric Staal, Sidney Crosby, Rick Nash and Jason Spezza.

Because he had been dominant in Europe during the lockout and was the oldest, Nash was selected for the team. As the youngest, Crosby was left off. The other two were put on the taxi squad to be available if someone got hurt.

The controversy over the naming of the team paled into insignificance compared to the controversy that erupted a few days before the team was to leave for Italy.

There weren't many dark days in Wayne Gretzky's career, but he had a stretch of them in February when the so-called "gambling scandal" broke.

It should be made perfectly clear right from the start that there was never a Wayne Gretzky gambling scandal. The media blew the story far out of proportion, implicated him by association and besmirched the pristine reputation he had worked so hard to establish.

Even today, there are occasional foolish snide remarks in the media about gambling in the Gretzky household, but he did not gamble on sports and never would.

The reports of a massive New Jersey gambling ring had hardly surfaced when a full-scale media feeding frenzy broke out, accusing Gretzky; his wife, Janet; his agent, Mike Barnett; Phoenix Coyotes assistant coach Rick Tocchet; and "over a hundred NHL players" of being involved in the ring.

At the time, I was covering the annual meeting of the NHL general managers—which was, ironically, held in a suburb of Las Vegas. I quickly caught a flight to Phoenix where Gretzky was to coach his Coyotes that night. The team had announced that under no circumstances would Gretzky talk to anyone in the media before that night's game. Nonetheless, I went to the rink in the latter part of the afternoon, and when Gretzky came in, flanked by two burly security guards, I started to approach him.

The security guards were about to block me, but Gretzky stretched out his hand. "Hey Strach," he said. "What's up?"

When I told him that I'd been dispatched there at the order of a disconcerted sports editor at the *Toronto Sun,* he quickly filled me in on the situation. He gave me the real story, not the one that was flooding the media.

He started by saying, "I didn't do it," and added that he was "one hundred per cent innocent."

Of course, it was possible that he was lying. But if you know Wayne Gretzky, then you know he was telling the truth. At one point when I was doing research for this book, I spoke to Mike Keenan about an incident during Gretzky's days with the Blues. Keenan didn't remember exactly what had happened, so I told him Gretzky's version.

"Well, if Wayne said it, that's the way it happened," said Keenan. "If Wayne says it, you can take it to the bank."

When the gambling allegations broke, Gretzky was four days away from leaving for Turin. Many among the Canadian media representatives already in Italy—and working on nothing but hearsay—were demanding that he step down and stay at home.

"No way," he said when I asked him about it. "I haven't done anything wrong. Why would I step down?

"I would never embarrass Team Canada or the country or hockey. If there was any truth to this, I would phone Gary Bettman and [Hockey Canada president] Bob Nicholson right now and say, 'You know what? I resign. It's over.' Even if I made a one-dollar bet. But I didn't. I would never do that. That's the bottom line. The bottom line is I didn't do it."

At the time, Gretzky didn't deny that Janet and Tocchet made bets on the National Football League, but did not concede that to do so was illegal. Tocchet was already on an indefinite leave of absence and was facing charges, but Janet was accused of nothing more than betting on football games.

Anyone who knew Gretzky at all would know that someone like him, a man always fully aware of the implications of his actions, wouldn't dream of being personally involved in sports betting. "I have never bet on sports in my life," he said.

He admitted that even though he rarely gambles, he had occasionally done so in Las Vegas casinos. But he added that even in those surroundings, where gambling is legal, he made a point of never entering the area where sports bets are placed.

"I wouldn't even walk into a sports book in Vegas," he said. "Even though it's legal, I would never do that. That's how serious I am about it."

Later that day, Janet issued a statement, backing up her husband's assertions.

"At no time did I ever place a wager on my husband's behalf," she said. "Other than the occasional horse race, my husband does not bet on sports."

What Janet didn't say was that in most of the cases when Gretzky bet on a horse, he owned it.

As we stood there in the bowels of the arena, Gretzky continued to stress his innocence of the charges.

"If I had done it, I would say so," he said. "If I had done something wrong, I would admit it."

"If I did one thing that would embarrass Team Canada or the country or hockey," he said, "I would resign. It didn't happen."

But as the media piled on accusation after accusation, there had even been suggestions that Gretzky was an integral part of the illegal ring. Despite being disturbed by the situation in which he found himself at the time, he had to smile.

"Come on," he said. "There are going to be so many innuendoes. I'm not aware of any kind of ring."

After the game, Gretzky held the promised press conference and repeated his assertion that he was innocent. When it was over, he invited me back to his house for a beer or two. At that time, four of his children were back in the Los Angeles area with Janet, but his eldest son, Ty, who was fifteen, was there.

As we stood around the kitchen counter talking about the furore, Ty was listening intently. "I would never bet on sports," said Gretzky, "but Janet is from St. Louis. She was betting on the NFL long before she met me. I keep telling her not to, but she does it. What are you going to do? Anyone who's married knows the answer to that."

At that point, Ty, who doesn't say an awful lot, spoke up. "That's right, Dad," he said. "When she gets on the phone with Rick, you go like this"—he threw his arms up and let out a huge sigh of exasperation—"and walk out of the room."

It was such a perfect imitation that we all laughed. Anyone who was there and had doubts about Gretzky's innocence would have cast aside those doubts on the spot.

Eventually, the matter wound its way through the courts. Six months after the allegations surfaced, former New Jersey state trooper James Harney pleaded guilty to conspiracy, promoting gambling and official misconduct. Four months after that, another New Jersey man, James Ulmer, pleaded guilty to conspiracy and promoting gambling.

Eighteen months after the furore, Tocchet was sentenced to two years' probation for having been a minor player in the conspiracy. He returned to the NHL in 2008 as an assistant coach, and as of this writing, was a highly regarded analyst on TV in Philadelphia.

Janet was never charged with anything. What all the media sharks had failed to notice was that it is not against the law to place a bet in New Jersey, even with an illegal betting ring.

Mike Barnett was never charged, either.

The "hundreds of players" who were supposed to have been involved were never found.

If any of the media members who rushed to judgment ever apologized to Gretzky, either in person or through their respective media outlets, it has been a well-kept secret.

The aspect of the whole affair that Gretzky will not talk about is its impact on his relationship with Bettman, a relationship that had not been great ever since Bettman did everything he could to sabotage Gretzky's 1994 goodwill tour of Scandinavia. But according to a reliable source, Bettman's actions regarding the gambling allegations widened a rift that has never healed.

The source, a close friend of Gretzky, said that on the night before the allegations became public, Gretzky called Bettman to assure him of his innocence. He said that Janet and Tocchet would be implicated to widely different degrees, but that he himself had not taken any part whatsoever in the placing of bets.

Gretzky knew that Bettman would have to respond to the media the next day, and he wanted him to say that he had faith that he was not involved. Bettman, however, did no such thing. He said he was retaining the league's own independent investigator—apparently the New Jersey authorities weren't good enough—and that everyone was under suspicion, including Gretzky.

Gretzky was furious, and reportedly has never forgiven Bettman. Considering the value which Gretzky places on having a good reputation, he probably never will.

Gretzky went to Italy, leaving one media storm only to shortly find himself in the midst of another. To say that the result of all the meticulous Olympic planning was a failure would be to put it mildly. Canada did manage to beat Germany and Italy in the opening round, but that hardly came as a surprise. The Canadians also managed to get past the Czech Republic 3–2. But they got shut out by Finland, which did not sit well with their fans, and shut out by Switzerland, which was seen as a total disaster. They barely managed to qualify for the quarter-finals.

That was as far as they got. In the opening game of the playdowns, they got shut out again, this time by Russia. The defending champions hadn't even made the final four! They finished seventh.

Canadians were outraged. All the second-guessers were beside themselves. Everyone had an idea as to what Gretzky and his staff should have done, and most of these views, valid or not, were given media exposure.

Some were downright idiotic, such as the radio announcer who suggested in one breath that Kris Draper should not have been on the team because his scoring numbers weren't exceptional and in the next breath that the management team should have placed a greater premium on speed. At the time, there was probably no faster skater in the league than Draper. He didn't score much because he was a premier penalty killer. It wasn't his job to score.

Other observations were not quite as ludicrous, but most of them were badly flawed. The most common criticism was that the team should have placed a much greater emphasis on youth. That was a marginally acceptable observation after the fact, but there was nothing in the twenty-year string of excellence provided by a succession of Team Canadas to support the contention.

Nash was the youngest player. He had already won an NHL scoring title and had been superb in the world championships. To say that he wasn't very good in the Olympics would be a generous understatement. Yet, after the fact, the critics suggested that the inclusion of more young players would have changed the result. But Nash hadn't helped the cause; why would the others?

The one player the critics seemed to want the most was Staal—certainly an excellent player now, but at the time, he had only two-thirds of an NHL season under his belt and had never played in a major tournament—not even at the junior level.

It was suggested in hindsight that, in view of the three shutouts, the team needed more scoring, so the league's top scorers should have been selected without regard for other factors, especially experience. That approach had been tried before by national teams—and by the New York Rangers, for that matter—and had been found to be sadly lacking. Furthermore, if the gold-medal 2002 team had been picked that way, it wouldn't have had either Mario Lemieux or Steve Yzerman, both of whom had missed part of the NHL season but excelled in the Olympics.

Many second-guessers were critical of the selection of Todd

Bertuzzi—and, after the fact, could justify their stance. But in the first two games of the Olympics, Bertuzzi was Canada's best forward. Then a twenty-million-dollar civil lawsuit landed on him and, all of a sudden, his game dried up. Gretzky could hardly have been expected to anticipate an ideal situation being negated by a lawyer, even though there's ample precedent.

As Gretzky himself had said before the Games began, the only way he could be proved right would be to come back with a gold medal. Anything else would be considered a failure.

Bobby Clarke, part of the troika that had handled the 1998 team, blamed Canada's loss on the international rules makers. They had cracked down on what they perceived as "violence," he said, and taken away the seminal aspect of the Canadian game—physical domination.

"I think the Europeans had a tremendous amount of respect for that part of the Canadian game—and some fear," he said. "Now you go over and everybody is the same. There is no difference.

"In fact, if you watched the Olympic hockey, the women's hockey actually allowed more stick checking than the men's. It did! I'm serious.

"The incidental stuff got called in the men's and it didn't get called in the women's."

Even though Clarke had resigned after the 1998 loss, he felt that Gretzky should be kept on after 2006. "Gretzky is a long way above the rest of us," he said. "I think Gretzky should have another kick at the can because I think he got blindsided.

"They've got five guys skating backward through the mid-zone. It's the exact opposite of what Canadian hockey has always been. But that's what won."

Clarke's opinion carried no weight. When the management team for the 2010 Olympic team was announced, the general manager was Steve Yzerman.

CHAPTER TWENTY-NINE

Retiring as a player in 1999 did not take Gretzky out of hockey. He was immediately bombarded with offers from teams that wanted him to work for their organization in some capacity—either as coach, high-level executive or even owner.

He looked at all the offers, gave them serious consideration and then, in 2000, became involved with the Phoenix Coyotes. At that time, the team played in a downtown dump that worked fairly well for basketball but certainly not for hockey.

The future, according to Coyotes owner Steve Ellman, was to be different. He was going to build a hockey arena as part of a complex in the suburb of Glendale. Alongside would be a new domed stadium for the Arizona Cardinals of the National Football League as well as stores, restaurants, bars, theatres and even apartment buildings.

In return for his involvement, Gretzky would get not only 10 per cent of the hockey team but 10 per cent of the whole complex.

Over the next few years, while he was acting as executive director of two Canadian Olympic hockey teams and fulfilling a number of other obligations to his corporate sponsors, Gretzky was also trying to make the Coyotes viable. He lined up other investors, brought in Cliff Fletcher as a caretaker general manager until his old friend Mike Barnett became available, and finally, in 2004, took over the coaching reins himself.

The franchise has been successful at times. Very few times. It was never a good team to start with, having originally been the Winnipeg Jets, winners of only two playoff series in the seventeen years they existed in the NHL before moving to Phoenix in 1996.

Barnett did nothing to make the team better, and by 2007, even Gretzky had to accept that his longtime friend hadn't done a satisfactory job. It was a team that had never had a superstar—and, to date, still hasn't. The Coyote with the most talent when Barnett arrived was probably Danny Briere. He was traded away for Chris Gratton, a workmanlike player who had very little potential and failed to live up to it.

In Gretzky's four years as a coach, the Coyotes never made the playoffs. But it must also be said that no intelligent hockey observers found that to be a surprise, considering the calibre of the players on his roster.

In recent years, with Don Maloney as GM, the Coyotes have been better. In 2012, when they advanced as far as the Western Conference final, hockey was the talk of the town and their home games were sold out. But for the most part, the Coyotes have been a dismal failure, their books always showing even more red than their uniforms.

Ellman sold his majority share of the team to Jerry Moyes in 2006, but the financial situation didn't improve, and in 2009, after Moyes had filed for bankruptcy, the NHL had to step in and assume ownership of the team until new owners took over in July 2013.

Gretzky had already signed a five-year contract extension, but because he was tangled up in the corporate web that lawyers create in such situations, he had to step down as coach and head of the Coyotes' hockey operations. He has had no direct involvement with the National Hockey League ever since.

He took over the coaching duties in Phoenix even though most of his friends advised against the idea, but his explanation was simple. "I love the game. I want to get back down to the ice and be among the players."

He's not there as of this writing, but until the path is cleared for his return, he continues to be as close to hockey as he can get. He is not only Canadian hockey's greatest ambassador, he is hockey's greatest ambassador.

In 1999, just seven months after his retirement, he was inducted into the Hockey Hall of Fame. The standard mandatory three-year waiting period had been waived.

Three months later, his number was retired by the NHL, a singular honour. "When I started wearing this number in junior hockey in 1977," he said, "I didn't expect that one day, they wouldn't let anybody else wear it. It's a great honour."

In 2002, when Queen Elizabeth II agreed to drop the puck for the ceremonial faceoff at the opening of Vancouver's GM Place, Canucks owner John McCaw asked Gretzky to be a part of the proceedings. The two had developed a friendship while waiting in vain for their functionaries to work out a contract for Gretzky in 1996.

Gretzky escorted the Queen onto the ice for the ceremonial face off, then sat beside her for the period of the game that she watched.

"She was really nice," Gretzky said. "She was trying to watch the game and she was really curious about the game. She was very impressed by the goaltenders. She thought the goaltenders were extremely quick and maybe the best athletes on the ice, in her mind.

"She was curious about icing and penalties. She was good. She really enjoyed herself."

Gretzky's only moment of concern came during the pre-game ceremony. "We walked down the ice and she tried to get closer to the young kids so she could wave to them," he said. "I was getting a little nervous because she was getting away from the carpet, but she was just trying to get closer to the kids."

In 2003, when the bidding to host the 2010 Olympics was coming down to the wire, Gretzky jumped on board to help the Canadian cause. He went to Prague, where the decision was to be announced, to try to seal the bid for Canada. "I'll just try to sell them on how great Canada is," he said, "how much people enjoy the Olympic games in Canada, how Vancouver is ready to support the Olympic Games and how it's the right city and the right choice for them.

"I've done a bunch of different things just trying to promote Canada and Vancouver," he said. "Whatever they ask me to do, I try to help them. I think it's the right place to have it. I think it's the next best thing for American TV, if it's not in the U.S., to have it in Canada. With the time zones, that helps a lot.

"With the venues they have for ice hockey, figure skating, curling and skiing, it's the perfect place. I hope they can get it."

They got it. Whether Gretzky had an impact on the decision-making is hard to say, but he certainly didn't hurt the cause.

In 2005, the last active link to the magical days of the Edmonton dynasty was severed when Mark Messier retired after twenty-five years in the NHL. Messier and Gretzky had been close in the dynasty years, they remained close when Gretzky left Edmonton and they're still close today.

For four years, they lived in the same apartment building. They won four Stanley Cups together. Their parents were friends. They were children in Wonderland, kids barely out of high school, conquering the hockey world.

"His family are great people," said Gretzky, "and they lived in Edmonton, which was great. His grandmother used to come to every game, every team function, every Christmas party.

"It was a pretty special group. He was a big leader of it. He was a unique person.

"He really truly enjoyed every part of being a hockey player—being with the guys, being in the locker room, being in the back of the bus, enjoying a big win. Everything you could conceivably think about as being a part of hockey, he loved.

"I've never seen a guy like that, except maybe Gordie Howe. Gordie didn't ever want to retire, and that's how Mark was: 'I want to play forever.' He never wanted to quit."

Like Gretzky, Messier started his professional career as a teenager. "When Mess came in to the league from the WHA at eighteen, he was kind of raw," Gretzky said. "He was just power and speed. But he developed soft hands and really learned the game, and passing the puck. When Glen moved him from left wing to centre, his career really went to a different level. We didn't have a guy to match up against Bryan Trottier. That always hurt us. Mess was able to stand up to that challenge, and that was a huge reason that we ended up winning.

"He really made himself into a playmaker. At first, he was more a goal scorer—go down the wing and snap the puck—but he became a good playmaking centreman. One of the reasons he was able to play so many years was that he developed into such a talent. I don't think he had that natural ability at the beginning."

Messier was a leader of legendary proportions and probably the first true power forward in today's sense of the phrase. "He used to scare me in practice," Gretzky said with a laugh. "He played with such a fierce competitiveness that sometimes I'd think, 'Geez, I hope he doesn't forget it's practice.'"

In 2010, either out of gratitude, or because he had been overlooked as flag bearer in previous Olympics, or maybe just because of an attack of plain old common sense, the Canadian Olympic Committee finally got it right and picked Gretzky to light the flame to open the Vancouver Olympics.

In September 2012, even though he had said he would never play in old-timers' games, he relented and took part in a two-game exhibition series in Russia. Two famous hockey events—the 1972 Summit Series and the 1987 Canada Cup—were commemorated, it being their fortieth and twenty-fifth anniversaries, respectively. Also, the series was a memorial for the victims of the plane crash that had claimed the lives of the entire Yaroslavl Lokomotiv team on September 7, 2011.

Gretzky had expected the games to provide a few laughs and a relaxed time. "That was the idea," he said in 2013. "It was supposed to be just a fun trip because we don't play a lot of hockey any more. But as soon as we got into the games and the fans got into it, the whole level changed.

"We were all thinking, 'What did we get ourselves into here?' We were just supposed to have fun and all of a sudden, everybody is trying hard to win."

The Russian team featured recently retired players like Alexander Mogilny, Igor Larionov and Alexei Yashin, whereas the Canadians were mostly of an earlier vintage. Even Ken Dryden and Phil Esposito were involved.

Once the Russians started double-shifting their better players, the Canadians knew they were in for a tough time. They lost the opener 6–5, an appropriate score for an anniversary of the 1987 Canada Cup.

But Mark Messier (who else?) told the team that he did not expect to lose the second game, and sure enough, on a goal by Brett Hull, Canada won 4–3. No one was churlish enough to point out that in every international game he ever played, Hull was on Team USA, not Team Canada.

"I always wanted to play in Russia," Gretzky said, "and I wish I could have done it twenty years ago. But for our age, I think the level of play was pretty good and everyone was trying, so that made it fun."

Even so, Gretzky later said that no one should expect to see him on the old-timers' tour. Events like the Russian series will be a rarity, if they happen at all.

"I work for the TD Bank [doing promotional work] ten days a year," he said in 2013. "I've got my restaurant [in downtown Toronto] and my wine company. Other than that, it's pretty quiet. I don't do a whole lot."

And he tries to be a good father to five kids—three boys and two girls. "You can only do so much," he said. "All you can do is try your best, and then the rest is up to them."

As California kids in 2013, they're heavily into the social media. Gretzky, of course, is not. With a laugh and a shake of his head, he says, "I always tell my kids, 'I spent thirty years trying not to let people know what I was doing, and you guys spend every day telling everybody exactly what I'm doing.'"

For the most part, Gretzky skates only at his annual fantasy camp. The first was held in Los Angeles beginning in 2003, but when Gretzky went to Phoenix, so did the camp. Once Gretzky left the Coyotes, the camp moved to Las Vegas. What better place to stage a fantasy?

It's not cheap—$11,999 per person—but it gives well-heeled fans a chance to experience an NHL training camp and is so highly regarded that there is no need for advertising. For Gretzky, it's an opportunity to raise money for the Wayne Gretzky Foundation, the charitable organization he founded in 2002, which provides less fortunate youth with a chance to experience hockey. The foundation has donated more than a million dollars towards equipment and ice time on the premise that playing hockey instills positive values in young people.

The fantasy camp not only helps the charity but gives Gretzky an opportunity to do something he loves. "I really enjoy being around people, especially people who love hockey," he said. "When people come to the camp, they're excited about it, so I'm excited as well."

Other players of Gretzky's era take part, and the coach of the 2013 version was Mike Keenan. As would be the case in the pro ranks, equipment, meals and lodging are all provided. But there are also a couple of Las Vegas evenings that would never get the approval of Gary Bettman.

Even with the camp, Gretzky's life today is a far cry from the hectic lifestyle he had when he was playing hockey for nine or more months a year and trying to satisfy a demanding fan base the rest of the time.

"I look back at that and there are some days when I miss it and there are days when I don't," he said in 2013. "But I've got no plans to get back into hockey at the moment. I think it's time to take a break."

Then he laughed and said, "The Kings wanted me to get involved with their team the summer before last, and I didn't. Maybe I should have. I could have got my name on another Stanley Cup."

I told him that when I retired, I didn't miss the travel or the job, but

I do miss the camaraderie, especially the part that comes after the job is over for the day.

"That's the part you can't replace," agreed Gretzky. "Being with the guys. Even when I was coaching in Phoenix, one of the best parts was having dinners with the trainers or assistant coaches. That's the part I miss. Just sitting around with guys I played with and guys I worked with and guys like you, and sitting around and hearing the stories of hockey and all the players over the years."

Gretzky still watches a lot of games. Over the course of an extended conversation, he makes references to specific players, and it's clear that he's every bit as conversant with the league now as he was when he played and coached.

"I love the game now," he said. "I think the game is a good game. I think the players are better than we were. I think the equipment is better. I like the refereeing. I think the hooking and holding are pretty much out of the game. If you can't skate, you can't play."

Even so, there must be changes that he would like to see.

"I think the biggest thing is the sticks," he said. "I think the graphite sticks have taken out a little bit of the feel. I know the shots are harder, and it's rougher on the goalies. But I think that these players are so good, if they went back to wood sticks, they'd have more feel of the stick. Consequently, there would be way more plays. They don't have the same feel we had."

When asked if he would ban those sticks if it were within his power, his answer was quick and unequivocal. "I would," he said.

He's not critical of today's players, just some of their equipment. "From an overall aspect, these guys are so much better than we were," he said. "That's not a knock, because when I grew up, we put the chubby kid in net. Now, these goaltenders are the best athletes on the team. Grant Fuhr kind of started that, then Patrick Roy and Martin Brodeur. The goalies now are all such good athletes. That's the biggest difference in the game. You don't score from centre ice any more."

I suggested to him that if today's rules were in place when he was in his prime, he would have left his existing single-season records of 96 goals and 215 points in the dust. It's not unreasonable to assume that he could have had something in the neighbourhood of 130 goals and perhaps even 300 points.

He didn't argue. After all, brilliant though he was when the teams were at full strength, he was devastating when the Oilers had a power play. If they got a five-on-three, you didn't wonder if they'd score, you wondered how long it would take them.

"We used to get a five-on-three every ten games," he said. "You can get two five-on-threes a game now. When I played, you'd have to brutalize a guy to get that second penalty.

"Now, you get six to ten power plays a game. Your power play has to be so good now because you can really capitalize on power plays. Sometimes we'd go three games with just one power play a game. That's the biggest difference."

He didn't have to do the arithmetic, but it was there. In his prime, he played an eighty-game season. Surely if all today's extra power plays were awarded, he would be involved in an average of one extra power-play goal a game. Assume that he scored one-third of those goals and got an assist on the others. Add those numbers to his best season and you get 123 goals and 295 points. And that's just allowing for power-play increases. It does not take into account how many more points he'd have by virtue of not being hooked and grabbed all night long as he was in the 1980s.

As for today's rules, he's fairly satisfied. While many hockey people, especially those who are offensively oriented, would like to see a reduction in the size of goaltenders' equipment, Gretzky concedes that a modification wouldn't be easy to implement.

"It's hard to do that because every goalie is a different size," he said. "You can't say that a guy who's six foot six has to wear the same equipment as a guy who's five foot eleven. That's hard to enforce or monitor."

And when it comes to making the nets larger, he's totally opposed. "No chance," he says vehemently. "That would be criminal."

But there is one rule today that bothers him.

"I think it's a real art to carry the puck up the ice and into the zone on a power play," he said. "Guys like Ray Bourque and Paul Coffey and Brian Leetch and Denis Potvin all could do that. Now, when you get a power play, the rule says you start it in their end. I'm not a big believer in that rule.

"Carrying the puck is a skill. Guys like Brian Campbell in Florida, that's what they do. But you don't get to see it as much any more because you start every power play now in the offensive zone. That's the other thing I'd change."

When he makes these observations, he's talking about professional hockey. For the youngsters, he has a different plan, one he has formulated over the years. We often talked about it in his playing days and we did so again in 2013.

"I'll tell you this, and I've been telling Bob Nicholson for years," he said. "When kids play, they should have a smaller net. It doesn't make sense to me that a ten-year-old goalie should have to defend the same goal as Marty Brodeur. If they made the nets smaller for the kids, it would teach the shooters more accuracy.

"In baseball, my twelve-year-old son doesn't play with the same bases as my nineteen-year-old son. In little-league football, they use a smaller ball. The younger kids are smaller people. I think the nets for those kids should be smaller, because the way it is now, the goalies are so small compared to the nets that some shots, they have no chance on. I'd put in a lighter puck for kids and smaller nets."

He feels that, instead of four feet by six, kids' nets should be three feet by five. The puck should be an ounce or two lighter. "With the smaller nets," he said, "the kids would have more fun, and the puck would be smaller so they could shoot it harder."

He would also like to see less structure—more opportunity for the kids to just go out there and play without adult involvement. "Bobby Orr and Guy Lafleur and Gordie Howe and Jean Beliveau, these guys all grew up on outdoor rinks and ponds," he said. (And, for that matter, so did Wayne Gretzky.)

"They all got together with other kids and played pond hockey. We've sort of lost the imagination in the game a little bit. Everything is so structured now at a young age that we've lost a little bit of that creativity. That's where their imagination all came from, but now everything is so structured and not just in hockey.

"I see it in baseball too. We used to go down and play baseball with just eight people, just barely enough for a game. But now, if the kids don't have nine players on each team and a coach, they're a little bit lost."

He once told me he was watching a kids' hockey practice near his California home one day and was amazed. "I was sitting there with my brother-in-law (the late Mike Brown) and said, 'Wow, these kids are ten years old.' I was really impressed. These are ten-year-olds in L.A. and they were flying around and around, backward and forward. I thought, 'There's something wrong here. I don't know what it is, but there's something wrong.'

"Then they threw a puck out, and the pace dropped by 50 per cent. The Europeans, every drill they do, they do with the puck," Gretzky says. "With the majority of our kids, as soon as the coaches come on the ice, they put the pucks away. When it comes time to handle the puck at full speed, the kids can't do it.

"When we were kids, we'd go out to the pond or the river or the rink, and the first thing we did was get out a puck. Everybody wanted to carry a puck.

"Nowadays, if you get fifteen or twenty kids and say, 'Okay, we're going to play five-a-side pond hockey; change when you're tired,' I'll bet you 90 per cent of the kids would say, 'What position do you want me to play?'

"They don't just go. We used to just go. Now, everything has to be so organized for these kids, they don't know what to do."

If there is something happening in hockey at any level that Wayne Gretzky doesn't know about, it isn't worth knowing. Hockey has been his life, and the game has been well rewarded for his involvement. As the game's best player, always subjected to the scrutiny of a relentless spotlight, he did nothing more controversial during his career than call the New Jersey Devils a Mickey Mouse team.

The fact that he was right didn't seem to matter to anybody. The Oilers were so much better than the Devils that the score would have been one-sided no matter who was in the nets for New Jersey. But Gretzky was upset that a close friend had to suffer the embarrassment of being the goaltender.

"The silly thing about it is that I was protecting my old friend and teammate Ron Low that we beat 13–3 that night," he explained. "Had he not been in net, it would never have happened."

With today's media being what they are, Gretzky couldn't get through life unscathed. He took some underserved hits during the so-called gambling scandal, and he came in for criticism for the job he did with the 2006 Olympic team, much of it from the same people who had been disparaging of his job with the 2002 team until it came together in the final week and won the gold medal.

Oddly enough, a large proportion of his criticism has come from Edmonton, even though he did more than anyone to put the city on the map. Not long before Gretzky retired, his longtime teammate Craig MacTavish became embroiled in a heated discussion with some members of the Edmonton media who had been critical of Gretzky.

It's an exchange that bears repeating because MacTavish is representative of almost everyone who has ever met or played with Gretzky—even most members of the Edmonton media.

When MacTavish, an assistant coach with the New York Rangers at that point, confronted them about their stance, one asked, "Do you think that Gretzky should never be criticized?"

"I do," replied MacTavish. "What has he ever done that he deserves criticism? He has never put money ahead of the game. He never missed a training camp or a practice. He was always there to play for Team Canada.

You get other players kicking and screaming that they want this guaranteed and that guaranteed before they'll play. Some of them won't play under any circumstances. Gretz has never shirked his responsibility. He just shows up and plays for his country every time.

"Don't you think he would have liked a summer off like everybody else? He is the greatest ambassador the game has ever seen. In hockey, we're in competition with all the other sports, and until he came along, hockey was almost unnoticed. Then he was so remarkable that he got all kinds of publicity for hockey.

"The guy almost transcends the game itself. The things he has done for the game of hockey—and all the players who have played the game of hockey in his era—speak for themselves."

To this day, Gretzky has the highest Q Score of any hockey player. That means that, worldwide, no hockey name is more recognizable than his. There will be other great players in the game, and some of his records will be broken. But most likely, so many of his records will prove unassailable that a new set of benchmarks—those established in the post-Gretzky era—will be established.

Gretzky didn't merely break records, he shattered them. At the time, it was assumed that Gretzky was just the latest step in hockey's evolution and that, before long, others would surpass his marks. But as of this writing he has been gone from the game for fourteen years, and there is no indication whatsoever that his important records are in any danger. The NHL norm has slipped back to the levels that existed prior to Gretzky. In some cases, it has even slipped well below levels that preceded Gretzky.

And at the risk of belabouring the point, even though it was mentioned earlier, it is so important that it deserves mentioning again. No matter how great a hockey player he might have been, he is every bit as great a human being.

ACKNOWLEDGEMENTS

A book like this can't be written without a lot of assistance, and the amount given by Wayne Gretzky was virtually limitless.

Over the years, he has been unfailingly helpful, and I feel tremendously fortunate to have been able to count him as a friend.

This is the section that allows an author to thank those who helped him write his book, but in this case, the acknowledgement goes much further than that. Without Wayne's help, there would have been no book.

There were also many others who contributed to the cause. Marian Strachan once again applied her eagle eye and sharp pen – or whatever the computer equivalent of the latter might be – to the raw product and got it to the point that we could turn it over to Lloyd Davis at Random House.

I've never quite understood people who can meticulously question every statement they read, but I am absolutely delighted that Lloyd is such a person. He saved me from tremendous embarrassment on a number of occasions by catching a lot more errors than I would like to admit I made. But I made them and Lloyd caught them.

Steve Ludzik and Mike Keenan provided some superb reminiscences of their interaction with Wayne. Scott Morrison, a friend for many years, also played an important role when we talked to Wayne about his last game.

Another friend, Bob Goodenow, supplied not only some memories but also a number of ideas and a fair amount of guidance. All of it was valuable and appreciated.

Lucie Leduc was kind enough to put aside whatever was going on in her life to give priority to the book, almost all of which was written in Florida when more pleasant pastimes were beckoning. Gail MacDonald and Dave Carter were also in Florida, and, as usual, they helped keep me on course.

Roy MacGregor, who has writing skills I can only covet, once again generously contributed a wonderful foreword and shared some memories of our time with Wayne in Europe.

Jenny Bradshaw is the kind of editor that every author longs for: intelligent, supportive and understanding, even in the face of incessant whining.

On the business side, Brian Wood generated the concept and made sure those who made commitments lived up to them – including me. And if, despite all this help, the book still contains errors, don't blame any of these people. The fault is mine.

PHOTOGRAPHIC CREDITS

FIRST INSERT:

Page 1: © Bruce Bennett/Getty Images
Page 2: © Lane Stewart/Sports Illustrated Classic/Getty Images
Page 3: © Bruce Bennett/Getty Images
Page 4: © Bruce Bennett/Getty Images
Page 5: © Bruce Edwards/The Canadian Press
Page 6: (top) © Bruce Bennett/Getty Images; (bottom) © Focus on Sport/Getty Images
Page 7: © Focus on Sport/Getty Images
Page 8: © Bruce Bennett/Getty Images

SECOND INSERT:

Page 1: Courtesy of the author
Page 2: (top) © Denis Brodeur/ Getty Images; (bottom) © Blaise Edwards/The Canadian Press
Page 3: (top) © John D. Hanlon/ Sports Illustrated/Getty Images; (bottom) © Time Life Pictures/Getty Images

INDEX

99: number retired by Kings, 173;
number retired by NHL, 9, 298

advertising: 3-D commercial, 153; Gretzky's
endorsements, 144, 147–48, 152–55,
301; hockey's acceptance in, 152–53
All-Star Game: 1979 (WHA), 144; 1999
(NHL), 16
American Express, 153
Anaheim Mighty Ducks, 9, 10, 215
Anderson, Arnold, 6
Anderson, Glenn: 1981–82 season, 39;
1983 playoffs, 59; 1986 playoffs, 88;
joins Oilers, 44; skill, 73
Anderson, Jean, 6
Anschutz Entertainment Group, 200–201
Anschutz, Philip, 192
Arbour, Al, 59, 63
Arizona Cardinals, 296
Art Ross Trophy: Dionne's 1980 win, 45;
wins by Gretzky, 9
assists: Gretzky records, 57, 95, 141

Badali, Gus, 44
Baizley, Don, 120
Barber, Bill, 47

Barnett, Mike: and 1994 goodwill tour,
175–77, 179; as Coyotes GM, 297;
contract negotiations for Gretzky, 118,
188, 191–92, 194, 199, 202, 217–18;
"gambling scandal", 289, 292; and
Gretzky endorsements, 153–54; and
Gretzky's retirement, 16
Baron, Murray, 211
Bassett, John, 35
Baumgartner, Ken, 30, 41
Beckham, David, 115
Belarus, 282–83
Belfour, Ed, 276
Beliveau, Jean, 80
Berg, Bill, 161
Berrigan, Ian, 118
Bertuzzi, Todd, 294–95
Bettman, Gary: 1994 lockout, 174, 180;
and 2002 Olympics, 268–69;
animosity with Gretzky, 180, 182;
animosity with Keenan, 193; Fischler's
backing of, 181; and Gretzky "gam-
bling scandal", 9, 290, 292–93;
propensity for lockouts, 46, 189; vetoes
McCaw's purchase of Gretzky, 216
Bird, Larry, 240

313